CW00540385

ARCHIE MACPHERSON was born and raised end of Glasgow. He was headteacher of Sv before he began his broadcasting career at the BBC in 1969. It was there that he became the principal commentator and presenter on *Sportscene*. He has since worked with STV, Eurosport, Talksport, Radio Clyde and Setanta. He has commentated on various key sporting events including several FIFA World Cups. In 2005 he received a Scottish BAFTA for special contribution to Scottish broadcasting and was inducted into Scottish football's Hall of Fame in 2017.

By the same author:

*Adventures in the Golden Age: Scotland in the World Cup Finals 1974–1998,* Black and White Publishing, 2018
*Silent Thunder,* Ringwood, 2014
*Undefeated: The Life and Times of Jimmy Johnstone,* Celtic FC, 2010
*A Game of Two Halves: The Autobiography,* Black and White Publishing, 2009
*Flower of Scotland? A Scottish Football Odyssey,* Highdown, 2005
*Jock Stein: The Definitive Biography,* Highdown, 2004
*Action Replays,* Chapmans Publishers, 1991
*The Great Derbies: Blue and Green, Rangers Versus Celtic,* BBC Books, 1989

# More Than a Game
## Living With the Old Firm

ARCHIE MACPHERSON

**Luath** Press Limited
EDINBURGH
www.luath.co.uk

First published 2020

ISBN: 978-1-913025-74-8

The author's right to be identified as authors of this book
under the Copyright, Designs and Patents Act 1988 has been asserted.

The paper used in this book is recyclable.
It is made from low chlorine pulps produced in a low energy,
low emissions manner from renewable forests.

Printed and bound by
Bell & Bain Ltd, Glasgow

Typeset in 11 point Sabon
by Main Point Books, Edinburgh

All images reproduced courtesy of the *Daily Record* except where indicated

# Contents

To my wife Jess

# Acknowledgements

THIS BOOK HAS a cast of hundreds but I would like to single out some of the people who helped marshal these numbers into formation for me. I would like to thank the following Old Firm players who were eager to relive their memories of a controversial day: Derek Johnstone, Davy Provan, Gordon Smith, Roy Aitken and Danny McGrain. I could not have gathered much of my information without the assistance of the Glasgow Police Museum and the many Strathclyde officers who contributed to the narrative but particularly to Gary Mitchell of the Scottish Police Federation who was constantly on points duty for me during my research. I am deeply grateful to Dave Scott of Nil by Mouth for his constant advice and access to valuable files. Dr Gerry Hassan's advice on the social issues arising in the book is greatly appreciated.

I would especially like to thank the former First Minister of Scotland Lord Jack McConnell for his contribution and invaluable advice, particularly on the social issues arising from Scottish football's controversies. Thank you to Cara Henderson, founder of Nil by Mouth, who took time out of her busy life in Switzerland to remind me of her significant foray into sectarianism, without which the narrative would have been the poorer. And thank you to Eric Craig and Elaine Mudie who went out of their way to help me portray a hero and a heroine. I'd like to thank others who helped or encouraged me along the way: Tom Brown, formerly of the *Daily Record*, football biographer Alex Montgomery and Pat Woods for his customary foraging through history. Special thanks to Graham Lister of the *Daily Record* picture desk.

# Timeline

1888    28 May, first Old Firm match

1949    27 August, Cox and Tully clash at Celtic Park

1963    16 May, Archie Macpherson's first Old Firm Cup Final as a
reporter

1965    Jock Stein wins Scottish League Cup v Rangers

1966    27 April, Rangers win Scottish Cup in replay v Celtic through
Kai Johansen goal

1967    25 May, Celtic become the first British club to win the
European Cup in Lisbon

1971    2 January, 66 people lose their lives in the Ibrox disaster
when a staircase collapses

1972    24 May, police and Rangers supporters clash in pitch
invasion in Barcelona; Rangers win the European Cup
Winners' Cup

1980    10 May, many are injured in the riot at Hampden park

1981    1 February, the Criminal Justice (Scotland) Act 1980 comes
into effect, banning the consumption of alcohol in Scottish
football stadiums and on trains and coaches carrying
spectators to and from these stadiums

1985    25 July, the Sporting Events (Control of Alcohol etc) Act bans
the consumption of alcohol within sight of football grounds
in England and Wales

1988    12 April, four Old Firm players end up in court charged with
conduct likely to cause a breach of the peace: trial of Terry
Butcher, Chris Woods and Graham Roberts of Rangers, and
Frank McAvennie of Celtic
23 November, David Murray buys Rangers

| | |
|---|---|
| 1989 | 10 July, Mo Johnston startles the footballing world by joining Rangers |
| 1994 | 4 March, Fergus McCann saves Celtic |
| 1995 | 7 October, Mark Scott murdered in a Bridgeton street |
| 2000 | Nil By Mouth anti-sectarian charity founded by Cara Henderson in response to the sectarian murder of her friend Mark Scott |
| 2002 | First Minister Jack McConnell's speech on 'Scotland's Secret Shame' |
| 2012 | 14 February, Rangers in administration<br>31 October, Rangers in liquidation |
| 2014 | 18 September, referendum on Scottish independence |
| 2020 | 13 March, all Scottish football brought to a close because of COVID-19 |

# Preface

*I watched from a very safe distance under a table or behind a chair, when my parents played football in the hall. Frances represented the Celtics and Jim the Rangers. For a long time they had no idea how much noise they made. Thump, thump, whack, crash! Several shrill shrieks, a man's rough roar, more crashes, a series of screams. THUMP, CRASH. Mrs Principal light keeper was grim. 'It goes on much too often, I really must insist that my husband speak to Jim.'*
*'Mama likes Daddy to beat her,' I piped up. 'She tries to beat him too, but he wins 'cause he kicks the hardest and she runs away.'*
*It seemed the neighbours were never quite sure how to take the explanation of the football games.*
Ruth Dickson, *Strangers to the Land:*
*Memoirs of a Lighthouse Keeper's Daughter on the May Island*

RUTH WAS AN observer of a domestic fracas, played on a tiny fragment of rock off the coast of Fife, that regularly adopted the identity of a Rangers-Celtic match. The Isle of May (near where the German fleet surrendered to the allies at the end of the First World War) still lends asylum to seals, puffins, cormorants, terns and, in Ruth's tender years during the 1930s, a handful of humans. Two of these were subject to the Corryvreckan-like pull of a football rivalry played far away in the West of Scotland. Such was the intensity of their battle of the sexes, focused on a small ball, in one of the most elegant and expansive lighthouses along the UK coastline, that the neighbours interpreted the bruises shown on the legs of the wife as clear evidence of domestic abuse. Indeed, it may have been that the game acted as a convenient way to express a hostility that festered below the surface of the relationship. However, Ruth leaves no indication of that as she simply describes an idyllic and happy childhood.

No, the game was the thing; the role-playing was the thing; the need to vanquish was the thing. Then life went on again. It was entirely separated from the daily grind. It was Ibrox Stadium and Celtic Park imported into a tranquil spot – with scant regard for the parochial conventions of a tiny island. It mattered to husband and wife in a way that neither the inhabitants of the island nor indeed anybody from there to Timbuktu (with the exceptions of the global spread of Glaswegian exiles) would fully understand. Out there, where the distant horizon of the North Sea could invite dreams of travel to distant lands, they had opted on travelling, via fevered imaginations, to the city of Glasgow. Two people, switching from their domestic relationship into a seemingly cutthroat duel was a dramatic act of reverence for the traditional fixture itself.

It could seem at first a trivial tale. Yet, it reveals how this form of tribalism could seep into the bloodstream anywhere, like Strontium-90 from a nuclear fall-out. It persists, because the two factions feed off each other to re-energise the historic enmity in ways which are quite unique. Yes there are other traditional derbies of great intensity around the world, but none which draw strength from social and political history – the study of which ought to be the preserve of academics. The Rangers-Celtic struggle has taken to the streets with stubborn values which deeply offend many, but also encourage multitudes. It adopts the historic, social and political turmoil of another island, swallows their stories as eagerly as a crystal meth addict and filters them into the mind through virulent oral traditions which resound with the songs and chants from days of yore.

Of course, when writing this book there was ample inspiration in other aspects of Scottish football. The era of Sir Alex at Pittodrie and Jim MacLean at Tannadice which produced the New Firm, for instance. A label attached by the media to their successes, in the hope that a new dynamic was being offered to Scottish football. But that age was fated never to last. Its roots weren't wide or deep enough to completely undermine the older, socially entrenched tradition. Eventually, with the disappearance of Sir Alex and Jim MacLean from the scene, the New Firm was to rehabilitate the Old, who were to become even stronger and more commanding than they had ever been. Let us not forget, as well, that around the world more fatal explosions of violence surrounding football matches have shocked us all from time to time. And, yes, there is probably a majority of people who regard the relationship of these two clubs as a continual corrosion of Scottish values and might cry 'A plague on both your houses!'. Of course, thousands would have attended these games since the inception of the Old Firm enmity on 28 May 1888, returning to their loved ones without breaking any law, or expressing any sectarian sentiment, and only wishing to see a good game of football. Indeed, I know some even now. The fact, though, is that everyone who has attended these games is complicit in the enduring rivalry. Which is one of clamorous hostility.

And it is the special one, the Big Bang at Hampden, that still resounds in the head. The Riot. The Old Firm Scottish Cup Final of 10 May 1980. It altered much; although sadly not everything about the Old Firm traditions. It would dramatically change how we would watch our football in any part of the country and initiate a political controversy which has lasted to this day. The scenes of that day were eventually watched by the biggest television audience the Old firm fixture had drawn up till then – for all the wrong reasons. For after the final whistle we were all preparing to wrap up and go home, unaware. But as the events unfolded that day a whole life's experience came flashing through my mind.

This book is my odyssey through half-a-century of broadcasting, through the games and issues that bound two historic clubs together in a self-perpetuating rivalry. It reflects on the changing values surrounding the clubs – the nervous role of the administrators, the hovering, attentive media and of how I witnessed television cover all of this – from the days when games were filmed in black and white celluloid and edited with razor-blades, right through to the dubious splendour of VAR. All along the way people have hated each other with an intensity which could suck the oxygen out of any stadium.

I have been swept along by the Old Firm like a piece of flotsam, borne on a rushing tide. From one side or the other, you were branded as indelibly as a Texan longhorn steer in the resolute belief on the terracing that nobody, but nobody, could be neutral. Of course, my experience of living with the Old Firm as if I belonged intimately within a continually warring family circle wasn't all violence and flying bottles. It was perhaps even worse than that at times, in the sinister atmosphere of mistrust and enmity, the efforts at one-upmanship and point-scoring to discredit the other. There are many sides to this story and I have tried to make sense of them all. The day when the tribes went to war would affect so many different people: football legislators, politicians, journalists, broadcasters, police, ambulance workers, A&E

medics. Their voices are heard here in their own words – mine included. Only the police horses were unable to recount how their derring-do saved the day. But there were others aplenty who could.

The Riot: Roots and Realities

10 May 1980, Hampden Park

# CHAPTER I

# Duel in the Sun

10 MAY 1980. Standing at the tunnel-mouth of the main enclosure, Chief Superintendent Hamish MacBean, Commander of the 'F' Division, City of Glasgow Police, and regular Match Commander at Hampden Park was beginning to relax. The normal tensions surrounding a Cup Final involving the Old Firm were beginning to fade. The sun was out. The world seemed a great place for one section of the crowd, a hellish aggravation for the other. The match had just reached its conclusion, after extra time. Not in a superbly dramatic style for the football that day had been fraught with nerves and most of the players had been affected by the extremes of tension. This had come from the torrents of abuse hurled from one end of the terracings to the other. Fanatical support can sometimes depress as well as inspire. Make a mistake and you let a whole community down, a community that regards its superiority as being confirmed by triumph. But on the whole, the game was only passably entertaining. In the 107th minute a stabbed shot by the Celtic captain Danny McGrain was redirected by a leg stuck out more in hope than anything else by Celtic's George McCluskey; the sudden deflection sent the tall, lanky Rangers goalkeeper Peter McCloy in the wrong direction and the cup was won. They thought it was all over.

It wasn't. As McGrain ran with his team towards the Celtic end of Hampden Park, with the cup, something made Chief Superintendent MacBean instinctively turn away from that particular scene of jubilation to look at the area just below the royal box in the main stand. What he saw sent a chill through even his experienced veins. For there, in the most expensive seats, reserved for the more affluent of the Old Firm support, punches were being thrown and necks being wrung. Men in '£500 Crombie coats were battering the hell out of each other.' Bodies were clashing and faces were pummelled as vitriolic anger tipped over into outright violence. Inspector Willie McMaster, who was now beside

MacBean, also expressed astonishment at this spectacle. But MacBean, turning back to the pitch, stiffened at what he now saw: 'Never mind what's happening in the stand. Look what's going on out there!' The crowd were surging on to the pitch. From either end they were now charging at each other.

High above all this, safe and secure on the commentary platform which was slung below the Hampden press-box, I made the fairly reasonable assumption that when the hordes would meet about the half-way line, they would not be joining hands around the centre-circle to sing 'Amazing Grace'. I was spectacularly correct. The attacks began. My comment which seemed to come from the depths of my bowels, might be seen, in retrospect, as absurdly obvious:

At the end of the day, let's not kid ourselves. These supporters hate each other.

But it was, I would claim, the neatest summary of decades of sectarian history you could pack into two sentences. It was no time for a Mary Beard-like lecture on the archaeology of bitterness.

Remote though I was to the scenes below, I was certainly no stranger to the hatred, the passion, the constant mutual eyeballing of these two clubs, at both boardroom and terracing level. The fact is, I wasn't all that shocked by what I was seeing. It was as if I had been waiting for this sort of thing all my life – this was an eruption which had the shape of destiny about it.

\* \* \* \*

I had been born only a couple of miles from Celtic Park, back when there were still gaslights in our tenement close in Shettleston. From my window high on the building I could watch the streams of colour sluicing their way down the pavements, as crowds moved towards Parkhead. On the days when the Old Firm were playing people just seemed different – talking incessantly all around me as if they were under threat from an unseen force. Call it fear of losing, of being made to feel like you might end up as a pallbearer for your own tradition. Even when I pushed the clothes-packed laundry-pram up the hill to the steamie for my grannie I would hear some of the old women refer to it. I recall one old biddy saying,

He's gaun tae the gemme. Christ, I hope he doesnae go near Deans's before he comes back.

Deans being a pub of renown in the area, a veritable den of iniquity in the eyes of womenfolk. The smell of cordite was competing with the aroma of Parazone in that steamie. Neither was there any hush to that day for us. We could actually hear what was happening.

When we played out our fantasies in bounce games on the windswept ash pitches of Shettleston Hill during Old Firm days, tidal waves of sound from Celtic Park would sweep towards us, like a grumbling monster demanding attention. We knew when a goal was scored. That noise was special. Coming at you sharper, like a ripping of the heavens. We would stop in our tracks. But who the fuck had scored? Free from family constraints we enjoyed swearing like troupers, especially when we were held in limbo at these moments, not knowing what was occurring in that cauldron just a couple of miles away. We wouldn't know until we saw the faces coming back down Shettleston Road. Oh, you could tell then all right, without asking, who had won. The aftermath of those days was largely benign in our area though. Yes, there was banter. Of course, there was sullen withdrawal, stoicism and silent drinking by the defeated. And there was plenty of unexpected geniality extended towards you from the victorious. All was now right for them in this best of possible worlds. And they all mixed. Indeed, my abiding memories are of the respective, staunch Old Firm supporters working actively together in politics. Everybody knew which foot anybody kicked with, but the allegiance to parties of the left, in the very early days supporting the ILP, then principally for the Labour Party and even the existing Communist Party, completely neutered any sectarian sensitivities. They bonded because of their unbridled hatred of the Tories. (Of whom it must be said, were even scarcer in Shettleston than Inuits in the Democratic Republic of the Congo.) Then they would separate into their own self-defined social networks and of course would never stand together at an Old Firm match.

This was despite the fact that we were just emerging from the effects of a world war. The carnage involved in beating Adolf Hitler seemed to have had little effect on those who encouraged the belief that on Old Firm match days the brotherhood of man was an impossible concept. Segregation was a word better known in Glasgow than anywhere outside the American Deep South. Supporters benignly accepted separate entrances and terraces in a way which astonished outsiders at the time, but which is now almost universal practice throughout the world of football. The war had done nothing to narrow the chasm between the two tribes. I had only a kind of dull awareness and acceptance of that until an incident sharpened my understanding of the toxic nature of that divide. A single day changed my whole perception of this fixture and of the simmering unrest that can lie just underneath the surface.

In 1949, a few days after an Old Firm game at Ibrox, I was on a local bus travelling northwards from Shettleston towards Carntyne. It was packed and hot on that clammy August day. Many of the men were obviously going to the well-known greyhound-track. I suddenly became aware of an argument swelling up at the front of the bus. Four men were at odds with each other, to say the least. Two in front, two behind. Perhaps it had been going on for some time before the voices were raised. When that happens in a confined space there is a counterbalance of eerie silence from the stunned on-lookers. The words were crisp, abusive, sectarian, heading towards a climax and I suddenly knew what it was all about. Cox and Tully.

These two names were being shot about like cannonballs. (The passing of time now makes the two names read like a legal firm rather than two footballers who sparked a riot.) The two had been all over the newspapers in the previous few days to my fateful bus ride. It had been alleged that in front of no less than 95,000 witnesses at Ibrox Park, on 27 August 1949. Cox had effectively assaulted Tully, and with the referee taking no action, had provoked a terracing revolt at the Celtic end, near which the alleged offence had been committed. A delusional accusation, or barefaced robbery, depending at which end you stood in the stadium. And these four men on the bus were contesting the issue to such an extent that we knew a non-aggression pact was not going to be signed before they reached the dog-track. Suddenly, they rose and went at each other which, in the confined space, meant that four shapes merged into one brawling heap. There were screams from some of the women and my stomach began to rebel. Then, charging at them, came the clippie, the Glasgow conductress, representing a species which could operate either with the tenderness of a Mother Theresa or the resolution of a King Kong. She was of the latter disposition and I recall her grabbing one of them round the neck and screaming at them as she tried to haul one to his senses. She was aided by some of the other men who rushed up and intervened as the caterwauling of 'Fenian' and 'Orange' bastard swirled around the bus.

At the time it seemed to last an eternity, although it may have only taken a couple of minutes or so before the four were separated, the bus stopped, and the four of them shoved off it to pursue God knows what. But it had made its mark. I wasn't mature enough to be making profound judgements, but the incident stayed with me, nay, haunted me for years.

So on that Cup Final day at Hampden, looking down at the milling throng, I remembered that first fight, that first surfacing of violence, like I had been through an initiation rite that had blooded me into the rougher realities of my neighbourhood. Of course even before I had left primary school I had heard all about the past: the 1909 riot at Hampden when both sides had ganged up to wreak destruction on the sleekit Scottish Football Association (SFA) trying to con them into paying for a replay of the final; of the social changes shaping a new relationship between the two clubs brought about by the influx of workers from Belfast into the Clyde shipyards and the extenuating Protestant-Catholic polarisation in the public mind; 1690, the Easter Uprising, the lot. But all that was distant then. The Cox-Tully controversy put names, faces, flesh and blood on the incoherent, abstract rages of sectarianism around me.

I have long wanted to trace this controversy back and investigate the circumstances of that day at Ibrox which set fire to the terracings. It was when I was within the BBC, decades later, in the mid–'80s that the opportunity was presented to me to do such a thing. I grabbed it. At the very least, for my starting point, I could boast that I had seen both Cox and Tully play in my mid-teens. These were certainly fragmentary memories, but allied to other pictures, and the recollections of supporters, I could claim my descriptions of both men were fundamentally sound.

They had little in common. Cox was a beautifully balanced defender who had a tackle like a trap snapping; Tully was a dawdling, meandering ball player of genius. Cox could have marketed Brylcreem as successfully as Johnny Haynes of Fulham in a later era, while Tully wore a dishevelled look that itself seemed suited to his cavalier approach to the game. Cox belonged to, and was a direct product of, that age of supremacy engineered through the powerful influence of Rangers' manager Bill Struth whose face still stares down the Ibrox trophy room, etched with awesome self-assurance; Tully was an import who represented the most formidable challenge to Rangers since the end of the war. Cox was an Ayrshire Protestant; Tully was a Belfast Catholic. On the terracings they could easily be identified as tribal icons. And Rangers were in ascendancy.

The statistics of the post-war era offer adequate explanation for their commanding status, and Celtic's frustration. In three seasons, from 1946 to 1949, in 12 matches, Rangers had won nine victories to Celtic's two, with one drawn. Then had come Charles Patrick Tully, for a fee of £8,000 from Belfast Celtic to Parkhead, something like a young, bold Lochinvar 'riding out of the west' to inspire his new club to an unexpected but wholly deserved 3-2 victory at Celtic Park in the first leg of sectional League Cup trophy. Two weeks later they made for Ibrox for the return game, with the thought uppermost in Celtic supporters' minds that it was conceivable that the Struth era of invincibility was drawing to a close.

But there was an obvious problem for my investigation. The passing of time. On my first step I learned that Charlie Tully had sadly died, 27 July 1971. Sammy Cox, I learned, was in rude health, but living in Canada. Try as I may, I was not pinning him down. Perhaps, in any case, he would be reluctant to answer questions about his alleged offence. Not the best start. But there were others around at the time who would make credible witnesses if they were still alive. And these indeed were the players who were fielded that July day:

RANGERS: Brown, Young, Shaw, Cox, Woodburn, Rae, Waddell, Findlay, Thornton, Duncanson, Rutherford.

CELTIC: Miller, Mallan, Baillie, Evans, Boden, McAuley, Collins, McPhail, Johnston, Tully, Haughey.

As I listened to the first voices, I couldn't help but feel, however much I was pursuing the origins of a day of violence, that in footballing terms I was hearing of an age of innocence compared to succeeding generations of tactical complexities. Here is the late Willie Thornton describing the make-up and ethos of the great Rangers side of the immediate post-war period, whose famed defence was called the Iron Curtain:

> To be honest I got fed up hearing about the Iron Curtain. All
> right, we had a great defence. I know that. But, in fact, if you
> look back, Rangers also had one of the best forward-lines in their
> history. We didn't score as many goals as some other eras, but we
> scored when it mattered and that's what counts, surely. That day
> we got the normal brief talk from Bill Struth. As usual he advised
> us to kick with the wind, if we won the toss and he reminded us
> about the bonus. He never forgot to mention the bonus. That
> was the extent of our team talk.

And from John McPhail, a great Celtic player whom I watched from
the schoolboys' enclosure scoring the only goal of the game to beat
Motherwell in the 1951 Scottish Cup Final, came words that seem like
from another planet compared to Mourinho psycho-babble, no matter
how successful that may have been:

> Jimmy McGrory, our manager, was one of nature's gentlemen
> and said very little to us. He was much less of an influence on us
> in the dressing room than Bob Kelly, the chairman. Bob could be
> a very stern man when he liked and autocratic, but he was also
> a wonderful man when you were in a crisis and he had a simple
> belief that football should be played with two wingers and a man
> going through the middle. There wasn't really much discussion.
> And, of course, we were always reminded that we were playing
> for the jerseys above all else.

That last comment resonates now with sincerity and purity compared
to the later eras of the mercenaries' creed, 'Have boots will travel'. But
it also suggests the strength of a colour, of identity, of a cause, of the
desperate need to satisfy the desires of the tribe. It was community
thinking. And that Celtic community was well represented at Ibrox in
the eye-watering crowd of 95,000 in 1949. They were delighted with
their team's start. According to a contemporary report:

> Celtic looked as if they were playing in somebody's benefit match.
> Their inter-passing was delightful.

This was hardly an unusual pattern and seems to have been repeated countless numbers of times during that decade. But, almost habitually, Celtic's ability to entertain was far removed from their capacity to win.

For me to investigate this properly, outside of reading reports from other sources, I had to talk to Cox personally, although my search was beginning to resemble the later hunt for Lord Lucan, as the former Ranger was permanently domiciled in Canada. I needed the ultimate witness, reliable or otherwise. Of course, I could imagine his reluctance to talk about an incident which he was accused of initiating and which sparked off an unprecedented terracing uproar at the Celtic end. I also knew that the conspiracy theorists in the press-box (yes, they are a hardy breed as contemporary records show) had already, prior to kick off, surmised that something in the Ibrox team selection revealed something of a sinister plan afoot. It showed that Cox would switch from his very customary position on the left defence to right-half. Why? The theory that swept through the press was that since Tully had bamboozled Rangers defence in the previous game Struth had decided to play the uncompromisingly hard-tackling Cox in that area to 'sort him out', as defined by the *cognoscenti*.

So, what did happen?

Twenty minutes into the game and Celtic were clearly in the ascendency and looked the more likely to score. Cox and Tully, racing after the ball inside the Rangers penalty area, clashed nearer the Celtic end. It was then that Cox was seen to turn and kick Tully deliberately. The Celtic player writhed on the ground and the western-side of Ibrox Park erupted in anger which rapidly intensified, as it seemed that the referee, AR Gebbie, from Hamilton, was apparently turning a blind-eye to it. This was a signal for revolt by supporters who saw it as an unprovoked attack on an irreproachable idol. As Tully lay writhing bottles started to fly. As one report had it, 'Bottles were merrily doing their "Pennies from Heaven"' act. Swathes of fighting broke out. The anger became so unbridled that the supporters were simply fighting among themselves. It became so intense that a section of the crowd near the track decided, for safety's sake, to spill over the boundary wall. In the unstable atmosphere this gave the impression that the pitch was about to be invaded, and Mr Gebbie, conspicuously indifferent to the incident on the park, must have been shaken to the core by that sight. Jack McGinn, future president of the SFA and future Celtic chairman, was in the crowd as a young teenager and ran to the top of the terracing; he recalls an old man saying, 'If you run they'll think you threw a bottle. Take it easy.' He also remembers that

> the sky was black with flying glass. We just had to duck and hope for the best.

John McPhail was standing some distance away, beside his marker Willie Woodburn, the Rangers' centre-half:

> I said to Ben [Woodburn's nick-name], 'In the name of God! If they get on the park, I bet I can beat you to the dressing room!'

Ibrox Stadium had been adequately policed this time and they stormed into action, clearing the younger elements off the track and diving in to arrest the bottle-throwers at the top of the terracing. Order was eventually restored and the game restarted after several minutes. John McPhail recalled:

> We just got on with the game. There might have been more dig in the tackles but honestly nobody really went out of control – but as you know, if you're getting a lot of aggro from the terracings it can sometimes look worse than it is. I think what did happen, though, is that we lost our rhythm. No doubt about that and certainly not surprisingly Charlie became less effective. I began to get the old feelings in the bones again that the tide was going to run against us.

It did. Rangers were to go on to win 2-0 with goals by Findlay and Waddell. So, had Tully been sorted out? Had he been taught to mind his manners? Was he being informed in the most positive way that Govan ruled? Had a Belfast man from what was perceived to be an alien culture been put in his place? That was the full flood of Celtic thinking on the spot and thereafter. Although there was widespread condemnation in the press for the bottle-throwing by some of the Celtic support, *The Glasgow Herald*'s judgement on the game reflected the view of the entire press-corps when their correspondent wrote:

There is no doubt at all as to what caused the trouble, the foul committed by Cox on Tully after 20 minutes play and the astonishing attitude of the referee in ignoring the offence and waving play on.

They also went on to remind their readers of recent history. After disorderly behaviour by the Celtic support in a game at Ibrox on 6 September 1941, Celtic Park had been closed down for a month by SFA edict, with warnings posted about future behaviour. For the modern proponents of strict liability (the closure of a stadium because of support misbehaviour) it probably would have been Ibrox that was closed. Not Celtic Park. The Celtic argument then was as crystal clear as it would be today. Why should a club whose players had behaved impeccably on the field be held hostage by a minority of hooligans? What then happened was not to placate those in the Celtic community who had cried 'Injustice!'.

The Referees' Committee of the SFA, a day after an inquiry into the incidents, announced they were

> satisfied that the rowdyism on the terracings were incited by two players S Cox of Rangers and C Tully of Celtic and also, to some measure, to an error of judgement by the referee.

Again, *The Glasgow Herald*'s take on that was almost one of stupefaction:

> It is no exaggeration to say that even Rangers followers were convinced – at the same time astonished – that their player, by his foul on his opponent was primarily responsible.

And went on to say of the SFA's conclusions that

> their finding implies that both players were equally to blame; that, so far as those who saw the incident can reason, was not the case.

All this furore about the imbalance and the unfairness of that adjudication swung the attention on Sammy Cox. At that time in the '80s I couldn't find anything he might have declared about the issue.

Perhaps not unexpectedly. It looked at first as if I was going to lose out on him. Then fortune turned in my favour. Rangers had been invited to play a summer tournament in Canada in 1980 against European and South American opposition only a month after their Cup Final defeat. From out of the blue I received an invite by Canadian Television to be the principal commentator for the event, so I travelled with the official party to Toronto with a rapidly growing conviction that Rangers playing in Canada would attract Scottish exiles, including one Sammy Cox. A friend of a friend of a friend then got a message to him somewhere in the Ontario province, and by return I received a message that he would come to my hotel and be interviewed.

I was in the splendid King Edward Hotel, made even more splendid for meeting and chatting for hours with the great Sir Stanley Matthews, on vacation, then almost 70, a fitness fanatic who would swim several lengths in the hotel pool, and afterwards run through the streets of the city for miles, and all before breakfast, putting my much younger self to shame. Coincidentally, he had played against Sammy Cox for England against Scotland in April 1949, in the famous 3-1 victory for the Scots. The impression I still carry is one of the greatest ever wingers expressing nothing but professional admiration for this stern defender.

When Cox eventually walked in it was difficult to imagine him as the cause of the fight on a Glasgow bus almost 30 years before. He was immaculately dressed, crisply spoken, with only the slightest twang of a transatlantic accent and above all he looked like one of these fortunate mortals who never seemed to age. Time had been kind to him. Indeed, he would live until he was 91. He could not have been more courteous even though by now he must have known what I would ask him. I eased into my interview with him by firstly raising the suspicion of that game, that Rangers had switched his customary position so that he could 'get at' Tully. He was politely dismissive of that:

An hour before kick-off Ian McColl walked into the dressing room wearing a big heavy coat and a muffler round his neck. Remember this was August and the weather was marvellous. He announced he had a terrible cold and wasn't fit enough to play. He hadn't even phoned in to warn us about it. We couldn't believe it. Mr Struth took one look at me and said, 'Sam, move over to right-half and get Willie Rae out of the stand in your position'. Now we all knew that Willie, realising earlier that he wasn't going to be playing, had something like a 16-course meal at the Ivy restaurant before the match, so you can imagine he was in a right good condition for it! But it had to be done. That's how I came to be playing right-half that day.

Almost without much prompting from me he slipped into an explanation of the 'incident', quietly and calmly, as if he were telling a kid a bedtime story.

> I went after the ball and turned, wanting to push it out of the penalty area. I knew Tully was close by me and I was certainly determined not to give him the freedom Ian McColl had given him at Celtic Park. But as I kicked it, I felt this sharp dig on my ankle and knew it was Charlie. I turned and kicked him. I admit that. I kicked him just above the shin-guard and said, 'Don't do that to me again'. It was a jab with the toe more than anything else and I was surprised to see him rolling about the ground as if I had booted him in the family jewels. Then I knew the crowd had reacted.

According to the stories circulating among the Celtic support, with a strength of conviction that seemed to suggest its source came from on the field of play itself, was the allegation that Cox had uttered something less than amiable to Tully. So, I had to ask him about that specific allegation:

Did you call him a Fenian bastard?

He recoiled at that, even though I'm sure he had been well acquainted with the accusation. It was visible indignation.

> I never said anything of a religious nature to Charlie Tully. I know the story got around that I did, but I deny it. I never did to anyone during these games. I played hard, and why shouldn't I have. The Celtic players did as well.

The pity is that I couldn't hear Tully's version, but in general terms other players were not familiar to such abuse. John McPhail told me:

Never at any time in my entire career did I hear a single religious remark made to me by any Rangers player. Sure, we were desperate to win. But it stayed at that.

The late Bobby Collins, the diminutive powerhouse of Celtic in the '50s, endorsed that view to me:

Religion? Nobody gave it a thought. If we had really been like some of our supporters it would have been mayhem every game and, of course, it was nothing of the kind.

Although clearly, he does not claim immunity from how such an atmosphere can play on the emotions and super-charge effort.

And Tully's reaction to the kick? Collins reflected on Tully's personality:

I doubt if he was totally blameless. I remember he could easily drive you up the wall. He once caused me to lose my temper on the golf-course when he deliberately made me miss a putt in a needle game. I almost went for him with my putter, then I burst out laughing. I just don't think Cox would have kicked him for nothing.

But kick him he did. And no punishment ensued. It was an incident which fortified the Celtic belief that the establishment could not give them a fair deal; that the partisan nature of the various authorities, from the referee on the day, to the SFA themselves, sprung from social attitudes towards a club which flew the tricolour and boasted proudly of their Irish origins. In short, there was institutional prejudice. Their opponents then threw the word 'paranoia' at them through the generations in the unceasing ebb and flow of charge and counter charge. The Cox-Tully saga contains a mix of fact, rumour, injustice and even myth. A highly combustible concoction.

\* \* \* \* \*

So down there on the Hampden pitch, these same elements had caught fire on 10 May 1980. A different age. A new generation. But a timeless squabble. And for me, with a familiarity that had now bred the ultimate contempt. It was loudly echoing that bitter clash which occurred on that bus going to Carntyne. This time, though, with spectacular choreography. The battle had commenced, and I found myself asking this question aloud to the now huge television audience:

And where are the police? For heaven's sake, where are the police?

# CHAPTER 2

# Call to Action

PC KENNY MALGARIN, later to become an Inspector, was sitting in a transit police van with five other uniformed officers of the Pollokshaws Support Group near Cathcart Road some distance from Hampden Park. They had been given duties which departed from the normal routine. They were to operate in that area instead of close to the stadium:

> We were there in case of any potential trouble that arose with people coming away from the stadium.

But Kenny added his own interpretation:

> I think it's possible their thinking was that if fewer police were in and around the stadium itself then the public would respond by behaving themselves, that it was about trust. And remember the IRA were very prominent at that time and being a major public occasion, we did a lot of patrolling in and around certain areas.

So, for the duration of the game Malgarin and his colleagues stayed in that vicinity keeping an eye on potential flashpoints particularly near well-known pubs. They were having, in fact, a relatively tranquil afternoon until they were stopped in their tracks later in the day. Malgarin recalls the words that were beamed out of Hampden.

'All stations outside Hampden go to the stadium IMMEDIATELY!' It was a cry for help and in itself an admission that something had gone badly wrong. That appeal was heard around the city where any policeman was in radio contact.

PC Jim Buchanan was in a car travelling to the Southern General Hospital with a prisoner who was to receive medical treatment. The prisoner was hardly at death's door, but he had to be seen by a doctor, and that was Buchanan's first priority. But while he was supervising the man in A&E, he received the same frantic call to drop everything and get to Hampden and could hardly ignore the urgency of the message on the radio:

> I told them I had a prisoner with me. They just told me in no uncertain manner to leave him and get to Hampden. So, I hand-cuffed the prisoner to a bed, and I bolted for Hampden. And, do you know, because of what happened next, I have no idea what became of that prisoner. For all I know he's still there handcuffed to a bed.

Twenty-two-year-old PC Willie Allan, who was to become a Match-Commander at St Mirren's ground in Paisley in later life, was a part of a detail named Panda Delta patrolling the southside of the city. He had been a member of the British Judo team at one stage of his career, which was not an inappropriate ability in his line of work. F429 was his number, which he recalls like an ex-serviceman reciting their army numbers, even years later. They were early shift, starting at 7am. They had been busy, having caught five housebreakers and booked a man for urinating in the street. A humdrum day in many ways. He was looking forward to an evening off since the other late shift would take over from them. But late afternoon, came a call. He remembers it as 'All resources get to Hampden Park NOW!' Whatever the variation of words, in his mind it came with the same urgency felt by the others. They sped to Hampden, the klaxon serenading the streets.

Twenty-three-year-old PC Tom McLeod had started his duties at Hampden at noon, having been driven over with others from Cranstonhill police station. He was part of a total force of almost 300 inside Hampden on the day. His first duty was at one of the 129 turnstiles, where he had to be watchful for anybody appearing to be under the influence, or to be sneaking in any form of alcohol. Beside him was what you might have called the sinbin, into which bottles or cans would be deposited if discovered. And that was the problem, as he pointed out to me:

> This being Glasgow, people were very cunning about how to get booze into a stadium. We couldn't search them then. All we

would say is, 'If you don't put it in the bin, then you don't get in'. Simple. Then some of them would walk away to find a spot where they could guzzle it down before coming back. Not ideal. So, we just had to go with instinct I suppose. Our powers were limited.

In fact, 70,303 did go through the turnstiles and Hampden from then on was awash in booze. McLeod, just before the game started, took up his post on the track at the Celtic end where he was eventually to make a crucial decision about the crowd pressing to get on to the pitch.

WPC Elaine Mudie was at the front entrance of Hampden, having been stationed thereabouts since early in the day. She was different from the others; she was on a horse. Before the day was out the pair of them were about to shunt the Lone Ranger and Silver out of the minds of cinema devotees.

Match Commander Hamish MacBean, on the track near the halfway-line, was no soft touch. Before he had been promoted to his current level of policing, he had enjoyed a spell with the Criminal Investigation Department (CID) which he confessed to me was one of the most rewarding of his career. He could claim that on one occasion he had looked down the barrel of a gun pointed at him by a murderer who had just blown a man's brains out, but had succeeded in staring him out calmly into laying down the weapon; a crisis which more than adequately prepared him to take on drunks at a football match, or the varied breaches of the peace that would occasionally occur in that area. But, as the crowds flooded on to the pitch, he was the first to realise that the Glasgow Police, famed for their handling of large crowds in the city, were looking mighty vulnerable.

*****

Glaswegians, for as long as I could remember, have been almost boastful to others of how their city's police are adept at crowd control. Justifiably so. I go back to a memory as a kid being taken on VE night into George Square, where tumultuous crowds had gathered to celebrate the end of the war in Europe, and of the police controlling a multitude which could easily have got out of hand. Countless times

I had been in crowds, around the Glasgow stadiums, never feeling any anxiety, because the uniforms were around as pillars of navigation and control. They seemed to have the knack of being where and when they were needed. So, it was an oddity, even to me, that I had to utter such a question about their apparent absence. Indeed, MacBean was quite adamant about that in later years:

> I can tell you that normally Old Firm games were easy to police inside the stadium. They were separated. The [Celtic and Rangers fans] were herded into different areas. I mean inside it, not outside in the streets. And I can admit that the biggest problems we had were when Rangers played Aberdeen. It was then we had our work cut out.

Nevertheless, because of the magnitude of the crowds assembled to watch them you could not help but feel at any time that you were sitting on the edge of a volcano ready to erupt.

However, I had built a resistance to it, after notching up about 20 of their meetings by 1980. My first Old Firm Cup Final, on 4 May 1963, as a humble BBC reporter, was as if I had volunteered to serve in the trenches. Even the press around me looked like snipers ready to take aim at me if I so much as raised my head above the ramparts and said something of which they did not approve. This was at the embryonic stage of televised football coverage by the BBC, everything on black and white film, except for a final like this when proper outside broadcast cameras were used. At the same time the Corporation was seen as a threat to the established print hegemony, and I was one of its insects only suitable for crushing. For some of their loudly aired comments about the Corporation at the time were as if they were referring to a cult that practised unmentionable rituals and had to be stamped out. Arthur Mountford of *Scotsport* and myself were new kids on the block and were considered threats to the printed press. Although our early and recurring mishaps in filming, which lent us the kind of Mack Sennett silent movie feel to our output might have allayed any fears about our superseding them. However, I can still feel the hostility to this day. But it wasn't just that which made the game so significant to me now. I was in at the start of something big, something that would fundamentally alter the thinking of one club in particular, for humiliation can be one of the strongest of motivations for radical change. On that Wednesday evening replay in 1963 after a 1-1 draw on the Saturday, Celtic were humiliated.

The club, dominated by the unflinching personality of Robert Kelly, must have been aware of the deep sense of frustration that existed among their supporters. They were unable to solidify their position in Scottish football in the aftermath of their famous 7-1 drubbing of Rangers in the Scottish League Cup Final of 1957. Anger and frustration go hand in hand, and at that stage Celtic supporters imagined that kind of negative twinning would go on for some time. Rather than reaching bedrock they had apparently left Hampden after that final and based themselves on quicksand, for compared to their great rivals they seemed to sink without trace over the next seven years. From that October day in 1957 until April 1965, Celtic went without a major trophy win, while Rangers picked up four League titles, four League Cups and four Scottish Cups.

So, the 1-1 draw on the Saturday, had simply been a stay of execution. For if you considered how they were handling themselves internally, it wasn't just Rangers v Celtic. It was stability v chaos. The only thing the two clubs had in common at that time was that their managers would only have worn tracksuits at a Halloween party. Not for them the coal face. They saw management in terms of distancing themselves from the hard grind. Jimmy McGrory of Celtic was one of the most genial men I ever met in football management. Always courteous, even to myself as a novice in the business, despite the various pressures heaped upon him. He carried the aura of a Celtic hero, with his British record of having scored 550 goals, including 55 hat-tricks in all senior competitions. You could interpret that as an insurance policy, because he was not delivering the league title to a hungry support even though they had won the Saint Mungo Cup in 1951 and the prestigious Coronation Cup in 1953. Indeed, at that time our commentary platform was just in front of the director's box in the former enclosure at Celtic Park. We were underneath the flight path of some of the most horrendous abuse I've ever heard at a football match, as insults were hurled at the directors, and particularly at the chairman Bob Kelly.

One story told to me by John McPhail gave an insight into the chaos that would eventually precede this final of 1963. He admitted that the directors used to go into the toilets in the away dressing room when they were away from Celtic Park, to make the final team selection before kick-off. There was one occasion when he was sure he would not be picked, because he had put on weight and knew he wasn't performing well. It was near the end of his career. But, to his astonishment, when Jimmy McGrory emerged from the toilets and read out the team, he had been selected. As the chairman had been delayed inside, for what McPhail interpreted was a bowel problem, the manager had read out the wrong team. McPhail stripped, and was on the park before it could be changed. A man's constipation had apparently determined the team selection.

The opposition, by comparison, had an air of invincibility about them. You could feel that any time you talked to their manager Scot Symon. When I first interviewed him inside Ibrox he was softly distant, like he feared contamination of a sort. An all-round sportsman he had represented Scotland at both football and cricket. I was new to the business then, and he was conscious of that. There was nothing chummy about him, even after he got to know who I was. He was cool to the extent that I felt like wearing thermal underwear to survive the process. It was more like meeting the curator of a richly endowed museum than a football manager. Even in the dressing room his displeasure could be introverted. Davy Wilson, who was on the left side of a famous Rangers forward-line of Henderson, McMillan, Millar, Brand and Wilson, once related to me what it was like after that first final game was drawn:

> The boss Scot Symon wasn't too happy with us. I can tell you. He was a remarkable man. He got very uptight about everything. I recall him at half-time in one game trying to drink a cup of tea, but it was spilling all over the place because his hands were shaking with tension. And that was Stirling Albion we were playing. So, you can imagine what it was like against Celtic. He didn't say much to us before the replay. He never did. It was just a case of something like, 'Well, you know what to do. You wouldn't be where you are if I didn't think you could do a job. Go out and do it.'

Contrast that with the thinking on the other side of the city. On the Saturday they had played a tiny little ginger-headed figure called Jimmy Johnstone who had impressed me, and virtually everyone else in the stadium, including the famous Fleet Street journalist Peter Wilson of the *Daily Mirror*, who wrote:

> The red-haired, featherweight imp who ranged up and down the wing and cat-footed it around the penalty box, his clown-white face a-jump with excitement, as he chased the ball in a manner reminiscent of Harpo Marx chasing blondes in his palmy days!

Eureka, he might have added! Indeed, it was such a fresh, invigorating performance that on that basis, Celtic promptly dropped him. They brought in a journeyman, by comparison, Bobby Craig, a veteran inside-forward, who had never played on the right-wing before, to replace him. This led the late and great Bobby Murdoch, who was 18 at the time, to tell me:

> To be honest, I think the team selection for the replay was a disgrace. Now I was a young lad, but I know the senior players could not believe that they had brought in Bobby Craig. I just felt then that we had missed our chance.

Rangers were superior in a manner that was barely reflected in the score-line of 3-0. Goals by Brand (two) and Wilson barely hints at their superiority. Celtic had got off lightly. To this day witnesses at the Rangers end deplored the fact that their superiority was not converted into a real trouncing to revenge their 7-1 thrashing in that League Cup Final. For they were facing up to Jim Baxter in his prime. He was tattooing his name over a city with deeds of style on the park and legends of socialising off it. He taunted and tortured Celtic that evening with an almost larcenous arrogance. It was a cabaret act. It was a performance of both elegance and ridicule. The thin as a rake midfielder with a right foot only for standing on, shoved the ball up his jersey at the end of the game and strolled off as if he had been playing in a dads v kids game at a Sunday school picnic, accentuating the hurt felt on the Celtic terracings.

You could sense their anger rising, although had the contest been balanced, and their team within touching distance of Rangers, the reaction might have been more incendiary. Although they could just-ifiably claim massive self-restraint, I think a telling factor was the utter disenchantment with the entire club at that time, meaning that full-throated protest at Baxter, was now beyond them. But it did not go down well with others. Bobby Murdoch, who was to develop into a massive force in midfield for the club, found it difficult to comprehend this:

> We were angry, to say the least. Me, especially, because at that stage of the game they had put me up front and all I was doing was running around chasing shadows getting nowhere as they kept passing the ball amongst themselves without any intention of coming near our goal again.

It incensed another man, as the Rangers captain Bobby Shearer admitted to me, when they returned to the dressing room to be greeted by their manager Scot Symon:

> I expected at least a hug. All I got was the manager coming straight at me, his eyes blazing: 'What right had you to humiliate these Celtic players? That was outrageous'. At first, I thought he was kidding, but he wasn't. 'You'll never do that again, believe you me.' He didn't say anything directly to Jim Baxter because, to be honest, the manager treated him differently from the rest. He had to get at him through me. If you had this sort of talent, I suppose you become a law unto yourself.

Baxter led an exceptional life which burned him out after two liver transplants. And sadly, I sat with him and Jimmy 'Jinky' Johnstone on separate occasions only weeks before either died. The Rangers player was at a Christmas ball in a Glasgow hotel in 2000, a mere husk of a man who barely spoke through the whole evening, and remained rooted to the spot, as if the chair had shackled him more effectively than any defender ever had. He had the disturbing pallor of imminent death about him. In 2006 five years after Baxter died I talked to 'Jinky' in the living room of his house in Lanarkshire. By that time he was suffering the excruciating symptoms of motor neuron disease at its terminal stage. Fellow sufferer historian Tony Judt described his experience of the disease as

> like being put in prison for life, no parole, and the prison is shrinking

by six inches every week. I know that at some point in the future it's going to crush me to death, but I don't know exactly when.

'Jinky' was barely able to speak, I could not associate the wrecked shape with the twisting wonderment of his football skills. He and Baxter were masters of all they surveyed in their prime. And I doubt if we will ever see their likes again. That, selfishly, doesn't pain me. I want to continue to boast I witnessed something unique, not only in their abilities, but in the praise they could draw from opposing fans. Amidst sectarian obduracy they provided a swapping of admiration among fans that broke through the barriers. And still do, to this day.

But we left the stadium that night of the Scottish Cup replay in 1963 in the absolute belief that the imbalanced relationship between the two clubs was beyond reversal. And, in dealing with Jimmy McGrory, you could not help but sympathise with this man for the dignified way he had taken a series of hammerings by the great rivals. Even so, there was a paradox contained in that evening. For as Rangers decided to toy with their opponents, they were sowing the seeds of their own downfall. They had gone too far. That ignominious defeat clearly bit deeper into the Celtic psyche than it ever had before. Something had to change. It didn't happen overnight, as it should have. It was to take another couple of years before their traditional thinking dramatically changed. The effect of that I encountered for the first time at the main entrance to Hampden one night in the autumn of 1965 at a game Celtic were involved in. Jock Stein had arrived at Parkhead in the previous March. The first time he addressed me at the front door of the stadium became my Darth Vader moment.

As former captain of the club and then reserve coach at Celtic, he had been told he would never rise any further than that level within the club, without anybody needing to spell out to him the reason why. But that impasse was defined more bluntly to me once by Billy McNeill his former captain:

Let's not beat about the bush. They were reluctant to give him full control because he was a Protestant.

This was backed up by Jim Conway, the player who helped Stein win his first trophy at Celtic Park in command of the reserve team when they beat Rangers 8-2 on aggregate in the reserve Cup Final of 1958. He told *Backpass* football magazine in the summer of 2017:

> Jock told me the chairman had said that he could not go any further because of his religion. He was quite upset and so was I. I could not believe it.

So that night of our first encounter, the dark figure appeared out of the bright lights of the interior of the Hampden foyer, his famous black coat making him appear as if out of a spectral mist, silhouetted menacingly and spitting fury. He scalded me with a torrent of words. I had said something about his defenders in a recent game which had touched him on the raw. I stood there rather like a schoolboy being addressed by his headmaster for being caught smoking in the school lavvies. Then came the technique which I was to become accustomed to when he was angered. As you opened your mouth to make some sort of reply he would simply turn on his heel and walk off, leaving you feeling like you had just been mugged. I felt a tension in the air by his very presence that was staggeringly new. McGrory and Symon had been ambassadors to the court of St James by comparison, although the Rangers manager did treat much of the media with undisguised disdain. We simply were not to know the impact Stein would make even within a few months. In terms of the powerplay between the two clubs, as personified by the two managers, we were about to enter a significantly new era.

Jock Stein had just driven a coach and horses through an old tradition. A man who had been enmeshed in a Rangers culture as a youth was now totally in charge of a previously anarchic Celtic. But whilst this was to inspire many changes in Scottish football it would certainly make little impact on the ancient rivalry which years later was now about to enact a bitterness in an unprecedented manner.

# CHAPTER 3

# A Blast From the Past

ON THAT DAY in 1980 Stein had only five years of his life left. He was now Scotland's manager, but his legacy was still an enduring factor in the minds of the managers on the respective benches. On one sat John Grieg who, as a player, had suffered countless frustrations during the Stein domination. Here was a chance to salve much of that hurt in one fell swoop. On the other, Billy McNeill had replaced a man whom many had thought irreplaceable. Here was an opportunity to show dynastic continuity with his great predecessor. The massed terracings were fully aware of that personal duel which only heightened the tensions among people whose passions on that warm, sunny day, had been fuelled by more than the traditional songs and chants. For it would become clear, eventually, that the alcohol bins at the turnstiles had been as effective a barrier against intoxication as a sandcastle facing a tsunami.

Legions had come through the turnstiles armed to the teeth, many of whom were hardly unskilled in the various uses of a bottle of beer. PC Tom McLeod had now moved his position to the track at the Celtic end where he would strictly adhere to the conventional policing technique, which was not completely surprising. He told me:

> We were never to watch the game. Our eyes had to be on the terracing throughout. But early on, even before the real trouble started, I noticed something that began to bother me. Something I thought could be potentially dangerous.

His identification of the fence as, paradoxically, a potential problem, in all probability saved lives.

PC Willie Allan's patrol car came across officers on their emergency rush to the stadium who simply did not know what was happening, because not all police had radio communication. What made it more

43

agonising was that their sense of urgency was dampened by the reality of getting into Hampden. As they left their vehicle in the Hampden carpark and dashed out to get on to the pitch they were faced by an immoveable mass of people at the entrances. They were either static or trying to get out. Allan and his colleagues felt helpless and they were now fully aware that all hell had broken out.

PC Kenny Malgarin, who had sped to the call for added resources, had now made it to the stadium but agonisingly was stymied by the same mass of folk. He couldn't reach the pitch initially. When eventually he met up with his superiors who were now actively involved organising matters at the stadium, he came across the Chief Constable of Strathclyde, Patrick Hamill. He'll never forget that moment:

> His face was white and strained. It was almost as if he was telling himself, 'My God, my career is at stake here'.

\* \* \* \* \*

However, what was occurring was not entirely unique to him. One of his predecessors as Chief Constable, James Robertson, had to engage himself with another invasion which I also witnessed, in one of my first assignments with the BBC as a radio reporter. Perhaps not on the same scale, but an occasion which made us worry about the image of Scottish football that was being presented to the world on television, even then. It was the Old Firm League Cup Final at Hampden on 23 October 1965 played in front of 107,609, the largest ever attendance for that final then. It was a sour game. *The Glasgow Herald* headlined it thus: 'LEAGUE CUP FINAL AN ORGY OF CRUDENESS'. You could picture their correspondent Raymond Jacobs foaming at the mouth during the game, by simply reading his assessment:

> The physical aspect of the match must take precedence over any other because that is what the match was all about. There was only a passing nod to the most elementary skills of the game and that largely came from Rangers. Power, stamina and scarcely containable vigour rode roughshod over any consideration of disciplined and thoughtful football. Man went for man. Tripping, hacking and jersey-pulling were rife. How can Scottish football raise its hands

piously in horror against the same gambits of continental players, when the two leading teams in the country indulge in the orgy of crudeness which made this so unpalatable a spectacle.

And from the words of Billy McNeill you could tell that Jacobs was far from indulging in a fantasy, when the Celtic captain told me years later:

> That was one of the worst finals I have ever played in. It was so tense if was frightening. Both sides were so scared of losing. You don't like to lose to Rangers at the best of times, but on this occasion Jock's first major Old Firm final, Rangers wanting to slap him down so early in his career, his newfound reputation on the line, all that got through to the players. We couldn't avoid it.

And I recall the Celtic director James Farrell saying publicly before the game, 'We will fight fire with fire', which led the late Alex Cameron, then of the *Daily Mail*, to say to me later, 'We should have gone to that match wearing tin helmets.'

This was exemplified by the narrative told to me by Billy McNeill about what happened in the very first minute.

> Ian Young clattered Willie Johnston. He went down as if he wasn't going to get back up again. He got booked for it and so did Johnston for retaliation, but the winger wasn't the same for the rest of the game. Big Jock had identified Johnston as the main threat to us and he told Young that his first tackle had to really matter. And he told him in no uncertain manner. Ian just went out and walloped him.

Celtic won 2-1 with the aid of two penalties, one of which, a tackle by David Provan on Jimmy Johnstone from behind, was hotly contested by the Rangers players, thus inflaming even more a wildly excited crowd. Raymond Jacobs in *The Glasgow Herald* had an interpretation of that incident which perhaps reflects on the negative reaction at one end of Hampden:

> when Celtic were given their second penalty award, the congratulations bestowed upon one another by McBride and

Johnstone were not only provocative but implied the referee had been cleverly deceived.

The subsequent events were astonishing, and for me, up in my radio booth, where I had to do reports near the press area, it was unprecedented and confusing. Celtic returned to the pitch for a lap of honour with their trophy. But, so did a couple of thousand Rangers supporters spilling on to the field in response. What was baffling is that we could not comprehend what they intended to do. They advanced, at first with obvious relish, and then as if they had put a brake on themselves, seeming to slow down when getting near the Celtic players, but in a defiant celebratory scarf-waving hysteria. Bobby Lennox, in his last ever game for the club, only recalls his own reaction.

I was quick on the park at the best of times. But I was never as quick as when I ran across the park to get up the tunnel out of the way. So, I never really saw what then happened.

Gair Henderson the *Evening Times'* chief football writer, and writing not far away from my position in the broadcasting box, seemed to interpret it as I did:

I have the impression that the entire trouble was caused by supporters who were little more than schoolchildren. When they invaded the field, they were waving Rangers scarves, but I did not see them armed with bottles or stones to commit harm to the Celtic players. But the damage has been done. Scottish football has been branded once again and you can be sure that highly coloured stories of the Hampden 'riot' will now be on their way to Italy – our next World Cup opponents. And they will say that the fans of Roma are little Lord Fauntleroys compared to the gangster thugs of Glasgow.

Hugh Keevins, as a boy, simply watching the game, long before he started to report on these fixtures, as one of Scotland's best-known journalists and broadcasters, clearly identified one element:

I definitely saw the Rangers supporters getting right up to the

Celtic players and noticed Ian Young actually throw the cup into the air which was caught by another player further away.

I would conclude that had any actual assault had been committed and observed, there would have been immediate repercussions from the other end. But my recollection is somewhat similar to Henderson's, and that while these supporters were entirely out of order, I witnessed no attempt to attack any Celtic player, although clearly there was unacceptable intimidation. With the help of some research by Jim Craig, the Lisbon Lion, I was able to read the following report in *The Times*.

Young, the right back was struck and knocked down. So too was the trainer Mochan, before the police rescued the players.

I'm sceptical about that report largely because it is anonymous. It has no journalistic byline attached. Nor have I come across anyone who can validate such an extreme act. Indeed, here is another take from *The Glasgow Herald*, on the invasion, which reinforces the idea that the incursion stopped short of assault:

More than one Celtic player came close to being assaulted and if any one attack had succeeded the subsequent events do not bear thinking about.

You have to wonder if in the Old Firm context, that in any controversy, you see what you want to see.

In fact, it is important to emphasise there was absolutely no response from the Celtic end, angered though their supporters justifiably were, watching basic hooliganism. It was a massive act of self-restraint, although if they had seen an assault I am sure it would have tipped them over the edge. The pitch was then cleared, but the memories of the day certainly were not. That same night the Chief Constable was called from a dinner he was attending, after fights had broken out between Rangers and Celtic supporters in the Burns and Laird steamer *Royal Ulsterman* taking supporters back to Belfast. He had to stay on the quay and supervise the operation which ended up with 19 Glasgow policemen travelling across the water to prevent a mutiny at sea. It was one of those charming reminders that the warring links between these two cities were virtually indissoluble.

But suddenly, within Ibrox there was a new awareness of how one man was threatening to reconfigure the landscape. In different ways Stein had elevated both Dunfermline and Hibernian to different levels of performance and success. Now he had a Scottish Cup and a League Cup to his credit for Celtic, and had the press paying court to him already. However, Ibrox's most hopeful analysis of Stein was that he would suffer the fate of a meteorite, scorching its way into view and then inevitably burning out quickly.

They might have thought there was evidence of that on the night of 27 April 1966. It produced a goal which placed a foreigner in the pantheons of Rangers greats, as the late Lisbon Lion Tommy Gemmell put it this way to me some years ago:

> I swear to you that even now I can go into pubs and get into banter with Rangers supporters and some of them will shout out to me. 'Well, what about Johansen then? What did he do to Celtic then?' And these people are in their late teens or early 20s. They couldn't possibly have seen him play and they certainly would not have been at the game that made him famous. And yet they remember him and keep casting him up to me.

Gemmell was referring to the Scottish Cup Final replay of that night when a Danish import called Kai Johansen scored the only goal of the game for Rangers. We were in the south enclosure at Hampden filming the final. George Davidson was on commentary. I was there to pick up interviews, if any. It was always a dire position, from which to talk about any game, because our platform was so much lower than the level of the pitch that we were almost subterranean. Thus, our filming, under very poor floodlights, would have drawn praise from Jacques Cousteau. I commentated from there on Rangers beating Kilmarnock in a League Cup Semi-Final 6-4, 6 October 1965, but if you saw our programme that night it was a 1-1 draw. It was in our Keystone Cups era when transferring celluloid film to a television programme was fraught with all kind of problems.

On that replayed Scottish Cup Final there was only one goal to contend with on a night of shadows. That's all they seemed to be from our position, particularly on the far side of the pitch. Rangers, with their darker jerseys were especially difficult to identify. And indeed, Celtic were chasing shadows. They had gained impetus from having beaten Rangers in that Scottish League Cup Final in the autumn and the roles had been reversed, with Celtic now on the front foot as the hunters. Except they couldn't snare their prey. Because of the huge impact Stein had already made in such a short time we all expected him to come away with a win. They continually surged forward in a way that Gemmell painfully reminisced about with me:

> To be honest I thought we had given them a right going over in both games but couldn't put the ball in the net. After the Saturday game we were confident we could take them in the second game.

That confidence was clearly apparent. But without the end product. Rangers did find it, striking against the tide. On that far side of the pitch a shadow called Kai Johansen, who had had a torrid time against John Hughes in the first game, and whose position with the club at that time was on a 'shoogly peg', pounced on a ball from a goal-line clearance from Murdoch and from 25 yards swept it past Simpson for the first goal he had ever scored in Scotland. Time – 70 minutes. The darker shadows had won. Although triumphalism rent the dark Hampden night, as per usual for the Rangers element in the 96,862 crowd, it did not dispel the sense of realism which was developing among some on the Ibrox board. A victory, yes. But a victory that had a dramatic rescue-act attached to it. They had seen Rangers outplayed for most of the game, and that icy reality was enough to chill the champagne for some board members who walked up the marble staircase at Ibrox every week.

Stein was a bad loser. 'A bear with a sore head', his friend Tony Queen used to say of him. Many managers I knew were of the same stock. He snapped at us that night. Clearly, by the percentage of possession Celtic commanded, he thought they should have won, although it was the fourth successive game Celtic had failed to score. But there was barely a soul I talked to among the press, who thought that a bubble had been burst. Stein simply seemed too well-grounded for that. And at least some across the city thought so too. Although Symon would take Rangers to a European Cup Winners' Cup Final in 1967 at Nuremburg against Bayern Munich, just after Celtic's triumph in Lisbon, but they lost 1-0, in a game where they had clear-cut chances to win. There was a growing feeling within the club that the tracksuited manager of their rivals represented a contest between a moderniser and a traditionalist. It was clear that Ibrox was in the early stages of what might be described as the 'Stein dementia'. They were beginning to forget all the previous achievements of their manager because of the new force banging at their gates.

So, I recall those times as a period of readjustment within the entire media. They were in general agreement that Scot Symon had been an outstanding manager for Rangers helping them to harvest six League championships, five Scottish Cups and four League Cups during his tenure. Of course, the stain of having lost a Scottish Cup game down at Berwick in January of 1967 had been ignominious but, outside that, his other record made him look unassailable, in any kind of reckoning. But football management is judged on elements which rarely mirror business norms. You do not need to acquire a qualification from the Harvard Business School to realise that inside a football boardroom sentiment can trump everything. What might have helped Symon was a sympathetic press, who could have found the words to curry support among the fans beginning to doubt his ability to take on Stein. But since he largely treated the pressmen with all the affection of a traffic warden booking a motorist on a double yellow line, it was not forthcoming. It was once claimed of him that a journalist had phoned to ask about a possible postponement of a particular game because of bad weather. 'Is there fog at Ibrox at the moment?' After the characteristic hesitation, the reply came, 'No comment!' Stein, by contrast, had them eating out of his hand only weeks after coming back to Glasgow.

Symon was eventually informed he was being sacked, in November 1967, by accountant Alex McBain who visited him on his sick bed with the decision, even though, at that stage, Rangers were top of the league. Given the rigid policy that kept Ibrox free from incursion by Catholics, leaving you to assume that even the tea ladies at Ibrox had to undergo clearance, McBain merited a news story in *The Glasgow Herald* on the 28 December 1989 when he died at the age of 94. For although he was an important asset to Rangers chairman John Lawrence's building company, and a member of the Kirk, he also did such valuable work for the Catholic Church in terms of their pension scheme for priests, that he was awarded a Papal Knighthood for his services: only the second non-Catholic Scot to have attained that at the time. However, that day of the sacking he was the agent of a transaction which did not carry too much Christian charity with it, for the modern equivalent of that transaction would be a sacking by email.

And, yes, there was an upsurge of sympathy for him, even from men whom he had held mostly in disdain. That week of his dismissal, I had invited Rangers inside-forward Ian McMillan to our BBC television programme. Without too much prompting from me, he proceeded to lash out against Symon. This, coming from a normally polite figure who avoided controversy, was astonishing. He talked about the time Rangers had been thrashed 6-1 by Eintracht Frankfurt in the European Cup in 1960. He quietly demolished him as a man from the wrong generation, by recounting that at half-time in that game, with the score 1-1 but with the writing on the wall, given the Germans' dominance, Symon had done nothing more than simply sip a cup of tea in the corner of the dressing room, at a time when the side badly needed some tactical discussion to withstand the German onslaught. Two days after that programme, quite coincidentally I bumped into Symon in the Isle of Skye hotel in Perth on the way up to a Dundee game. He looked me up and down from his restaurant seat like I was the bringer of plague, icy anger in his eyes, but said calmly, with masterly self-restraint that was itself threatening:

If my wife had got hold of you on Saturday night, she would have torn your eyes out.

He was referring to my pointed questioning of McMillan. He then added, 'However, you are entitled to your opinion'. And turned to his scallops, as if I wasn't there. In its calm, dignified fury, it stunned me. Had he struck me with the tall saltcellar he had had in his hand at the time, I could not have been more affected. Afterwards, something else struck me about his calm demeanour: that he was probably relieved to be free from having to compete with this new force that had entered the scene. Put on a tracksuit, like the other man, and muck about on a training ground? That was never going to be Symon.

So, you could say Stein had claimed his first major victim. And, so began a period which made us aware that a new political climate had opened up. It would be one of almost religiously observed scrutiny by a man whose sectarian experiences had imbued him with a passion to gain credit and respect from the media and the general public for his club, which he felt historically had been lumbered by prejudice. He had astonishing reach. He had, within an amazingly short period of time, a cadre of informers, seemingly the length and breadth of the land. You really had to watch what you were saying, publicly, at any given time. Once when a journalist cracked a tasteless joke about a helicopter misdirecting itself and ploughing into Celtic supporters at Hampden. Within half-an-hour of uttering that to a group of colleagues, he received a withering phone call from Stein which haunted him for the rest of his professional life. Some people who watched a transmission of an Aberdeen–Rangers game privately within the BBC with me one day, had uttered complimentary remarks about Rangers' subsequent victory. By the end of the day Stein knew about every word that had been uttered and phoned in his displeasure about bias, with that distinctive husky voice of his, which carried such menace. In fact, in his early days he would go so far as adopting a false name to call the BBC, because he was aware that storm cones had been hoisted within the Corporation, to warn anybody that he could turn you to jelly with his aggression.

He did regard the BBC during that period as principal purveyors of anti-Celtic sentiment, a view based principally on the fact that the second-half of the 1957 Scottish League Cup 7-1 victory by Celtic over Rangers was never broadcast, because when the technician in charge of the operation in London went for a cup of tea at half-time when the score was 1-1, he forgot to take the dust-cap off the recording camera. Trying to explain that to Stein through the years was like trying to tell him there were fairies at the bottom of the garden. So, given all this engagement with the media, where stood Rangers?

They appointed Scot Symon's assistant David White as manager that November of 1967. A tidy and intelligent wing-half with Clyde and then their manager, he was always interesting to listen to on football. He was certainly a tracksuit man and seemed to fit the measurements of a progressive thinker. But that wasn't enough. Beside Stein he seemed diminutive. At a function once, at the BBC, we overheard Stein encouraging White not to be scared to go on television to debate anything with him, as he would not 'savage' him. Very considerate. But also, very patronising. And an accurate reflection of the public's perception that White was no match, in any sense, with the more physically impressive rival. He did not get the results expected of him and was sacked on Thursday 27 November 1969 after continuing failures. The following Wednesday, a man working as a journalist for the Scottish *Daily Express*, Willie Waddell, an iconic figure from the '40s and '50s as a superb winger for the club, was appointed manager. This was just days before he had perpetrated the proverbial hatchet job in his article, headed, 'THE BOY DAVID MUST GO'. It remains one of the seminal headlines of that era. That had been his short, and abrupt manifesto for taking on this job in which he would develop into one of the strongest and most influential managers in the history of the Scottish game.

Stein in one corner. 'Deedle' Waddell in the other. Producing a turbulence that was like shooting the rapids. Exciting, provocative, controversial. As each tried to grab the headlines in the almost weekly effort to upstage the other, you were taught lessons on how to compose pieces that would be a balancing act. Every day you were asked to face your Maker. It was an education that bolstered us for future professional life. If you could cope with them, then it prepared you for other tussles with the likes of other barnstormers like Sir Alex. When I was a kid my father used to take me to see the fights at various boxing booths in the city where the noble art could produce the whiff of the abattoir in all its gore. Stein's tangling with Waddell reminded me of those days when the baying mobs used to surround the booths hoping one or the other in the ring would hit the canvas and never get up again. To me, their personal duel carried the primitivism of the boxing booths, because it was largely uninfluenced by foreign talent, or the flagrant manipulation of finances, that would seep into the game in the future. It was between two earthy Lanarkshire men who came from the same sort of culture: one who, steeped to such an extent in Rangers tradition, sounded at times like a southern senator in the States, steadfastly segregationist but knowing he could not cling on to that belief for too much longer in a rapidly changing world; the other brought up in that culture, but now aggressively disdainful of it; both of them managing local boys who did not need tutored in how apocalyptic a defeat could feel on an Old Firm match day. These were breathless times.

Not that the Greig–McNeill duel lacked its own substance. That day in 1980 they were as fired up as at any other time as managers.

The New Firm, Aberdeen and Dundee United, had invaded traditional territory and looked like camping there. So, this final had new meaning. But, unlike some of the tensions I had experienced in that previous generation, I never felt I was being sucked into something bitterly personal as in the Stein–Waddell era. When I interviewed both managers days before the final, they seemed both unaffected by the hype. They both had great respect for one another. We filmed Greig in front of his neatly displayed trophy cabinet as if he hadn't a care in the world. After all he had heard Celtic had serious injury problems. You wouldn't have thought so at the McNeill household. Yet, the father of the house was even more laid back. We couldn't find some of his medals for us to film, including the European Cup Winners' Medal. After a search we discovered his daughters had taken them to use as currency to play 'shops' with the kids from next door! Stein and Waddell wouldn't have let us in the front door.

What they both hoped was that someone would rise from the ranks at Hampden that day in May and achieve sainthood in the canon of football folklore. But someone upstaged them.

CHAPTER 4

# A Girl on a White Horse

WPC ELAINE MUDIE would ride on to Hampden Park that afternoon little realising that before the day was out, people throughout Europe would see her as a kind of Joan of Arc battling battalions of evil. She was riding what was technically called a grey gelding, but so prominent and unexpected was her presence there, that to this day, I still visualise her horse as a shining white beacon of hope set against the murkiness of sectarian violence. She was in her early years of the force, having joined just after she had turned 18 in 1976. Policing was in her DNA, as her great-uncle had risen in the Metropolitan Police to become the personal bodyguard to the newly abdicated king, Edward VIII, the Duke of Windsor. In her middle age, and long retired from the police, she no longer sat on horses but occasionally on a tractor clearing snow from the runways at Glasgow Airport in her customer service job. She was adamant that clearing snow was a great deal easier than shunting angry men off a football pitch. She spoke to me with an articulate self-assurance that reflects on the resilience she showed in coping with initial disappointments in her attempts to qualify for the force, but still talks affectionately of that period.

> A girl in the office where I was working at the time decided to join the police and eventually when she walked in with her uniform I thought it was so smart I thought I'd like to be part of that too. But since I wasn't the brightest academically it took me three attempts to pass their tests, until the big sergeant in charge must have thought 'She's not going to go away, so we'll just let her in'.

Such self-effacement does not suggest a quality that would benefit her much in the hard business of policing.

She had joined when the police structure was only a year into radical changes, which meant that women were now patrolling with men. It was in these early days that she revealed her independence of spirit that would lead to her dramatic appearance at Hampden in later years, a result of dealing with an intensely masculine world. Even though her actions could have been interpreted as protective instinct on the part of her colleagues, she sometimes found it denigrating.

> When we went out with the men in Panda cars to an incident, they're first instinct was to say to me. 'Just stay in the car and listen to our radio.' But I'm not that sort of person. So, I would just get out of the car and join in. I resented it. But not as a feminist. I had joined the police to be in everything they did. But I was not an active feminist. I think that leads to too many complications.

She rejects any suggestion of being a pioneer of sorts. Perhaps not consciously. But the publicity she would eventually receive could only have helped ambitious women in any walk of life.

However, she had another passion which was to provide a clear-cut path for her in the force:

> I always loved horses. When I was much younger, I used to go up north to my grannie's and all my friends there had horses, so we would spend the whole summer riding them. They were just ponies, of course, but it meant we could all teach ourselves to ride. So, when I got into the Force my sergeant at Drumchapel helped me write my application for a riding test. I went out to the Pollock estate under the supervision of Inspector Hogg, a marvellous man who was on the pitch with me at Hampden that day. I was given two horses to ride. One was a big, fat lazy horse who wouldn't move. The second one was an ex-racehorse who, the minute you touched it, would bolt to the end of the field and spin and rear. I just found it hilarious. But when I had my interview with the Inspector, he said he'd been impressed with how calm I had been when the horse was rearing all over the place. So, they put me on a probation period of six months, and then kept me on to secure a permanent position in 1979 just less than a year before that day at Hampden.

She observed changes taking place in the mounties even during her time. At first there were only a handful of women on horse duty. Now they are up to about 90 per cent. But she regretted an element about that:

> When I started, I would go out on patrol with men mostly. We hardly talked. We got on with our business of looking around the streets. Then when more women came into my area you would get two women patrolling down the street and they would be gabbing to each other. They would be talking about clothes, about family, about the TV programmes they had been watching. My view was that we should look stern and on duty all the time.

You could tell from that she would be no blushing violet among the football fraternity. So, most of her early duties were at football grounds. And that day, she did feel some nerves about taking on her first Cup Final duties.

There were others trying to cloak any trace of nerves. You could have found that in two hotels in Ayrshire where the rivals were making their final preparations. Celtic at Seamill. Rangers in Troon. Those who were into reading that morning's newspapers, which some players would deliberately avoid anyway, would have been made aware that this final was shrouded in more than the usual conjecture. Celtic were depressed. They had blown a 9-point lead on Aberdeen and lost the league. The Rangers' cupboard was bare. They had ended up fifth in the league. They had been beaten 4-1 by St Mirren only days before. If they did not win this cup, they would miss a European competition for the first time in five years. Now McNeill and Greig, both of whom had been appointed only two years previously, were hardly in the last-chance saloon, although they seemed at least within easy reach of the spittoon. This all lent a special edge to the occasion. Something that did not influence Celtic's David Provan now ensconced as a Sky television stalwart. For he has barely anything good to say about this fixture at any time:

> I hated playing in these games. Detested them. They were toxic. The hatred surrounding them was unhealthy. You would only enjoy them if you were two goals up and the referee was looking at his watch. That was the only time.

By contrast, Gordon Smith of Rangers, who had joined the club three years before, actually had great affection for it:

It's the one game I always wanted to play in, after seeing Baxter in his prime when I was a schoolboy. But, of course, it had its consequences. I remember when we won the League Cup against Celtic, the season I joined, we went to a hotel to celebrate and there were Celtic fans there who recognised us and taunted us. Nothing wrong with that. But when I came back out, I discovered my car had been smashed up, windows all broken, tyres cut. And that gave me a clear indication of how much hatred surrounded this rivalry.

Roy Aitken, to be a future Celtic captain, simply loved it:

It was the greatest game for me. There was nothing like it. It always gave me a special buzz. And that day because we had injury problems and I was going to play out of position – I'd never felt more up for it.

They all travelled to Hampden on luxurious buses. WPC Elaine Mudie, on the other hand, trotted peacefully through the Glasgow streets from the city centre on a horse, which had been down that route so often it barely needed guidance. It had a name reeking of salty Ayrshire breezes and the lapping of the sea. Ballantrae. This was in keeping with the police tradition of associating Scottish landmarks with their horses like they were reminders of the land they policed. And, of course, it was big and white. 'I absolutely adored him', WPC Elaine Mudie still insists,

although he was a crabbit old bugger at times. He had a big long beard and we used to cut them, to keep the horses all tidy, but he wouldn't let us get near his. He was so obstinate. We had to get a vet out to dope him. So, we would put him to sleep on his feet. But as soon as the clippers made a sound he would wake up and resist. That was that. So, he still had his beard that day at Hampden.

Clearly horses could be as temperamental as some of the well-known players in the buses arriving at the stadium entrance that day. But when ridden by the mounted police they seemed to know instinctively what their duties clearly were. Obstinate though Ballantrae could be on occasion, it was a characteristic that might have helped him to display steadiness among crowds. Because of that, Elaine and her horse were stationed normally at the front entrances of stadiums. The animals were tried and trusted and were chosen with care as Elaine explained:

> We got our horses from all over the place. We took a good few from Ireland and from farmers in Scotland. And if they were good, we would keep them and then retire them up to a sort of rest home near Aboyne. We put them through a lot in their training. They used to produce a barrage of noises of all kinds testing them out and sometimes we'd even get a pipe band in to play around them. They wouldn't go out on the road unless we felt they were properly up for it, as he certainly was that day.

Being a Cup Final, readiness for horse and footballer were on a par. The meek perish in that atmosphere. Every sinew in the body is required. But Gordon Smith had a dilemma which he nursed privately. He admitted that at the time he wasn't sure if he was physically up for it:

> I'll be honest. There were several times in my career when I did this, but I remember this time particularly, because I declared myself fit when I don't think I was. I had a problem with my ankle, and I got fitness tests and the manager told me I would have to undergo one on the morning of the game. Well, I did. Now I certainly was feeling some pain after it. But I'll tell you what swayed me to play. I believed we were really going to win that day. I really did. Another thing was my grandfather had won two cup medals with Kilmarnock. I had two for Rangers. This would have been my third. It would have put me ahead of him. And I definitely thought we were going to win anyway. I was sure of it.

So did many others in the media. For Celtic were about to field a weakened team. David Provan talked about their improvisation:

We had lost our two central defenders, so Billy McNeill decided to play Roy Aitken at the back, who was a midfielder but was no stranger playing at the back. And he had to play another midfield player at centre-half, Mike Conroy, who was handed the task of the day to play against Derek Johnstone perhaps their most important player. So, all that added to a confidence issue that affected the club at the time because we had blown a 9-point lead on Aberdeen who went on to win the title. There was a real deflation about the club because of that. But, you know, I think improvisation can help players. They are being asked to step up and do a job and toe the line. So, the pressure was immense.

As Smith admitted, the first thing they had to cope with was the atmosphere:

I was given a great piece of advice by the Rangers physio once when I was playing in my first game against Celtic for the club. Remember, in those days we never went out to warm-up. We just went out five minutes before kick-off and played. So, he said to me, 'Go down the tunnel before the game and stick your head out and sample the atmosphere. If you don't, you'll get the shock of your life about what you see and hear, and you won't recover quickly. So, do it'.

With such recently insipid results, by either side, it was probably the general feeling amongst the media that Rangers were only marginally favourites, even though Celtic were minus key players, for reasons of injury and suspensions. McNeill's words of defiance, to counter the odds which seemed to be piling up against him, was balanced by Greig's bold assertion to me that Rangers would not end the season totally barren. It generated an atmosphere on the eve of the game which inspired Ian Paul of *The Glasgow Herald* to write an article infused with dramatic irony:

Such additional pressures, allied to the already terrifying obsessions which dominate confrontations between the teams, would, you think, guarantee a collision which ought to be staged by Mickey Duff [the boxing promoter] rather than Younger's Tartan.

This irony was intensified by the sponsorship of that brewery company, some of whose products were shortly to be used in very imaginative ways by its boisterous clientele. Nobody, though, could have predicted the tumult that would eventually occur. Nevertheless, mentally you were always prepared for any eventuality, for at any moment the event could be stricken by controversy. It was in the nature of the beast. Sitting at the edge of this affair, through the years, there was always the gut feeling that there was a judiciary out there noting every breath you took during commentary, let alone what words you used. I have to record, lest I convey a degree of exaggeration here, that on one occasion I was accused of calling Rangers players by their Christian names more often than the Celtic players. Not a jibe shouted at me from a pub door-mouth, although there were certainly fusillades of those, but from Jimmy Farrell a Celtic director who was then chairman of the Race Relations Board in Glasgow, where I thought there might have been more compelling issues to occupy his mind. That almost sinister obsessive scrutiny made me feel a bit like Winston Smith in *Nineteen Eighty-Four*.

Then there was Waddell. His vitriol was of a different order. It stemmed from an incident at Hampden on a day which should have had the entire Rangers community on cloud seven.

\* \* \* \* \*

It was the Scottish Cup Final of 1973. One which carried special significance. It was the first fruition of a tempestuous but successful partnership with Jock Wallace as manager. It also carried historic significance for them in Rangers' centenary year. It would be misinterpreting history to equate Waddell's relinquishing of management to his coach Jock Wallace in 1972, on the back of winning the UEFA Cup Winners' Cup, as a decline in his influence. He continued to command the corridors of Ibrox, during which period Wallace, as manager, went on to win two trebles in 1976 and 1978, the first Rangers manager to achieve that, and for which he deserves great credit. Although the media did not accord him the deserved merit, partly because we were all still dominated by the presence of Waddell. Any time you were around the club you could sense Waddell, in differing roles, was still a driving force. He had never given up on his desire to see Stein rendered impotent. Stein had mixed ancient admiration for Waddell, as a former great player, with a distaste for his continuing, 'Which school did you go to?' ethos, although at the same time exploiting that tunnel vision to his own advantage. On the other hand, he used to talk sympathetically of Wallace. He knew that the other, the ardent Struth disciple, was not an easy man to get on with. That, perhaps, is slightly understating the matter. However, they brought Rangers to Hampden that year, to face Celtic who had crushed Hibernian 6-1 in the previous year's final, under Stein.

We at the BBC were trying something new. We had brought Billy Connolly into the scheme of things, a lover of Celtic, whose popularity as an entertainer was beginning to swell. From the other side was ex-Rangers captain Bobby Shearer, who quite apart from being a redoubtable full-back, was something of a wit himself, which had turned him into a popular after-dinner speaker. They were beside me in the commentary position, which on this occasion was low down in the south enclosure, to offer us their thoughts before, at half-time and at the end of the game. Cosmetic? Certainly. But, in the sometimes the Grim Reaper analysis of this fixture, which can feel like you are discussing the collapse of society, it was at least an attempt at lightening the potential gloom for some of our audience. Indeed, at half-time I remember Connolly distinctly saying that he didn't need to eat the sandwich the BBC had handsomely provided as he had just devoured his fingernails through tension. As the devoted Celtic man he is, you could understand why. Rangers simply never looked like losing this one.

Sitting in the stand among the directors, Waddell was about to be reminded of the time when, for the first and last time as a manager, he humbled Stein. For he would have been keeping his eye on one of his favourite signings, Derek Johnstone. In 1971 the manager had shocked us all by giving the 16-year-old boy from Dundee his debut in the Scottish League Cup against their great rivals. It turned out to be a masterstroke: with a deft, classic header, the youngster had scored the only goal of the game to win the cup for Rangers. Waddell, at last, had put one over his adversary. Two years later with the score standing at 2-2, in a game which had fluctuated dramatically, there was the same boy, now much more mature, rising to head a free kick. Same action as in '71, same easy leap, same determination, except this time he hit the post. This is what made the resultant goal a collector's item. The ball trundled along the goal line with, it seemed at the time, the pace of a hedgehog trying to cross a road, it was just asking to be run over. First to it was the fierce Rangers defender Tom Forsyth. Except he didn't hit it, he trod on it and almost lost balance as a result. But with his studs on top of the ball he managed to shove it over the line. 3-2. Game over. Cup won. And whilst that was memorable enough, what happened after the final whistle could have been straight out of a pantomime when the villain is booed and hissed as he interlopes on a scene of merriment.

I had turned my back to the pitch at least 20 minutes after the final whistle to interview Billy Connolly and Bobby Shearer and I kept that position as one of our assistant producers hauled the winning manager Jock Wallace into a seat for interview. Wallace was never the most loquacious of interviewees, but he had an obvious sincerity, that made him appear solidly authentic, with his favourite phrase, 'You need character in a team', oft repeated. But, then, midway through the interview his eyes seemed to glaze over and he was now looking past me, not at me. I had no idea what was diverting his attention. He then started to rise from his seat to end the interview prematurely, so I swivelled round to look towards the pitch. There was an enraged Waddell on the track, looking as if several of his blood vessels were bursting. He was continually pointing to the ground in front of him, like a dog owner demanding the pet bring the stick back to feet. I am no lip reader but my rough translation of his lips moving in coordination with his irate body language was, 'Get your arse down here, pronto', omitting the expletives. He was treating his manager in front of press and television personnel like he was a lackey. Booing and hissing ought to have proceeded because he was intruding on Wallace's moment of deserved triumph, in having taken the trophy away from the man Waddell continually obsessed over. The Rangers manager, who had fought and been wounded fighting the Communist insurgence in British Malaya in the late '60s, was clearly acting with enormous self-restraint, when he apologised to us, then sloped off. Apparently, Waddell was looking for him to be presented to Princess Anne, who had been in attendance at the game. It was a master–slave vignette that hinted at even more turbulent times to come. When I approached Waddell later, to explain that he had interrupted an interview that was going out live to the nation, he snapped. His nose was close to mine and I recall him hissing words to the effect that I had become too close to Stein to offer any neutral views about his club. He had dragged me into his principal obsession. It was brief, brutal and from which our relationship never recovered. Although, to this day, I regard him as one of the most significant and influential figures in the Scottish game in the modern era.

The subservient or dignified way, depending on your interpretation, in which Wallace accepted such treatment received an almost poignant underscoring two days later, when in an interview in *The Glasgow Herald*, he spoke of his days in Wallyford village in the east of Scotland, and of how he would ask for a lift on a Rangers supporters' bus heading for Glasgow:

> Sometimes they did, sometimes they didn't. I had this friend and together we had a ball. He stood on the wing crossing them. He was Waddell. I stood and headed them in. I was Waddell.

His boyhood hero had ultimately become his nemesis. In later years, waiting inside Ibrox to interview a player downstairs in the marble foyer, I heard the clatter of voices, like cymbals being struck, coming from the top of the stairs. It was Wallace and Waddell screaming at each other in the landing above. It went on for at least ten minutes before I heard a door being slammed. The voices were unmistakeable, the evidence clear – silverware in the trophy room was no palliative to prevent a stormy relationship. You felt a fuse had been lit for an explosion that would finish only one of them off. Inevitably it did.

\* \* \* \* \*

However, by 1980 at Hampden that day, Waddell was now a peripheral figure. He was now called a consultant, which to many of us felt like he already had one foot out of the door at Ibrox. By comparison with his predecessor, John Greig did not suffer that form of oppression. He was his own man now. Paradoxically, Billy McNeill was developing an unstable relationship with his chairman Desmond White, which, eventually, would run on to the rocks. When I later employed Billy as a co-commentator, his description of his relationship with White clearly did not match the screaming intensity of the Waddell–Wallace one. It was more like that of Bob Cratchit with Scrooge.

So, two of Scottish football's greatest players were now squaring up to each other for the first time in a Scottish Cup Final as managers. It was an appetising prospect for all of us. But given what was to erupt after the final whistle, it was difficult to find the right words to use with them. Days later, asking them what they thought of the game itself, as I had to, made me feel like the person who might have asked, 'And what did you think of the play, Mrs Lincoln?'.

## CHAPTER 5

# Staircase 13

TRYING TO RECALL much of the game itself is difficult for most of us. It is shrouded in the downpouring of images of the riot, smothering many of the game's details, like Vesuvius' ash did for Pompeii. Even for the victors. Roy Aitken admitted to a block in his memory:

> I honestly can't remember much about it. I can recall the 1985 final against Dundee United much better than that. I don't know why that is.

Gordon Smith also treated it like a challenge to memory:

> It's difficult to look back on the game itself. Some games stick out in your mind. But with this one it was like just some few key moments I recall.

David Provan's primary remembrance was of relief when the final whistle went:

> I remember, above all, running down towards the Celtic end with the Cup. That stands out. The rest is blurred.

Derek Johnstone's comment reflected what most people thought of the quality overall:

> I thought it was one of the poorest Old Firm games I ever played in. Only one or two moments stick out like the great chance I had near the end when Davie Cooper crossed to Tam [Tommy] McLean who volleyed it to me. But I mistimed the flight of the ball at the far post, even though I was only a

couple of yards out and it just sailed past. That's about all.

But, of course, after some prompting, they all recall the goal. Who wouldn't in a Cup Final? The unlikely source was Danny McGrain. Unlikely in the sense that one of the best right-backs I have ever seen, harboured no desire to be the nation's primary goalscorer. His wonderful ventures down the right side of the field were characterised by speed, control and vision. But, around the opponents' penalty area, his whole instinct was to be a provider. In 17 years with Celtic he managed only four goals which for a man who invaded penalty areas with unceasing regularity, looks a meagre return. But that bare statistic tells you nothing of the rich harvest his side reaped off his play. That day, deep into extra time, he was sweating. And although everyone on the field at the time remembers the goal, they certainly didn't know what exactly was going through the mind of the Celtic captain, who at that stage in his life was triumphantly dealing with Type 1 diabetes. 'It was hot', he told me:

I thought it was getting to me and I was worried about getting cramp. That's what was going through my mind. We had won a corner-kick and I was well up the field for it. There must have been 20 players in that area. Remember it was extra time and just one goal would do it. Everybody knew that. I was just outside the penalty area myself and I was concerned about what would happen if Rangers counter attacked. There was nobody behind me except Peter Latchford in our goal. Somebody cleared it high out of the penalty area. So, the ball dropped out of the skies towards me. As I say, I was worried about my legs and getting cramp. So, my first thought was, 'How are my legs going to last if Rangers get hold of the ball'. My first instinct was to kick the ball out of the park, get it away from there to safety, anywhere so they wouldn't get hold of the ball. Now, it had been a tiring game, so like everybody else I was suffering. So, when it eventually reached me, I totally mistimed it. Rather than putting it out the park, out of play, anywhere, the ball struck the bottom of my leg and it went towards the 18-yard line. It was threatening nobody. However, George McCluskey was rushing out, just after the corner had been cleared. I saw him sticking out a leg diverting it away from Peter McCloy who was moving in the other direction. He had no chance. I tell you, when I saw the ball landing in the net after just trying to belt it anywhere for safety, I felt I had won the lottery.

Viewers who travel back in time on the magic carpet of YouTube might have looked at that goal and consider McGrain's interpretation of that moment, as modesty taken to extremes because. Even as I recorded it at the time, it looked a direct attempt at goal. 'Danny McGrain's shot', I clearly said instinctively. Indeed, the commentator on our rival channel credited him solely with the goal itself almost immediately. Overall, it does provide a moment of insight into how YouTube can play tricks with history. And, in any case, in all the years of knowing McGrain he has always spoken with absolute candour about anything he did on the field. Like admitting to me a mistake he had made in the Scotland–Yugoslavia World Cup game in 1974, which he believed had cost his team dearly.

The goal was watched high up in a BBC cabin at the Celtic end of the ground by our programme presenter Dougie Donnelly who is heard and seen around the world now on NBC's Golf Channel. He was housed with Jock Wallace and Bertie Auld, in the normal balancing act of analysing. Like his two guests he had been disappointed in the quality of the game, especially as this was the first time he had introduced the Cup Final Special direct from Hampden for the BBC. In a custom I had established in previous years, Dougie had bought a new suit for the occasion. Sunday best was *de rigueur* for the Cup Final. But it had all seemed something of a let-down for the three of them up there, as it dragged itself into extra time:

> I had been getting very little out of the pair of them until that goal went in. Looking down Hampden we had a perfect view of how it went in. It definitely was a deflection. And as soon as it went in, I got instructions to get on to the pitch and interview the winning captain. Little did I think that when I went down there I was about to get a ringside seat of mayhem.

So was Police Cadet Willie McAdam standing at the Celtic end. In later years as a Constable in the Govan district, he was to become friendly with Graeme Souness, sometimes sharing early morning cups of tea with him at Ibrox during his patrols. But he was there that day as a full-blown Celtic supporter. And on the scoring of the goal he became disorientated:

> Honestly, for about five minutes after that I couldn't see the game because of a dust-cloud that arose around us because of the excitement of the supporters dancing up and down on a really bad terracing that had seemed to have worn away with loose bits of concrete lying about.

On duty, PC Tom McLeod, the Rangers-supporting trackside officer at the Celtic end, at that moment noticed something that perturbed him.

> The youngsters right down at the front were being pressed against the 10 foot high fence that had been put up around the track. I began to get concerned about that.

The fence, unlike others in English grounds like Old Trafford, for instance, had no spiked overhang to deter climbing. The top of it was straight and graspable.

WPC Elaine Mudie with her other colleagues had just mounted their horses again which was the normal procedure about 15 minutes from the end of any game. Having heard the roar from inside, she did notice something:

> It had been a long wait. Then I saw some Rangers supporters leaving from the back of the stand and I just assumed it was all over and we could just supervise everybody leaving. Usually that would be no problem. Except eventually there was a hell of a noise still coming from inside and it seemed to get louder. It was unusual.

Match Commander Hamish MacBean was in radio communication, issuing instructions to his officers in different parts in and around the stadium. When the goal was scored, he alerted everybody to the expected mass evacuation of Rangers supporters. He had already deployed his resources to where he thought they would be most needed before the end of the first 90 minutes:

I was very happy the way things had gone although I had my reservations about the overall resources I had at my command. All we had to do now inside the stadium was to prepare for the cup presentation.

Which is exactly what we were preparing for in the BBC team. Perfectly straightforward. Rangers up first. Then Celtic for the cup itself. Twelve cameras had been positioned around the ground, including the pitch-level camera following Dougie Donnelly who had rushed from his interviewing position to reach pitchside for interviews. The goal itself was being replayed over and over again to the viewers, and as it was being analysed by Wallace and Auld, I couldn't help but think that posterity would identify this final only by one of the least glamorous goals in the stadium's history, and the final would recede into almost obscurity compared to other Celtic triumphs. That thought didn't last long. For that thought was before Danny McGrain ran with the cup to the east terracing to greet his own supporters, many of whom were kids pressed up against the high restraining fence around the track.

That he managed to break into a trot given the immense mental and physical effort he had put into the 120 minutes of play, which caused him to worry about cramp, only shows that triumph packs its own adrenalin. Nevertheless, looking down on the baking terraces, we were already missing a factor which had been staring us in the face. The guzzlers. Hugh Keevins, who was on one of his first assignments with his new paper *The Scotsman,* recounted that,

> as I travelled out to Hampden from the centre of the city you could see that all the traditional Celtic and Rangers pubs in the southside were packed. They were all sitting or standing outside in the glorious sun drinking heavily. The booze and the heat. What a lethal combination. That really did strike me at the time.

\* \* \* \*

It is not as if the authorities were ignorant of the potential trouble caused by drink. I recall the efforts that were made to counter that toxic factor through the years, but with little effect. As I reflect on that gloriously sunny day at Hampden it is nevertheless a winter's day that comes pushing its way into mind. The authorities had reached the conclusion that an Old Firm match on 1 January, after Hogmanay celebrations, when many might find it hard to remain vertical, was an intrinsic part of the problem. Tragically, this only led to a change of date. It was 2 January 1971.

New Year's Day had fallen on a Friday in 1971, but the game was to be played the following day. Tinkering with the calendar was about the best Scottish football could come up with to dampen passions fuelled by drinking. Admittedly, dealing with that state of spiritual and physical exhaustion on 1 January is an art form which few master, leading some of us to toy, temporarily, with the notion of total abstinence. Perhaps sobriety was imposed more by nature than anything else that day, for the weather was liverish itself. It bore a funereal greyness with a spectral mist hanging over the city. This did not augur well for the match because the Govan district of Glasgow, beside the River Clyde, could well have claimed to have been the world's cradle of fogs. To add to winter's dominance an overnight frost had set in throughout the land and hardened grounds everywhere.

In the light of subsequent events it is very difficult to avoid looking for portents, accentuating the wintry bitterness of the day, let alone that which existed on the opposing terraces. And yet with an eerie sense of foreboding, *The Glasgow Herald* of that very morning had produced an editorial, the main thrust of which was an expression of relief at having got 1970 behind us. It described the old year as

> a year of disasters including earthquakes in Peru, death and destruction on a monumental scale in Pakistan, a terrible fire at a French dance hall, and the loss of the Fraserburgh lifeboat.

No prophecy was contained, but in the reading of those words that morning, one might have been forgiven for feeling immensely secure in engaging in nothing more adventurous than going to a football match.

In a sense I was glad I was to be indoors on a day that would have chilled you to the marrow. I was to introduce the Scottish edition of *Grandstand* from the studio later that afternoon, with that ancient mariner, ex-sea captain George Davidson on the commentary platform at Ibrox. I never actually got to that studio.

Late in the afternoon our ears were to the radio, since no pictures were being beamed straight into Broadcasting House, and from it came the sound of a breakthrough at Ibrox. Celtic had scored with only a couple of minutes remaining. Jimmy Johnstone's goal. I imagined that at every sports desk around the country would have been concocting lyrical praises for another late and spectacular Jock Stein triumph. Until there was another blast from the radio. Rangers had equalised within a minute. Then, within seconds of that, the game was over, with the Head of Sport at the BBC at the time prancing around the room with gushing relief, as if divine intervention had allowed Colin Stein to equalise in the last second of the game. As we hurriedly tried to digest this, I went about my business preparing a script for the start of the programme. I can't recall how many minutes I had pored over this when I heard Frank Bough on a television set beside me announce that he was being informed that two deaths had been reported after that day's game at Ibrox. Everything stopped. We listened. Nothing of verification was coming from radio, the reason for which we couldn't fathom at the time. But we still churned on with our work, although with an air of mystery now suspended over us. Then came the words, which were uttered with an almost stunning ferocity, even though Bough spoke them in measured tones. Firstly, he said he wanted to correct that first report from Ibrox that he had read out. Then there came the words which enveloped the office in an eerie silence:

We have heard that many people have been killed in an accident at Ibrox. Latest reports say 22.

It was difficult to take in. My first thoughts were that there must have been a donnybrook, that the tribes had got at one another, even though Bough had used the word, 'accident'. It had to be that. What else could it be? Then, within the next 15 or so minutes, more information led us to believe that something calamitous had occurred within Ibrox. And, even though it still was not fully clear what had happened, the news began to worsen with Bough stressing that there were very likely to be many more fatalities. The mood in the office changed. Within about five minutes, before we went on the air, we decided to cancel our Scottish edition. How could we talk about football when it had been confirmed that we had a major disaster on our hands? This would have to be left to hard news reporting by other colleagues in Broadcasting House. For we had heard nothing from any of the BBC personnel at the ground itself. We had a whole television broadcasting team out there, but there came not a single word from any of them. Not even from the radio commentary team which had been broadcasting throughout the entire game. Why not? It was like a security blanket had been thrown over the entire area. Of course, there was a reason for this, which turned out to be one of the bizarre aspects of this tragedy, as we were to learn later. To this day I am unsure how *Grandstand* got their information out so quickly. It was then decided I should get to Ibrox, like a 'bat out of hell' I recall the editor saying to me.

I have had many bizarre taxi rides in my day but none as surreal as this one. Even before the advent of the smartphone and the internet you could get startling information flowing from a driver, given the potent grapevine that operated among the cabs, almost uncannily, throughout the city. You could get the latest on the stock exchange or hear who was sleeping with whom, depending on the driver you got. So, ironically, I found myself as a representative of a famous broadcasting institution, meant to be fully in touch with events, quizzing the driver about what he had heard, given the frustration I was feeling about being largely in the dark. He said one sentence to me which I cannot put out of my head even yet. 'Staircase 13. Lotta folk deid.' That's all. But they're still lodged with me. Silence after that, as my imagination ran riot, not really knowing what I would have to face up to when I got there. I had only been dropped off at the front entrance of the stadium only a minute or two before Jock Stein emerged, pale-faced, to confront a posse of the press. He was brusque. I recall him brushing past a journalist who had asked him something, not too coherently, about the game itself, to be reminded, bluntly, that there were people lying dead inside. Perhaps the most stunning post-match comment Stein ever made to the press.

Even bracing myself for what I might see inside, didn't prepare me for witnessing bodies lying in the track at Ibrox. It was bit like the sensation I used to experience when I would walk into the waters off the beach at Gourock as a boy, and when the iciness of the waters reached your midriff, you felt the breath was being taken from you. An icy numbing. But once you were out at Gourock you recovered quickly enough. Not this time. This creeping sensation lasted for months, every time the images forced their way into my mind. Many of the dead had blackened faces, as if in their death struggle for life they had been touched by some macabre cosmetic. They had been fighting desperately and unsuccessfully for air to breathe. They had taken some of the injured into the dressing rooms where the players had to make a quick evacuation, which was described to me later by Sandy Jardine:

> We were in the bath enjoying ourselves after getting the late equaliser when Jock Wallace came in and shouted for us to get out, there was an emergency. But even before we could start drying ourselves, they were bringing in the injured. In just a few minutes the floor was covered with people just lying there moaning. You would have thought there had been a war outside. Then we heard about the dead. We just went home, numb.

It was inside Ibrox that I began to learn of why there was such poor communication back to Broadcasting House. The accident had occurred on a far corner of Ibrox, on the staircase on the backside of the terracing. The radio commentators had simply wrapped up and left as soon as the game was over. Only one BBC reporter remained in the press-box, but he was high up on his own, at the opposite end of the ground where the tragedy happened. His remoteness in an almost empty press-box meant he knew nothing of what was occurring on that distant staircase, completely out of his view. An entire BBC outside broadcast crew, technicians, cameramen and director were stationed outside Ibrox at the Celtic end, where there was ample room to park large vans and well away from what was occurring at the Copland Road end. They had simply packed away their gear innocently and arrived back at their storage base in East Kilbride, entirely ignorant of what had occurred. One of Scotland's major newspapers, the *Daily Record*, was on strike, and had their usual journalists been around a great deal would have been clarified much sooner. However, John Burrowes, then news editor of the paper, decided to go out to Ibrox, to put together a report for that week's *Sunday Mail*. He had just returned from Vietnam after a tour of duty, but even he, hardened by the daily witness of the awfulness of war and the frequent sight of napalmed bodies, was peculiarly affected when, afterwards in a hospital, he saw one man bending over his dead friend, saying over and over again:

Jimmy, I promise as long as I live, we will never go to an Old Firm match again. Jimmy, I promise. I promise.

By that stage we all knew that 66 people had died. It was many months later that I received a graphic description of the aftermath, within Ibrox, from Detective Superintendent Joe Beattie, the man who had led the hunt for the notorious Glasgow murderer who even yet goes under the name 'Bible John', and who had gone home from the game, like many others, completely unaware that a tragedy had taken place. He then received a call from the Chief Constable of Glasgow, asking him to get back to Ibrox and take charge of the investigation. He had policed Ibrox many times before as Superintendent of the Govan Police office when attendances at Old Firm games were around the 80,000 mark. The traditional repercussions of those games made him a busy man, because almost inevitably often hundreds were arrested on a single day. Indeed, he used a phrase about Govan police station on those days, which I will never forget. He said, 'It was an area of mass sub normality'. But this was a change of circumstance. This was different. On Staircase 13 he found stark evidence of the spontaneous, violent force it had been subjected to by the crush of people exiting the ground. The central steel railings running down the middle of the staircase had been twisted in such a manner that they looked as formidable a buttress as burnt-out matchsticks. He was aware too of the historic record of accidents at the ground. In 1902 a collapsed stand resulted in 26 deaths and 550 injured. In 1961 crowd crush on that stairway led to 2 deaths and 50 injured. In 1969 a crowd crush on the stairway saw 24 injured. And now 66 dead and over 200 injured. This was all on his mind as he made his way towards the Ibrox boardroom.

It was in disarray. His first impression was that the directors were like 'headless chickens', as he put it, not knowing which way to turn and actually trying to distance themselves from the event by simply not talking about it. One director, who used to play junior football with Inspector Beattie, kept on reminiscing about their time in the game together. The policeman, to an extent, understood how shock can disorientate people, make them lapse into denial mode and that not talking about it would help. But he was anxious to get on with his first report to them, particularly wanting to know what matters had been taken in hand over the previous accidents on that same staircase. He was becoming impatient as they were all very vague about the previous police inspection of that staircase some months earlier. Nobody could remember who had accompanied the police on their inspection, and Joe Beattie was gaining the impression that some immediate buck-passing was going on. Then came clarity. Into the breach stepped Willie Waddell. Beattie immediately realised that the man from the dugout was now head and shoulders above the rest of his directors who were now looking like survivors in a lifeboat seeking rescue from anywhere. Waddell was now fully in charge.

What Waddell was to accomplish from that evening onwards would clearly identify him as a man with vision, of self-belief, of a determination to modernise the club, however flawed it might yet turn out to be under his tutelage. In my view he was no match for Stein as a tactician or motivator. But what he was forging from then on, was at a different level from the Celtic manager. He was now becoming more entrepreneur than football coach. No other person in the club at that time could have achieved what he did. Waddell was Rangers' salvation. He started by rallying the public, as the late Sandy Jardine explained to me once:

> The manager was brilliant. He did everything. I don't think he slept for months. He couldn't have with the amount of work he put in. We were all organised to go to the various funerals and to visit the injured in hospital. No training was done. The whole experience drained us. Then, when we played our first game back at Ibrox weeks after, it was like being in a trance. The atmosphere was unreal.

There was a postscript to the entire day which pained me, in a bizarre way. It made me realise that there were, within the hierarchy of the BBC at the time, lofty grandees who had no conception of how important football was to many of their own viewers, even to the extent of an insensitive disregard for the nature of the tragedy. For in a discussion, late that evening, when we were trying to decide what to show on the programme, given that the editor and I had decided the game itself would never be shown by the Corporation, and it never has been, one executive, believing our reaction within in our department to be excessive, asked me. 'How many were at the game?' 'Eighty-thousand,'

I replied. 'How many died?' he asked. 'Sixty-six,' I replied again. He paused then said, as God is my witness, 'Sixty-six out of 80,000, not all that many, is it?'

Over a year later with that question still ringing in my ears, with haunting regularity, I read the report which Lord Wheatley produced on the back of the disaster. The Safety of Sports Grounds Act of 1975 from which the report sprung, was well-meaning but legalistic, with glaring loopholes, but at least emphasising the need for grounds to be licensed by local authorities. This would mean that money would have to be spent on ground improvement especially in means of access and egress based on the horror of Staircase 13. How many clubs had the wherewithal to make significant changes? And how had all this affected Hampden in terms of security and safety on that sweltering day in May?

* * * * *

The one thing which was entirely noticeable was the 10-foot-high fence which had been erected around the track in 1976 to adhere to UEFA regulations, and particularly for the European Cup Final between Bayern Munich and Saint-Étienne of that year. And behind the fence, that day in 1980, was a crowd of 70,303, which was about to demonstrate beyond any conceivable doubt, that the wintry day of 1971 with its appalling disaster and the human toll it extracted, shaking the country to its core, had contributed nothing to snuff out the flames of sectarian hatred. On that bright day in May, few retained memories of the unprecedented gestures of Celtic and Rangers players signing autographs for fans after a memorial service in Glasgow Cathedral. Nor had it sunk in that Rangers players had attended a requiem mass in St Andrew's Cathedral and that a priest who had won thousands of pounds on the pools donated a considerable amount of money to the Ibrox disaster fund. All mere flimsy and fading postscripts, virtually dissolved by the passing of time and the resilience of intolerance. So once again on 10 May 1980 it was a time for the twinning of triumphalism and anger.

That fence, which Danny McGrain and some others of his players had advanced towards and which separated them from exultant fans, had already been shown to be entirely vulnerable. Long before kick-off we had been treated to a pre-match invasion; a warm-up that the police ought to have taken to heart. For not long after the gates had opened and the crowd admitted, some very young Celtic supporters managed to get over the fence, with green balloons, to frolic harmlessly on the edge of pitch. This was immediately followed by a response from the other end with Rangers youngsters scaling the fence, then running the full length of the pitch to chase their rivals off. All this so-called frivolous activity was being cheered on by the so-called more mature adults higher up the terracings, in a tit-for-tat rehearsal for what occurred later. To any mind, mature or otherwise, that fence was now demonstrably inadequate.

So McGrain and his colleagues were understandably anxious to show their appreciation of the support they had received through this long afternoon. And, equally naturally, that crowded terracing was in the mood for more intimacy with their players. Many of them were streaming down the terracing to get as close as they could. Some were trying to scale the fence, and I can recall, in the first instance, some bodies balancing themselves on top, like they were in troop training, before dropping over on to the track. But only a few. A trickle. Exuberance was beginning to banish any reservations about getting over the wall and the numbers began to increase. Not yet hundreds, but the potential for a deluge. Then came an intervention which to this day has not been fully appreciated, nor even officially recognised. It was made by one of the few men in Hampden that day who hadn't actually seen the winning goal being scored.

## CHAPTER 6

# A Financial Behemoth

PC TOM MCLEOD, as a football fan himself, was certainly interested in the game and its outcome. But duty called, so he kept his back to the play throughout as he surveyed the sun-drenched faces of the Celtic legions massed on the east terracing. Self-denial came with the job. David Bruce, former Chief Inspector of Hamilton and Match Commander at Fir Park, was at his first Old Firm game at the age of 18 and was standing in the south-west enclosure at the other end, simply as a fan. He certainly knew what that self-denial meant to a policeman. It was about keeping your wits about you. He spoke of an Old Firm technique:

> One of the worst experiences I ever had was at my first Old Firm game on duty. It was on 29 August, the first meeting of the 1987–8 season. Souness was sent off for a foul on Billy Stark. Well, there were about 400 cops on duty and nearly 200 arrests. But you wouldn't have known it was happening. It all looked orderly throughout. I was standing in the middle of the old Jungle at Celtic Park. Now you couldn't look at the game. You had to stand back to back throughout the match, for if you stood with your back to the crowd for too long, you would come out of there with spittle like phlegm covering your uniform.

His colleague McLeod, being on guard in textbook style, was nevertheless now feeling anxiety about the perimeter fence. He had seen young faces pressed against it from the outset. I remember as a kid being carried over the heads of the crowd, like in pass-the-parcel, until I arrived trackside during big games at Hampden. It was the accepted ritual when the stadium was a massive canyon of a place with over 100,000 at big games. McLeod, in future life after he retired, was to find himself in the area of juvenile crime, helping to prevent further offending by those he counselled in a disadvantaged neighbourhood in the city of Glasgow. On that day, by contrast, he was concerned about innocent young faces whose only excesses were adulation of their heroes. He felt distinctly uncomfortable:

> With the terracing in a terrible state there was a ready supply of rubble to pick up as ammunition. Missiles were being thrown occasionally from the older supporters at the back, near the end of the game, and they were landing in among their own supporters. I just didn't get it. Stones, bits of cement, things like that. You couldn't dare turn away from that. And then I saw a danger sign. After the Celtic players had come up close, the kids at the front were being pressed against the fence and I could see the panic in their faces. Apart from anything else they were trying to get out of the way of the missiles being thrown.

Remote as I was, from the commentary box I could still make out the logjam of bodies pushing towards the fence waiting their opportunity to get over. I certainly knew nothing of McLeod's next bold action. He recalled:

> I decided to open that gate beside me or else there could have been some serious damage done. I then dragged out one kid after the other, maybe about a dozen or so, but down came another surge, and scores began to get through. It was then I noticed that the other officer, further round the track, had taken his cue from me and did the same. Then the invasion was unstoppable.

McLeod is adamant that the action he and his colleague took, which certainly made it easier for the ultimate invasion, nevertheless prevented something potentially much worse. You need only look at two simple but crucial sentences from the Hillsborough report 32 years later, on the deaths at that FA Cup semi-final, to comprehend the validity of his action that day:

> There was a small *locked* [sic] gate at the front of each pen. The crush became unbearable and fans collapsed underfoot.

An avoidable tragedy on a massive scale unfolded at Sheffield Wednesday's ground that day. We cannot draw too many parallels with what happened in that English stadium, as conditions were certainly not totally similar, but it is conceivable a serious accident might have occurred had McLeod not opened that gate. The instant decision he made to open it, on a fence which was supposedly constructed to prevent such invasions, and then help drag kids out, was, you could claim, almost a heroic act. The fact that it was based on simple common sense could in no way detract from the way he acted under great pressure.

The first few hundreds were now on the pitch though. More were following. The entire east terracing seemed swarming with the desire to celebrate on the turf itself. I felt no alarm whatsoever at that stage. But I was puzzled as to why the invasion could not have been stopped, little realising that one humane act of a single Constable had coincidentally eased their passage, and that there had been a meagre police force down there anyway.

As soon as the Celtic players became aware of the presence of scores of their own supporters around them, they took off, as David Provan explained:

I vividly recall us close to the supporters, just to thank them for their support. But when so many began to come on, not with any malice aforethought, but just to celebrate, I think it was John Clark, Celtic's assistant manager, who said, 'We'd better get back to the dressing room'. But, as I went up the tunnel, I saw the pitch was beginning to swarm with supporters. That was the end of it for us. Honestly, I can tell you I knew absolutely nothing about what happened. You might not believe this, but I tell you I didn't know there had been a riot until I got home and saw it on the news.

Gordon Smith was so dejected at losing that he simply turned himself off, blanking everything:

I heard nothing, saw nothing. I didn't even look at the pitch when we went up to get our runners' up medals. I didn't know what had happened until I saw you talking about it on television that night.

Derek Johnstone did witness the start of it. He had gradually become aware of something special going on outside and went upstairs to the presentation area to look out on the milling throngs:

> I actually started to worry watching it. It's the first time at a football match I actually felt frightened because it passed through my mind that some of them might try to get up the tunnel and into the dressing room area which they could have done easily because I barely saw a policeman among the crowd.

Roy Aitken saw nothing after the cup presentation:

> I just went home. Honestly, my memories are hazy about the game as I said, but like most of the others I only saw the scenes later that night on the box. But there was one thing I kept asking myself and still do. Why were there so many Rangers supporters left in the stadium to have had the numbers to come back on the pitch? Surely there was enough time for them between the end of the game and the cup presentation and us going on the pitch, just to go, leave?

It is something echoed by Dougie Donnelly, close by the tunnel:

> It really was surprising how many Rangers supporters were still in the stadium. I mean after a team is beaten the fans usually just leave. But there were thousands still there even after the cup had been presented. That's something that puzzled me.

The response to that comes from the Match Commander, MacBean, drawing on his long experience, who analysed it this way:

> The winning goal came in extra time. Since there was only one goal in it, the Rangers supporters clearly hung on hoping for an equaliser, right through to the final whistle. Remember, it takes some time to clear a large attendance from a ground the size of Hampden, given the care that was taken after the Ibrox disaster. And yes, there were supporters making their way up towards the exits. I could see the gap between that movement and some of the young ones near the bottom just hanging on, defiant I suppose.

Although we could not have realised it at the time, one innocent celebratory gesture by the Celtic players was to catapult Scottish football into a new dimension of legislation. Willie McAdam, amidst the rejoicing Celtic fans, also recalled that crucial moment when his blood ran cold:

> I always remember the tension there was from the very beginning among the Celtic support. They were unusually subdued, not much singing, no great amounting of shouting. Real tension. I think maybe because of how they had blown the league. Honestly, there was none of the atmosphere you normally experienced at an Old Firm match. The fear was we were going to end up with nothing that season. I think that's what even lay behind the explosion at the end. Relief as well as anything. It seemed good-natured at first, and when we saw Celtic supporters getting on to the pitch my mates decided they would like to go on as well. We moved down the terracing. But when we got near the fence, I decided that it wasn't for me. I had been accepted as a Police Cadet and I just felt it wouldn't be right to do that, since the police down there were really up against it now. I definitely had sympathy for them. Then, out of the corner of my eye I saw the first Rangers supporters coming on at the other end, and I thought, 'Oh, no! Here we go!'.

Dougie Donnelly was at first so intent on doing his job that he did not see that first break-out:

> I had come to the pitch of course for interviews and then suddenly I felt, something is going wrong, badly wrong. Even though I was talking to McGrain I was aware of the pitch getting crowded. Then a steward grabbed me by the arm and told me to get up the tunnel for safety's sake. By that time the fans were close-by and I could see some skirmishing going on And as I heard you say in commentary, where were the police? There seemed so few of them. Right away, as it developed, I knew fine well this would now be a major international news story.

The Celtic fans were now deep into the Rangers' half of the field. They were getting closer to where David Bruce was standing in the south-west enclosure. What followed was to remain vividly in his memory, even though he was to face a much worse tragedy in his professional life. He was one of the first policemen to get to Lockerbie after the tragedy there, where he saw sights of victims still strapped into their passenger seats, propped on the roofs of the town. That permanently scarred his memory. But it has not blurred his recollection of that final. He and his mates felt that the advance of the Celtic supporters would trigger a reaction and decided they wanted no part of it. But not before they saw hostilities becoming vicious. He was stirred, almost poetically, as missiles began to take flight from around him at the Rangers end. As he put it:

> It was like that scene in the film of *Henry V* when Laurence Olivier as the King gives a hand signal and suddenly huge flights of arrows fly through the air at Agincourt.

To me, perhaps less poetically, the bottles were flying like flocks of starlings suddenly scared off a city building, for the battalions were now into unbridled collision. It was then that Hamish MacBean had made his clarion call throughout the city for immediate assistance and added to me, on reflection:

> From then on you had to keep your eyes on the sky. Anything would come down on you.

Tom McLeod was now on the move with his handful of colleagues:

> We were told to retreat from the fence and take up a position in front of the goalposts for safety's sake, because the missiles were now coming from everywhere. Then, when the Rangers supporters came on in big numbers, we were told to retreat to the centre line. Some of us facing one way, some the other. But, honestly, it was a very thin blue line.

Outside Hampden the horses had remained calm and idle, insulated from events inside. Then different sounds emerged. WPC Elaine Mudie began to sense a change in atmosphere:

The four of us has just patrolled around there at the front of the stadium waiting for the crowds to come out at the end of the game. There had been about 20 horses on duty that day, but they had been dispersed around other nearby areas especially to the train station at Mount Florida to help with the crowds which would obviously congregate there. I didn't have a radio, but I could hear others getting calls, and I saw this colleague I had been talking to reaching down to his left side where we have a long baton in a sheath. He was taking it in and out, the way we were told to practise before we would need to go into action with it. We had to make sure we could pull it out easily. Then he told me it looked as if we were actually going to ride on to the pitch and I started to laugh because I just couldn't believe it. Taking horses on to a football pitch, even to me then it just sounded so daft and I actually had a slight giggle about it. But not for too long. For our leader, Chief Inspector Hogg, sobered us up all right with the command 'Right! We're going in!' I really did feel a bit nervous then, thinking I wasn't going to like this. But off we trotted, two in front, two behind. Not really knowing what to expect.

From my high vantage point, the first Rangers terracing response had been sporadic. Then their first patrol got over the fence and secured itself just behind the goal at that end, and this encouraged others to follow. I could now see them flowing down the terracing with a reckless bravado. There was no one there to stop them. They seemed to mass behind their own goal before gaining confidence to launch their first assault. Although this was now scarcely believable, I had to take a grip of my senses and try to make something of a scene which now was beginning to look, from on high, like armies of ants scrabbling over a few crumbs on the floor. I have to emphasise that I arrived at Hampden that day armed with the usual clichés to describe and comment on a football match. Now, below me, was urban warfare. The transition was not all that easy. It was like a bassoonist turning up for an orchestral performance and then being expected to play first violin. In any case, even in the spontaneity of my response, the basic rule of thumb was keeping in mind the simple fact that viewers could see for themselves what was going on. The pictures themselves were telling graphic stories which required only an occasional intervention. But when they came, they had to count.

The Celtic supporters had innocently wished to salute their heroes, but they were now quite clearly into traditional goading as they advanced further. Although I cannot recall it myself, since there were now so many on the pitch prancing around in all directions, and making it awkward to focus on one particular area. Hugh Keevins, for *The Scotsman*, did spy something that pinpointed the extent of the Celtic advance:

> One youth clad in Celtic's green-and-white hooped strip appeared in front of the goal behind which the Rangers fans congregated. From somewhere he produced a ball and 'scored' a goal to the delight of his compatriots... that was the signal for the balloon to go up.

There had been a considerable reaction before that single incident, but the 'goal' was obviously not meant to placate the sloping terrace, still populated by a dejected, and now incensed legion. They accepted that gesture as an invite to join the party and responded, 'in kind', as MacBean succinctly put it afterwards. Thereafter followed a series of thrusts and counter-thrusts; an ebb and flow of sprinting figures with first one side then the other claiming territorial advantage. I saw bodies falling, heads being held in agony, kicks being aimed, occasional figures crumpled in a heap, and I recall the bottles which missed their targets bouncing merrily off the hard Hampden pitch as a reminder of how good the weather had been that day. But it wasn't only bottles. Tom MacLeod had identified that earlier. Weaponry was more varied than simply bottles. In fact, the stadium itself was providing them with some equally lethal ammunition. One man in the presentation area knew this better than anyone else; a man who regarded Hampden almost as his personal fiefdom, but who exactly 28 days later would receive news about the stadium which would affect him like a death in the family.

*\* \* \* \* \**

Ernie Walker, secretary of the SFA, knew Hampden was crumbling. Slowly. Inevitably. Broken bits of concrete lay about handily. PC Tom McAdam had already been the recipient of some of it during the

86

outburst. Walker was fully aware that for seven years there had been an unequal stand-off between the valiant Queen's Park officials, proudly sustaining their amateur values, and various public bodies, like the Westminster government, whose indifferences were turning this grand old place into a financial behemoth. The stadium required massive funding for radical reconstruction, quite beyond Queen's Park's financial capabilities. Hampden Park Ltd, had been set up as a cooperative effort by various agencies, including the SFA and the Scottish Sports Council, to encourage government funding that hopefully would amount to 50 per cent of the whole project. Meanwhile, it was as if both the public and the media were treating the ageing stadium like a failing family octogenarian, whom you visit from time to time, only to lend moral support. At the same time criticism of the dear old place was mounting.

The Old Firm, in different eras, dragged Hampden into their perpetual tug of war for dominant influence. Separately, and then eventually in tandem, their desire was to replace this stadium to the betterment of themselves; in effect, for the Scottish public to abandon Hampden. The predominant role was taken up firstly by Rangers, and then with equal enthusiasm by Celtic in later years. It was as if they were both jostling for poll position to deliver a fatal blow to an institution which on 10 May 1980 was certainly displaying some stark inadequacies. Accustomed to sitting on high on a television platform, I admit I developed an indifference to the plight of the average supporter, some of whom had to adopt the skills of the mountain goat to negotiate terracing that was disintegrating in places, particularly at the Celtic end. But still they came. That was all we cared about at that time. No matter that as you approached the stadium you were made to fear a moderate south-westerly could bring the whole edifice tumbling down. Willie McAdam's description of the 'dust storm' provoked by the Celtic goal illustrates accurately the potential dangers of a terracing with collapsing concrete steps and broken pieces of wood, all exposing the unsafe gravelly-footing underneath. The situation conveyed something of stasis in the Scottish game, of the inability to understand the importance of supporting a national focal point, as club football, particularly as Ibrox and Parkhead was flourishing through European competitions.

Nor was the national agency, the Scottish Sports Council, all that concerned. Set up to foster sports development throughout the land, its priorities lay principally with the so-called minority sports, underpinned by the general assumption that football, our national sport, as it were, could look after itself. Six years before that 1980 Cup Final day, in the spring of 1974, as a member of the Council, I attended its general meeting in the Beach Ballroom in Aberdeen and listened, as plans were being established to send representatives to the Commonwealth Games in New Zealand for a general inspection of its organisation and facilities. Not a word about Hampden and its state of dilapidation, until the meeting was about to close. Suffering a mild dose of astonishment at that apparent indifference, I hurriedly interjected under Any Other Business and pointed out to those shuffling their papers, getting ready for a quick exit, that there was a World Cup in Germany opening in a couple of months. Would it not be a good idea to send Council representatives to Germany and look at the newly built stadia there, which might provide ideas for a new Hampden, if ever anybody got around to doing anything about it? A freebie trip to Germany? They jumped at it, as I knew they would.

Some weeks later, on the eve of Scotland's opening game against Zaire, I met two Council members in Dortmund, the chairman at the time, and a colleague who was ex-RAF. They regaled me with some odd views they had of the world, including emitting a sudden paean of praise for German efficiency, as we mapped out their visitation of the various stadia. And guess who they thought exemplified the best of Teutonic values? None other than Adolf Hitler. I listened in disbelief. Here was a chairman of a public body and his colleague, who once had worn the Queen's uniform, lending praise to one of the worst creatures of the 20th century. It was an interlude which nagged at me for some time, as it was difficult to square this dark sophistry with a proposed period of Scottish football enlightenment. But at that stage, I was more concerned about preparing for a World Cup, hoping that, despite my distaste for the pair of them, they might actually come up with something productive. So, untidily, I put that conversation to the back of my mind as we looked at the pristine modern stadium of Borussia Dortmund.

Signal Iduna Park had been constructed into a box-like shape which conveyed a feeling of spacious intimacy. Stunning. They were impressed. So were others, including Rangers general manager Willie Waddell. What emerged from that visit, months later, were plans which offered three possibilities for a new Hampden: a mini, a midi and a maxi model. All three of these designs, with potential costs, were then touted around civic and political circles for years. Eventually the government relented and promised to dig into its coffers and assist. Almost exactly a month after the hordes had mounted their invasion of the stadium, on the morning of Friday 7 June 1980, the Scottish Sports Council and the SFA were informed that £5.5 million would be granted by the government for reconstruction. Devoted as he had been to fighting to achieve this, Ernie Walker was, as Socrates would have put it, 'over the moon'.

By midnight of that same day the offer seemed in great jeopardy. Unofficially a dead-duck. Gone, like a Tommy Cooper vanishing trick, but without the giggle. To me it always reads like a sordid tale which had the dramatic conclusion of a stiletto being stuck between the ribs in a dark alley. Walker's ribs, no less.

The climax had been at a boxing match that evening. It was a night when the glitterati of Scottish sport and the cream of the media were ringside to watch and report on Jim Watt defending his world-lightweight crown against Howard Davis Jr of the USA. On a drizzly night, I remember a steward handing around leaflets to the press before the contest. It contained a statement by the Rangers chairman, surgeon Rae Simpson. The Under-Secretary of State for Scotland Alex Fletcher had been a guest of Rangers that evening, and we had to conclude he had not been there to advise on transfer policy, for what we read was nakedly political. It was, in effect, telling the government not to waste its money on Hampden and that the continuing modernisation of Ibrox could conceivably allow it to suffice as a surrogate national stadium in future. On the one hand this seemed eminently sensible. Rangers were ploughing on with the project to make Ibrox the most modern stadium in the UK. And, of course, at one period, they most certainly achieved that. In strict commercial terms they were fully entitled to maximise the benefits from their asset, as Celtic would theirs, in a similar manner, in another decade. But the way in which political influence had obviously been sought by Rangers at the time – and the willingness of a free-marketeering Thatcher government to save a few pennies, and then withdraw their offer, at the chimes of midnight – seemed like a pronouncement of the death of Hampden Park. Although the official government announcement did not appear until ten days later, we all knew it had abandoned Hampden that night at Ibrox.

*The Glasgow Herald* chose to 'bury' this development on page seven of their broadsheet, devoting more space on their front page to Jim Watt's triumph in the ring. They did so with a quote from Rae Simpson saying simply, 'We are not campaigning for Ibrox to be the next national stadium'. Although further down that article they reported that Rangers were set to

> rebuild their centenary stand at a cost of £4 million. It will be based on the same design as the two stands built in the last two years and will make Ibrox Scotland's premier stadium.

You do not need to be shot through with cynicism to work out that, even by default, Scottish international games would most likely gravitate towards Ibrox, because of its then unparalleled modernity. Whatever interpretation you could put on it, Hampden, without financial support, was finished. I felt at the time, frankly, that the stadium had no future. Playing international games on a rotational basis around the country made financial sense. And, I noted the headline on the front page of *The Glasgow Herald* on 18 June 1980: 'HAMPDEN CASH GOES TO INDUSTRY', over a report that

> The £18 million needed... is to be spent on industrial regeneration in the West of Scotland.

God knows where it was actually spent. But it could not remain simply a governmental issue. It became an Old Firm one, inevitably.

For into the breach leapt Desmond White, chairman of Celtic. He went straight into attack, in a statement reported in the Glasgow *Evening Time* only two days after the Watt fight:

> Rangers do not seek the goal of Scottish football, but only a personal advantage – they want the top matches for Ibrox. The mumblings of advantage to others is only a camouflage of Rangers' real intent – personal profit.

Forty years later that scathing attack was dropped into the historical waste-bin when Celtic perfectly reasonably promoted their magnificent stadium, which hosted the Opening Ceremony of the 2014 Commonwealth Games, as a positive alternative to Hampden. There was little thought of charity on their minds. Anybody, like myself, who approved of a common sense and financially prudent rotational idea for the national side's games were seen to be really supporting Rangers in their bid to outsmart the other side of the city. It was another example of how you had to live with the most lurid of interpretations of your views from one side or the other. And in any case, through the years I did a huge about-turn on Hampden, stressing its neutrality in our deeply divided footballing society. And, on 10 May, Hampden seemed to be using its very dilapidation as a source of ammunition, to the dismay of the onlooking secretary of the SFA.

*****

Although Ernie Walker had no telepathic communication with me at any time, I feel assured now that at the height of the fracas he would have been doing exactly as I was at that juncture – starting to count the suffering casualties we could clearly see on the Hampden pitch. I found myself trying to make some measurement of what was to be the outcome. At a rough estimation it looked like a scoring draw, to put it in a way that they themselves would have understood down there. There seemed to be parity of injuries. Unless there was going to be a dramatic intervention, which at that stage seemed remote, would all this run out of steam, or would it end up in some sort of carnage, with one lot claiming supremacy? And in any case, who were the real aggressors? The Celtic fans, who converted justifiable celebration into a parade of mockery, or their counterparts at the other end, where a sizeable number gave the impression they would grasp at any excuse to get at their hated rivals? These questions, even yet, still hang in the air and are plucked from there depending which end you supported. But it was not only the slender police force who could possibly provide answers. The press cameramen, the 'snappers' down there with cameras, right in the thick of it, capturing the scenes for posterity, looked to me like their adrenalin was pumping so strongly that, with the opportunities of getting pictures of a lifetime, they had left their nervous systems outside in the car park.

# CHAPTER 7

# Toxic Anarchy

TO THE HUGE television audience and the affronted dignitaries and the indignant journalists and commentators, all of this looked like some kind of shipwreck. But, to the snappers, it was a shipwreck with gold bullion in the hold. Which self-respecting press-photographer would not have wished to be there, up to their necks in the turmoil, their shutters blinking remorselessly, capturing the myriad of violent images coming out of what they had previously thought would be plain sailing on a placid sea? Indeed, any photographer worth his salt would have known of Robert Capa, who snapped one of the great images of conflict when he captured the moment a Republican militiaman was gunned down on a battlefield during the Spanish Civil War. A startling image that was either a product of momentary genius or just the damned good luck of being in the right place at the right time. Or both. After all, he had held the camera above his head when he took it and had no idea of exactly what he had captured. But, from what I could observe, looking down on this scene, all of the snappers looked as if they could have been following Capa's maxim, 'If your pictures aren't good enough, you aren't close enough'.

So they were in the thick of it. Fully exposed to the toxic anarchy. Now, obviously, aiming a McEwan's Pale Ale bottle at somebody's cranium might not carry the same romantic cachet as the gunning down of a man in Andalusia. But for a photographer, the principle was the exactly the same. The challenge was to frame a picture of something special, something that would startle the onlooker because of the unexpected and alien nature of a battle being fought on a football field. It lent itself to capturing the extraordinary for posterity, and every photographer there was now in the hunt for exactly that, despite the risks involved, under a sky clouded with missiles.

Twenty-two year-old photographer Donald McLeod, newly appointed *by The Scotsman,* had joined the Edinburgh-based newspaper after working for the *Evening Express* in Aberdeen and was about to undergo a baptism of fire. Without wishing to discount the value of working in Aberdeen he now realised, as the scale of the explosion sucked him into activity, that he was now into another loftier dimension of his trade. His learning curve was to have the shape of the face of the Eiger. He was also discovering an almost spiritual belief in coping with hostile conditions, camera in hand:

> I was learning you live in your own wee bubble at these times and you find that you're less worried than perhaps you should be. It's all so surreal. You go into autopilot and you try to take images that reflect exactly what happened.

When the first invasion occurred, he took up his position right on the halfway-line but several yards on to the playing area itself. The scene was fertile territory for his favourite Nikon camera, with a constant swirl of action around that made him feel he was in the vortex of the action:

> What was happening in front of me then is exactly the kind of event any journalist would love to have covered. Quite surprisingly, right out of the blue, here was I having started my photographic career in Aberdeen, where there never had been any challenges remotely like this, and now I was watching Neanderthals knocking lumps out of each other at a football match. It was ferocious but with a curious mix to it. There were some celebrating on one side and the other side seemed to have a 'Gerrintae them' attitude.

He was tense and alert, and was entitled to be so, since his 'Neanderthal' analogy would probably have received some sympathy in a court of law. The invaders were now potential assailants. He saw a respected colleague, Kenny Lennox of the *Scottish Daily Express*, being attacked by a supporter who objected to being selected for publicity. His assailant had not reckoned on a camera being of more use than simply taking pictures. Lennox wielded his expensive and probably well-insured Nikon like a sledgehammer, and felled him with it. The camera survived, but, alas, painstaking research has not revealed the fate of the attacker. Perhaps Lennox was unfortunate, because in general the persistent danger to the snappers was not direct attack, but the random use of missiles of different kinds.

Stan Hunter also of the *Scottish Daily Express* was a victim of one of the most bizarre incidents. He had been in the midst of the battle, witnessed bottles striking heads and was on guard against such an assault. Suddenly he was struck from an unexpected source. A wheelchair. A supporter was on the field with an invalid sitting comfortingly on the chair, but it was being propelled like one of these Panzer tanks that almost thwarted the Americans in the Battle of the Bulge. It struck him amidships, although there is no record of what Hunter's reaction to that was. He still continued to snap.

Like Donald McLeod, nothing was to stop him in his work. He was able to capture a particular image which, compared to others he had captured, lent a droll alternative to the turmoil:

> I snapped a policeman trying to catch this supporter, who at the same time was trying to dodge away from him. They were in front of each other dummying one way or the other, and what I captured was a picture of two figures apparently jiving to music.

But the photographer could not fail to notice that the greatly outnumbered police looked to be chasing shadows. There seemed to be many uncoordinated pursuits of individuals, largely because he couldn't see too many police about. He doubted if the authorities were making any impact at all on the pitched battle.

PC Tom McLeod was now part of what he describes as a 'rather thin blue line', critically referring to the paucity of uniforms on the pitch. They were spread along the centre line, battling against the odds. He was suddenly faced with a situation that was almost farcical, were it not for the fact that there were victims of various assaults all around him:

> I saw this Rangers supporter running towards me and I got ready to take action. He suddenly stopped and looked me in the face and said, 'We're only on to give you a helping hand'. I told him to get outta there or else he'd end up in jail. He got off his mark.

Why not just arrest him? Remember if you arrested somebody, it would take two of you to take him to the charge bar. With limited resources the policy was quite clearly containment and clearing the pitch.

PC Willie Allan and his colleagues, who had instantly responded to the call for assistance, had now struggled their way onto the playing area itself. It had taken them longer than they had imagined to get through the crowds, and felt they were perhaps too late to make any material difference to what was going on:

We got in and I tell you it was raining bottles and cans. And I really believe they must have taken crates of beer on to the terracings. I don't know how, but that's what it seemed like, because there were so many coming down on us. It was really difficult to move further on. And of course it struck us right away, there weren't as many of our colleagues there as normally would be at an Old Firm Cup Final. Now, there was an overall plan for such contingencies. It was something I had to plan as a Match Commander myself in future years. If there was a pitch invasion, you would congregate your resources in the middle of the park and then work your way outwards. But on this day it was well beyond us being able to do that. So what we did was just chase people just to get them off the pitch. I'm sure the bosses who were there just saw it as making sense.

Of course, ultimately, there were many arrests.

PC John Staunton, on duty at the Celtic end, was a loyal supporter of that club, and felt so incensed at seeing his fellow fans pouring on to the pitch that he felt he had to resort to something to try to clear them off. He knew his baton was going to be ineffective, so he improvised. He pulled out one of the corner flags and started to lay about him with little compunction, clattering anybody in sight with what has always been seen as an innocuous artefact in the football culture. He could claim a policing first for that, and at the same time raising the question, could all the police be like him, utterly non-partisan in times of these conflicts?

It might sound a preposterous question, but one I have heard raised subsequently in that prolific Old Firm rumour factory, within which the police were perceived as an overwhelmingly Protestant organisation, leaving you to draw obvious conclusions. Who were they particularly chasing in fact? In the chaos, even if you had wanted to pursue a conspiracy theory, you would not have been able to tell. However, in seeking some clarity about this, PC Tom McLeod lends, at the very least, a practical analogy of a potentially instinctive partisan effect that actually rendered both him and his colleagues perplexed and somewhat amused.

> We were on duty at Celtic Park one day. There were eight of us in our group, four of the constables were Celtic supporters in fact. The other four were for Rangers. After the game, groups of both Celtic and Rangers supporters began a fight as they walked away from the ground. It became so serious so we decided we had to intervene. We gave chase and made arrests even though the groups had separated and were making off. When we came back with the folk we had arrested we discovered that the police who were Celtic fans, had arrested Rangers supporters and the Rangers sympathisers among us had Celtic fans under arrest. Work that one out.

It's an equation that could fit any conspiracy theory. But Hampden that day was so confusing there was no trail of arresting that led anywhere conclusively. This was clearly recognised by photographer Ian Torrance, working for the *Sunday Mirror*, who could see that all was chaos. He had started at the Rangers end, behind the goal where he left his equipment in order to join the posse of photographers following Danny McGrain with the trophy. Suddenly he realised that his gear would be exposed to the supporters who were starting to climb over the fence. As he hurtled back to recover it, the bottles thickened in the sky. He was running straight into a blitzkrieg:

> That's when it was getting very dangerous and I suppose I was fortunate not to have been hit. But I could see around me people who had been. And of course there were sectarian chants being shouted which was kind of stupid since the other lot at the Celtic end couldn't possibly have heard them. In any

case I wasn't put off or terrified I just kept working away and there was plenty to see. And yes, I saw some casualties who seemed badly hurt.

Many were already being treated by ambulance workers who certainly required the same nerve and disdain of danger as the photographers around them. Tom Donaldson, Deputy Commandant of the Scottish Ambulance service, was on the terracing at the Rangers end when Celtic scored the winning goal. He had been dealing with a lad who looked to have twisted his ankle, which was not the most surprising injury of the day, given the occasional bouts of hysteria which can break out on the terracings. It was then he became fully aware of a change in the atmosphere, especially when he saw Danny McGrain taking the cup to his supporters at the other end. He felt a surge of anger growing around him:

> The bottles started. They were coming down from behind us and were actually hitting their own people. It just didn't make any sense. So, after we had tended to this lad, we went back on to the track and then positioned ourselves in the goalmouth and kept our eyes on the surge of the crowd coming on all sides. We felt the net would give us some protection.

Out of approximately 60 of his colleagues, who were in teams of four circling the track at the start of proceedings, Donaldson was one of the most experienced. He had been at the Ibrox disaster tending the injured and had also helped to carry bodies on to the track after. He insists the images of that day do not haunt him, horrendous though they were, but they are nevertheless still vividly there; particularly his final view of Staircase 13:

> When we had taken everybody out of there, I looked down the staircase. It wasn't empty. There were jackets, scarves, shoes, bits of torn clothing just lying in a heap. And all down the stairs the mangled metal of the central barrier which had collapsed. It was all a bit like a jumble sale.

If anything had prepared him for a riot at Hampden it was that experience, because the ambulance volunteers found themselves being swamped by a mounting total of injuries:

> Some had injured themselves just by climbing over the fence. And then the bottles flying anywhere were taking their toll. And not just that. We saw what looked like bricks being used. Where the hell did they get them from? So we were dealing with serious cuts and bruises on the heads and hands in the main. A lot of blood about though. One or two had fainted and I remember one man had a fractured ankle down near the corner flag that we had to deal with. But thankfully, no matter how much anger there was out there, nobody attacked us. And that was helpful because, honestly, we were being swamped by people needing immediate attention.

Digging into my own recollections, and taking into account every-thing that occurred, I seem to have sensed a peak to the battle, a point in which you felt this could really get out of hand and that somebody out there could get killed. I could see some hand-to-hand wrestling going on but primarily the missile-throwing seemed to be self-perpetuating. A flight of bottles would be met by another. That was going on in droves. And, since there seemed to be plentiful ammunition to hand, the idea of a possible fatality down there was passing through my mind. Hyperbole being a commentator's frequent companion, an image passed through my mind which fitted the bill, or so I thought at the time. From my lips came this analogy, 'This is like a scene out of *Apocalypse Now*'. It was a subliminal response to Francis Ford Coppola's film, which had hit the screens a year before. It is now rated by *Sight & Sound* as the 14th best film ever made and is preserved in the American Library of Congress for its cultural significance. It is sometimes forgotten that it was based on Joseph Conrad's novella, *Heart of Darkness* – an expression I could equally have used for the scenes below me. *Apocalypse Now* made a huge impact on the public. All the knowledgeable cameramen at the BBC raved about the superb cinematography employed in the battle scenes, especially the flight of the helicopters going into battle to the accompaniment of Wagner's *Ride of the Valkyries*. Below them was a vision of hell. As was mine at that moment at Hampden. And I suppose at the time I didn't realise that there was a possibility that a single sentence could attach itself permanently to the event, like a password you could use to gain instant access to the memories of that day. Perhaps for some it has.

It was uttered with a degree of disgust at watching the casualties mount, some kneeling holding their heads, others lying on their sides with mates hovering over them, some still active but with blood on their faces. It wasn't any easier inside the stadium walls, in the ambulance room, which had never been designed for such a massive emergency. Even when the injured were being treated by the medical team they were still trying to attack each other and some had to be roughly handled to avoid any more blood flowing. Outside, with little sign of the clashes abating, Donald McLeod was still in the thick of it. Then something stirred him:

I heard this rumble but I just didn't know what it was until I saw it. It was the police horses coming on.

At long last. Match Commander McBean had been suffering acute frustration. Given the fact that the basic strategy had catastrophically failed, he realised that the mounted branch could be their saving grace, and his plea to them could only have been with tones of desperation. This was reflected in what he admitted to me many years later:

I sent out that command but the problem was getting the horses into the stadium through the two entrances at each end of the grandstand. They were being blocked by huge numbers of people, either trying to leave or just hanging about there. I don't know how many minutes it took for them to get on to the pitch, maybe just several minutes from my call. But it did seem like an eternity at the time.

What gave them confidence to enter the fray? Curiously, and perhaps coincidentally, only an hour before the game, Inspector Hogg had given an interview to Iain Gray of *The Glasgow Herald* about the tradition of the mounties, stating:

We find that horses are invaluable in crowd control situations like riots. In some countries, however, horses would not be acceptable and tear gas would be considered more efficient. I have also found that very few people are prepared to harm a horse. In fact, there have been many times where we have had to rescue a fan from others fans, after he had struck one of our horses.

His notion of Glaswegian tolerance to the species was about to be put to the test. The horses entered the stadium calmly, and on his command they proceeded four abreast to appear more formidable, and by that action announce their presence in a dramatic way. To WPC Elaine Mudie it was as if the weather had changed and the sun had been blotted out:

Honestly, I thought it had started raining. The sky was filled with missiles of all sorts. Remember I was just 21 and a bit naive. To me it was a horror show. It was hard to take in. There were fans and some police running about everywhere. You're trained for this though. You go into autopilot and get on with it. Now when we first appeared on the pitch a story eventually got around that I had led the charge.

Watching from where I was that did seem to be the case. Not so, as she explained:

The truth was that Ballantrae was hit in the backside by a toilet roll and it bolted. If you could have put my words in a bubble above my head it would have been, 'Whoa, stop!' because I couldn't hold him back. So, on I went. And I tell you I was oblivious to colours. It didn't matter to me whether green and white, or blue. They were just all thugs asking for it.

So, the least lethal missile thrown at Hampden that day had accidentally propelled the woman on the white horse into the public eye, with a sudden spurt that could have been accompanied by the cry of 'Hi ho, Silver', had there been a single soul there in the mood to make light of the reckless mess. But, there wasn't much levity about. The mounties were now intent of creating order, but four horses amidst this cauldron of unmitigated hatred was not enough. With a bigger number, they could have made a straight charge. What they found themselves performing was a kind of vacuuming process, sweeping over parts of the pitch, shoving at groups, showing more muscle than their outnumbered colleagues on foot. But they were finding it difficult to keep in formation. PC McLeod, still battling against the odds, was clearly delighted to see the reinforcements. He offered unstinting praise for the way the Glasgow police horses were trained in crowd management:

> My worst experience personally in a crowd at a football match was at Liverpool's ground for the famous Scotland–Wales game which qualified us for the World Cup in Argentina in 1978. Now I'm 6-feet but I was lifted off my feet by the police horses they used in Liverpool. Their technique was different down there. They didn't funnel a crowd into queues to get into games, and shape the crowd in an organised way, as our mounties do up here. They just jammed us against the stadium walls that night, and the pressure was so great I thought I was a gonner. They do things differently down there. We've got the right techniques in my view.

What the four mounties were doing was playing for time to an extent, waiting for additional resources which had now been called for by the Match Commander. Then they would launch a stronger line against the throngs. In any case, out of the sheaths came the batons. WPC Mudie recalled using hers for the first time ever:

> At first I wasn't sure whether I was to use it or not. Then I saw the Chief Inspector using his so I felt it would be OK for me as well. I really gave some of them a right banging. I had to. They either just fell over or ran away. But in honesty I don't think we hit all that many because the threat was enough. You know the horses' presence did have an immediate effect in itself. Just seeing us ready to go at them.

True. I could see the crowds scattering, not departing, just spreading out a bit more in ripples that didn't take them back over the fence, at least at that first entry. Our own BBC cameras were obviously in more static positions around the stadium. But, even though nobody had officially told me, I knew that our cameras were picking up marvellous panoramic views of the maelstrom which would be now watched by more than a domestic audience. Experience had enlightened me to the narrow, metropolitan ways of our BBC network colleagues in London. The FA Cup Final which they had been covering, and in which West Ham had beaten Arsenal 1-0, to become the first club outwith the topflight to win it, had long ended. Their interest switched to Scotland only for one reason, the riot. Of course, any sports or news editor anywhere in Europe would have done so, given they had access to the pictures, which very quickly became available everywhere. But I knew in the south they would be treating this as some kind of snapshot of Scottish delinquency, which hurt me more than anything else, even as I was describing it. I was fully aware that some of the senior sports management in London lent the impression we still painted our faces in blue woad. This annoyance of mine rose as our cameras were now focussing particularly on the horses, with inevitably the woman in the saddle startling people with her own dramatic invasion. For in the public's eyes, Elaine Mudie had crossed into a strongly perceived male preserve, with panache:

> I saw this officer wrestling with a ned on the ground. I was heading straight towards them. I shouted on him not to move, but he did. Unfortunately. As he dragged the man backwards I couldn't change my direction quickly enough. I rammed him. He went flat on his back. And would you believe I had just knocked out a police inspector.

It wasn't until later they realised that her colleague had broken his leg and ended up in hospital. Almost exploding into Hampden came the rest of the cavalry, including another two more women WPCs, Janet Messur and Mary Glen. They had galloped there from all parts around the stadium. WPC Mudie felt relieved:

> It was great to see them coming in. We now had about treble the force of mounties on the pitch. You could tell the very sight of extra horses coming to our support put the fear of death into some of them. But we still had work to do to clear the pitch.

I could see the gradual build-up of this new force at one end of Hampden. You could tell it was a well-practised manoeuvre, smooth, unflurried, brimming with serious intent. They could hardly disguise that they were now about to enact something quite dramatic. For suddenly a broad line of 12 horses galloped, batons raised, straight down the pitch. The effect was spectacular. It was like watching a glass plate being dropped suddenly from on high and the fragments flying everywhere. The tribes were fleeing as if for their very lives.

This was historic. It would ultimately be recognised as the first time Glasgow mounted police had charged a crowd since Black Friday of 31 January 1919 in George Square, when they ruthlessly attacked striking workers. This time, in 1980, it was purposeful, uncompromising, but I suspect less bitter than the previous one, which had clear political overtones. But it was certainly working. And now my mood had changed. I was actually beginning to be enthralled by the spectacle. It was like I had just been dropped into a mediaeval pageant. Nothing in the game itself could match the stuff of pounding hooves, batons waving, bodies falling. Somehow or other I began to feel I was watching the main show, and a game of football had merely been the warm-up act. The Scottish Cup Final match itself was now at the very start of a gradual process of being eclipsed into eventual oblivion. The separation of the factions could clearly be identified now, with the mounties pushing the Celtic supporters back to their own 'territory' and then turning in the other direction for another sweep to mop up the remaining detritus of the battle.

Unfortunately it had come too late for one man in particular; a man who had followed Capa's photography maxim to the letter, and had taken his camera up as close to the action as he could practically get. Thus, Eric Craig, Mackinlay's Whisky Photographer of the Year, was repaid for all his efforts with a half-drunk bottle of bubbly Pomagne, which plummeted from the heavens and landed directly on his skull.

## CHAPTER 8

# European Invasions

ERIC CRAIG WAS considered by his peers to be at the top of his profession. I knew him from working through the years at so many similar venues, including all six World Cups for which Scotland had qualified. I had enjoyed one or two libations in the company of Eric and his colleagues in those days, seeking refuge from the hazards of trying to make sense of Scotland's quixotic record in these competitions. By 1980 he was working as the principal sports photographer for the *Daily Record,* whose circulation at that time was in the region of 655,000, reflecting the days when some people would actually go out at midnight to buy the earliest editions of newspapers, such was the appetite for the printed press. There was fierce tabloid competition with the *Scottish Daily Express,* the formidable rival of his newspaper in that era, although I never saw much hostility between the respective photographers. There seemed to be a calculated camaraderie among them. So many people around the country would have seen the product of his skill in the pages of the *Daily Record* over the years as he fitted the needs of a popular paper perfectly. Skilled photography, after all, can induce people to read even the densest of text.

But you have to wonder if much of the wider public really knew what this man meant to photographic journalism. He was no ordinary photographer of sporting action. His picture of the boxer Walter McGowan doing a somersault in the ring after winning a title, was nominated for a Commonwealth Press Award in 1963 and was placed second in a fiercely competitive field. But it was never just a case of knowing how to handle the apertures of a lens. A sense of cunning, or timing, was useful if you pursued exclusivity, the holy grail of tabloid journalism. Despite knowing there might be trouble about snapping the irrepressible Jimmy Johnstone in a rowing boat after his embarrassing jaunt in the Clyde without oars just before the World Cup in Germany in 1974, and with the SFA hoping the press would keep quiet about it, his photograph revealed all, exclusively. He got it because he had taken the initiative to get to their hotel on the Clyde coast before any of his rivals had appeared. He knew there might be consequences from the SFA, but he was steeped in the aggressive culture of a publishing organisation, one of whose executives, Hugh Cudlipp, had published in 1953 a book using a title that became a clarion call for a bold free press: *Publish And Be Damned!*. So the image, to the envy of other photographers and the anger of the SFA, was splashed in his newspaper.

But, to uphold that blessed virtue, there had to be hard grafting. Craig rose through the ranks in a non-digital era when a photographer's role involved incredible efforts to get material on to the newspaper. Nowadays it can miraculously travel straight from a camera directly to a page. But in 1974 at the World Cup in Germany he was involved in an effort to get essential portraiture back to the *Daily Record*. The narrative of his efforts to succeed in that, has distinct echoes of a John le Carré plot, with added touches of farce. His newspaper had struck a deal with the Scottish players for a strictly exclusive squad photograph in their World Cup gear. The players, led by feisty chief negotiator Billy Bremner, could not agree the terms and stalled on the deal, until the players were actually in Germany within days of the tournament starting, where they eventually relented. To his disgust, as a perfectionist, Craig had to set up this session in the hotel with a sense of urgency, with little preparation, and in a cramped room with quite inadequate lighting. The players were squeezed in and the photographer did his duty, as best he could. Speed was of the essence now. His instruction was to fly from Frankfurt to London with the film and hand it physically to anyone on the next flight to Glasgow, explaining to them to pass the film, in a small package, to a *Daily Record* representative waiting at the airport. Craig spotted a girl heading to the departure lounge. She was wearing a distinctive red coat. That clear-cut identity seemed ideal. She smilingly agreed to help. So, he handed over the film, informed his office what he had arranged and returned to Frankfurt on his essential World Cup duties.

Back in Germany he was pleased with his laborious slog of a day. That reverie was interrupted when he received a call from the Glasgow office to tell him, in no uncertain terms, that no girl with a red coat had come off the London flight, and where the hell was the film, for which undoubtedly the newspaper had paid handsomely into the players' pool. He had no answer to that and panic ensued. Loss of face is sometimes more wounding than a wasted investment in that industry. The word would get out to their gleeful competitors, and it certainly would put the players' trust in the newspaper in some jeopardy. After hours of frantic calls throughout Europe they received a response. It came from the Metropolitan Police in London. They had the film. They had found it in the possession of a drug runner they had just arrested before boarding a flight to Glasgow. She was a girl in a red coat.

The photograph did eventually appear, but the story of how Craig had accidentally picked a drug-cartel mule, out of all the people in a crowded Heathrow Airport, was unsurprisingly binned.

\* \* \* \*

That bottle at Hampden on 10 May 1980 had felled one of the industry's notables and the news of his injury spread rapidly. His colleague Ian Torrance was informed by a rival: 'Eric's been hit'. Ian went in search of him, even as the field was still an area of confusion:

> He was being tended by an ambulance man just behind the goal at the Rangers end. I got a shock. Blood was streaming down his face but he was fully conscious, although really looking the worst for wear.

That man tending him was ambulance man Tom Donaldson:

> I suddenly recognised who he [Craig] was since I had met him at so many games around Glasgow. I was in nodding terms with him because he was so well-known. And yes, this was the most serious case we had come upon. He really had been hit badly on the head and we did all we could to clean him up. But it did look very serious.

As Craig looked at the dark bottle lying innocently by his side, he realised that it was probably one of the most lethal objects that could have travelled through the air. It had a thick glass base and still contained a substantial amount of the elixir. It could have felled an ox.

For the first time in that entire afternoon he had been forced to stop snapping. Around them supporters were beginning to disperse more quickly, but that did not allay the anxiety Torrance felt about his close colleague. The problem was that Craig showed little sign of leaving the area, even though having had treatment, blood was still pouring down his face. Craig does clearly remember though, the route that eventually put him in that painful cul-de-sac:

We were allowed to tour the park with the victorious team after the cup presentation. That had been decreed. So off we went. Now in those days we just didn't have what is common now, digital long-lenses that can provide close-ups from a distance. We had to be right up with them. So I was actually doing a lap of honour along with the team. I can't remember exactly when the first bottles started flying, it was just that I suddenly became aware of it and I started to keep one eye on the sky while I was working away, getting a lot of good shots and honestly I never thought for a moment about the danger involved. I just kept working on. And I was everywhere, all over the pitch and I thought I had got through it all right, because the mounties in particular had made a huge difference and they seemed to be getting order on the park at last. So I was just winding up. That's when I was struck. And it wasn't even a decent bottle of booze that got me. I just got down on one knee and felt my head. I suddenly realised there was a lot of blood there.

Tending him with all his expertise in dealing with injuries, Tom Donaldson nevertheless came to the conclusion that he needed medical attention and advised Craig that at the very least he would need to get stitches for the wound in his head. After Donaldson left, his colleague, Ian Torrance was keen to get him straight to hospital. But Craig was, at first, hesitant about that for a reason that still puzzles him.

'Curiously, although I had been stunned, the pain then wasn't really intense', he recalled,

but, importantly, I hadn't lost consciousness. As I learned later, if I had passed out, then it's possible, because of the actual serious damage, I might have become paralysed, or even died. But what

I did tell Ian, right away, was that there was something wrong with my hearing. Despite the turmoil going on all around me everything had become strangely dulled.

At that stage he was in no fit state to think back and analyse why he had ended up in hospital. A bottle had put him there, of course, but why had all this been allowed in the first place. He had in mind the police. However, he is still able to talk about them without a trace of bitterness. But certainly with regret. Logically it was their apparent lack of preparedness that had put his life in some jeopardy. That's why he was lying on his back in an ambulance heading for an unknown fate.

As we talked together in later years about the police policy that day, another image emerged almost spontaneously between us. Another day of turbulence lodged in both our memories. Craig and I had been at another venue, doing exactly as we had been doing that afternoon in 1980, when the police in a foreign place seemed to have a policy which was both mysterious and almost malevolent. We found ourselves reminiscing about another final which was to be utterly overshadowed by subsequent events. We had both witnessed in our different areas of work, inside a famous Spanish stadium, an experience which elicited from him the words that applied equally to that European night as to that afternoon at Hampden. 'Let's face it, the police got it badly wrong.' Eric Craig and I were thinking of Barcelona 1972.

\* \* \* \*

It all happened before Franco's downfall. Spain was still in the grip of dictatorship. Particularly oppressed was the Catalan population of Barcelona. Not that the evidence of this was highly visible to tourists along the Costas, who in any case were anesthetised against any scrutiny of the political system by drowning themselves in Cuba Libre, and that raging firewater Fundador, which could stun the brain for only a few pence. We all entered this marvellous city under a false prospectus. Barcelona seemed so awesomely handsome and welcoming. But, two years before this Scottish influx, Amnesty International had put up posters at airports in all parts of Europe, showing imprisoned faces on a backdrop of sandy beaches and blue skies. The National Union of Mineworkers had urged its members not to holiday in Spain. Few paid attention. Cheap access to the sun and the pouring of alcohol into glasses the size of goldfish bowls put paid to any moral uprising on the beaches against the ever present *Guardia Civil*. Many of the Rangers supporters who flooded into the area could well have been part of the huge growth in tourism from the UK that had bolstered the regime's finances in the few years previously. To a good proportion of them this area wasn't entirely alien. Lex McLean, for instance, the highly successful Scottish comedian and devoted Rangers supporter, always holidayed in Sitges, a resort only a stone's throw from Barcelona. But, that year, those Rangers fans were to learn in the most dramatic way that the Spanish hand reaching out to greet the visitor sometimes wore an iron glove. Rangers, on the fringe of possible European success, were certainly not escaping the parochialism of Glasgow just by passing through customs. There was that other matter. Lisbon. There would be comparisons, one occasion set against the other. It would be Barcelona v Lisbon.

The other side of the city had travelled to the Portuguese capital and turned that European Cup Final, five years previously, into something akin to a revolution in European football with ensuing celebrations in the Estádio Nacional that looked like a new monarch had gained the throne. How could that be matched? Underneath all the razzmatazz of reaching a European final, that parochial challenge could never be shooed away. Even though a European Cup Final was the secondary European tournament, it was clear Rangers had the opportunity to make it an achievement that was the equal of any. In tune with a good result the supporters would make it appear so. They had seen the Celtic support frolicking merrily on the Lisbon turf. They were after the same. The players knew that, and the inescapable thought went through some of their minds, they dare not fail. So despite the cosmopolitan context, the Old Firm nexus was clearly in evidence throughout the whole stay. Just as in the past in Europe.

For only six days after Celtic had lifted the cup in Lisbon in 1967, Rangers played Bayern Munich in Nuremburg in the European Cup Winners' Cup and lost narrowly 1-0 to an extra time goal. A German official actually said, of the Rangers performance, that they weren't just playing against his team, they were playing against Celtic as well, because of that stunning victory in Lisbon. In the German's view their rivals had put an extra burden on their shoulders which had proved too much for them.

It was very much the same in Barcelona in 1972. Rangers had won nothing that season. Celtic, on the other hand in 1967 had cleaned up everything domestically. And importantly Celtic went into their final against one of the great names in Europe, Inter Milan. Had they failed, it would not have ended the Stein era, merely stalled it. In short, they gave the clear impression they were relishing the role of playing audacious new kids on the block. That also excluded that hackneyed notion that they had nothing to lose. Simply, they exuded extraordinary confidence in themselves which you could almost reach out and touch. In their grand hotel outside Lisbon they gave no hint of being overawed by the occasion. It was also helping that the real pressure was on the team which had established *catenaccio,* and who were certainly favoured as winners throughout Europe. Rangers, by contrast, had looked stale by the end of that season, finishing in fourth place in the league, a whole 15 points behind their great rivals. The thought of defeat was more a conscious undercurrent. That was an important difference from Lisbon. I sensed this by having been close to the teams in their respective hotels. In Barcelona the media were making a kind of macabre joke. They had learned that in April 1972 the famous Hollywood actor George Sanders had committed suicide in a luxurious hotel in Castelldefels, just outside the city. The media hoped that the Rangers manager, Waddell, wouldn't contemplate such a way out if his team failed to beat the relatively unknown opposition, Dynamo Moscow.

Let us remember, Waddell was under great pressure which was starting to have an effect on him. He had taken the Ibrox disaster in his stride, bore the responsibility of handling everything connected with it and now was facing the possibility of a defeat in Europe on a grand stage. He also knew his old friends in the press would garrotte him if he failed. At one point in these few pre-match days, I recall having a conversation with Alex Cameron, now of the *Daily Record,* over a couple of Carlos Primeros. We both shuddered about the prospect of what might happen if they lost this. Booze and defeat. It didn't bear thinking about.

On the eve of the game, the city had given us a foretaste of how rowdy Barcelona could be. Part of the USA Mediterranean fleet were on shore leave and were seemingly trying remodel the city. In the narrow lanes leading off the famous Las Ramblas we saw police, and their own American shore-patrols to be fair, wading into groups of white uniformed sailors, who if they weren't being flattened, were vomiting indiscriminate plumes around the cobblestones. There was a certain relish in the baton swishes of the police which suggested that in their spare time they might be into sadomasochism. They certainly wouldn't be into turning a blind eye even to litter dropping. It was scary.

When we arrived at the stadium hours before kick-off, in broad daylight, many Rangers supporters were strolling around the pitch with impunity. Hundreds of them. Unaccountably, our commentary position for this particular game was down near pitchside rather than up high. But, at least I was right behind the very obvious hierarchy of the police, who looked completely unconcerned about this mild pitch invasion. You could see maw, paw and the weans bedecked in red, white and blue strolling over and around the pitch, as if they were there to simulate the Spanish evening tradition of *paseo*. So, at the outset, the police had established a condition of tolerance which was to be utterly deceptive. In the Estádio Nacional there was a considerable police presence; the Chief of the Public Security for Lisbon is quoted in the David Frier and Pat Woods book, *We'll Always Have Lisbon*, as saying:

We are calling in the crack police guard, the reputation of the Scots' exuberance has preceded them to Lisbon.

They had a plan mapped out and were prepared for some disorder. All I saw, around the Estádio Nacional, were smiling and generally corpulent officers with gun holsters, looking like giant carbuncles, but with no hint of menace. In Barcelona the police, as we will find out, operated on a hugely different policy, which had nothing to do with stadium control in itself. And, significantly, unlike the Lisbon police being from their own region, in the Spanish city the men ringing the Camp Nou were not Catalans.

It all seemed so civilised and chummy at that early stage. Preparing for commentary, I knew that the Scottish public would be making comparisons to that other event five years previously. The Barcelona final had little chance of competing with what we saw in Lisbon, played in glorious afternoon sunshine, in a stadium which looked revamped from a structure the Romans had left behind, all white and sparkling. The Barcelona final was held under floodlights in the evening, and in the vastness of a stadium that lent the impression it was cloaked in darkness. Lisbon had had a sheen that Barcelona simply could not match. The Portuguese venue might have been picked out by a theatrical impresario for a special staging, the Barcelona venue looked conventional by comparison, no matter how significant this game was. Then there was the other absolute contrast which tormented and frustrated us at the BBC in Barcelona.

Celtic's defeat of Inter Milan was shown live to Scottish viewers. Rangers' game against Dynamo Moscow was not. At that time the dogma of the SFA was that if there was a game of importance being played in Scotland on the same evening, then there would be no live transmissions of any other. Scotland were playing in an international that night at Hampden, and although we were virtually on our bended knees, like condemned men pleading for clemency, for the ban to be lifted, we were dealing with the secretary of the SFA, Willie Allan, who, as apparatchiks go, could have flourished inside the Kremlin. This decision not to show the game live looked like a downgrading. The whole BBC team, especially myself in the commentary position, faced the frightening prospect of covering a game whose outcome would be known before it hit the screens back home. This was not just an ordinary highlights package of several minutes, which I knew how to handle. This was a whole European game to be kept in cold storage until the final whistle. It cast a pall over us. Supposing Rangers were defeated. The recorded game would be watched only by their own masochists and Celtic supporters. It was like feeling you were entering a 100-metre dash wearing shackles around the ankles.

At first it seemed that Rangers were making this easier for us, since they went three up in the game only four minutes into the second-half, so the cup looked clearly theirs. We had noted though that after each Rangers goal there had been invasions of hundreds of their supporters, without any sign of interference by the police to stop them. All they did was gently shepherd them off. And then it became bizarre: the Russians scored twice, after which, with only seconds left, the referee blew for an infringement which the Rangers support thought was the end of the game and invaded, for the fourth time. It should not have been allowed and they had plenty resources to stop it. So what did that reluctance to act do? It simply gave licence to the Rangers fans who wanted to emulate Lisbon. The police were simply onlookers at that stage. But, in fact, they did have a strategy. One that was well known and feared by

Catalans throughout the city.

It came to our attention this way. The final whistle did eventually go, with Rangers, on tired and shaky legs winning 3-2. The crowd did come on, in such numbers that the players were swamped. I could vividly recall the invasion in Lisbon to set against what was about to occur. At that stage I could see no difference in comparison with post-game celebrations in Portugal. In the Estádio Nacional the police made the judgement that nothing could be done to stop the flood invading the pitch, and that taking chunks out of it for souvenirs was a price worth paying. So they let them be, even though in Dr Salazar's dictatorial regime the police were not noted for leniency. Indeed, the authorities came to me to make an announcement to my compatriots, on the PA system, to ask the Celtic supporters to please vacate the pitch, which had as much chance of succeeding as my asking them to sing, 'We'll Guard Old Derry's Walls'. The Portuguese got it right, they let them be. In the Camp Nou that night, by contrast, I could see the massive crowd which had now filled the pitch in front of the cup presentation area was faced by a line of police with batons at the ready. The supporters wanted to see the presentation of the cup, which the police obviously thought, for some bizarre reason, should not be allowed until the pitch was cleared. In Lisbon the crowd was so dense on the field that it became a struggle for an exhausted Billy McNeill to walk over to the presentation area just in front of us. With enormous display of strength, under the circumstances, he managed to climb the steep stairs to lift the trophy. Clearly a different mentality existed among the Portuguese constabulary. The Barcelona lot had no such accommodation in mind.

At pitch level I was very close to what happened next. The supporters were rooted to the spot. But not for long. I can still visualise the small officer in charge of the police on the ground, at the right-hand side of the line, lifting his hand and then abruptly lowering it like a man pulling a lever. It was the signal for action to commence. And it did, with a vengeance. The batons went into action, flailing violently. The supporters at the front were being battered. This happened so suddenly and unexpectedly that it was difficult to comprehend at first. The supporters then retreated to their own terracing where, apparently without so much as a cautionary thought, they began to break up seats to get some kind of weapons in their hands and proceeded to charge back at the police on the pitch.

This reaction was disgraceful, no matter what kind of complexion you put on it. It was also essentially suicidal, because they were faced by a force that apparently had no scruples on how to deal with disorder, as we had already seen in the streets of the city the previous night. It was a battle they were never going to win. By this time, I had climbed further up the stadium to get a panoramic view of the cut and thrust of the action. I came across the Reuter's correspondent for Catalonia, sitting at his typewriter, who I sensed was glad to meet a Scotsman who wasn't actually on the field. As soon as he started to speak to me I realised he was angry. But not for the reason I had anticipated. As soon as he started I asked him to pause, while I took out a notebook to take notes for a later report I had to do. He was very explicit and outspoken:

> What you are seeing down there is the fascist police in action. That is the only way they can handle any disturbance. They are the experts in ruthless suppression. They are not even local police. They are not Catalans. That is why they are so hated in this city. They are recruited in Castile and Murcia. Anywhere but Catalonia. They are in this area to maintain a dictatorship. They have regarded these supporters like an assault on the *caudillo*, Franco himself. That is how they are conditioned to act. Respond to command, don't think. These supporters simply do not understand their lives could be at risk.

In the immediacy of the event that interpretation did not reach other ears in the press area. They targeted the supporters without any compunction as any decent journalist would have done since the Rangers fans response had been utterly disgraceful. Alex Cameron in the *Daily Record* wrote:

> The sight of hordes of them racing out to attack a baton-charging line of police struck a new note in outright hooliganism.

Jim Parkinson of *The Glasgow Herald* recorded how he had been asked by young Rangers supporters to help them get out of the main gate to get away from the baton strikes of the police. He then added that the 'cancerous evil of hooligans' was damaging the image of Scottish football, and went on to say:

As our prestige soars at club and international level, our stock is
plunging crazily by this disease on the terracing.

All this was understandable and legitimate criticism of the alcohol-
fuelled reaction of the Rangers supporters.

But at that stage the police strategy was not under scrutiny. The
priority was to attach blame to a ransacking mob who were simply asking
for the criticism that was about to be heaped upon them. Nobody was of
an inclination to wonder why this had been allowed to happen. Because,
of course, it might reek of seeking some excuse for the wildness of much
of the Rangers support. That is the way the rest of Europe generally saw
it and how UEFA ultimately banned the club from European competition
for two years. It was reduced to one year after an appeal by the Rangers
manager, Willie Waddell. But our BBC team witnessed something we
considered sinister. The battle was reaching something of a crescendo
in the middle of the pitch, the police slashing away right, left and centre
and the supporters giving as good as they were getting. I was in full flow
about what I was seeing, when suddenly the main camera, whose pictures
I was talking to, swung away from the fighting and focused on an empty
street outside the stadium. This bewildered us. Why that manoeuvre?
We could only hazard a guess that somebody, somewhere in authority,
had passed on word that enough was enough and that they didn't want
to expose any further the violent conduct of their own police. However,
any professional in the television business would have seen this riot as
spectacular. Even in a partisan way they could have shown up the wild
conduct of the foreign supporters. On a night of extremes I believe we
had just experienced a television producer in a totalitarian state being
told from afar where to point his cameras.

I still wonder, had that little man in uniform not given the fatal hand
signal and just kept it in his pocket, as the complacent force seemed to
be doing earlier in the day, the scenes that rightly outraged the continent
would not have occurred. Eric Craig, calm, camera in hand, saw
much of that like myself, and was even in the Rangers dressing room
to photograph John Greig being handed the European Cup Winners'
Cup trophy by an official, with all the pomp and circumstance of being
handed a cup of tea. But Craig never looks back at Hampden without
thinking of how, out in the vast Nou Camp, the police had got it so
wrong as well.

\* \* \* \* \*

By the time Craig was able to leave Hampden in May 1980, to be taken to hospital, most of the pitch had been cleared. There were still stragglers about but the bulk had taken flight back from whence they came. Some of them might have been struggling with their consciences after what they had been dragged into. Who is to tell? But order had been restored. Not that the hatred had evaporated. I could still hear isolated offensive chants floating up to me, a reminder that the battle might have ended, but the sectarian war would continue in all its perverse forms.

# CHAPTER 9

# City on Alert

THE HORSES HAD done it. The sight of them, the sound of them, the flourishing gallop of them. That had saved the day. And there were patrons who were greatly appreciative of their efforts and wanted to demonstrate that. When they did, the sight and sound of it struck WPC Elaine Mudie like a tidal wave which almost overwhelmed her:

> There had been chaos on the pitch with people and police running everywhere. But now with so many horses there and more police who had managed to get to the stadium and get on to the pitch, some of them too late, of course, it was time for us to organise ourselves and get the horses into proper order. So we formed into twos, so that we could ride out nice and smart and disciplined. And as we trotted past the stand I noticed it was full of people, absolutely packed. I had thought they would have gone, but no. They must have just been sitting there watching all that fighting on the pitch. So when we reached there everyone stood and applauded us. Everyone. I can still see that so vividly. I filled up. I felt choked. My eyes ran. That's why one of the newspapers had a headline, 'THE TEARS OF THE HAMPDEN HEROINE', when one of them asked me about it afterwards. And yes, I had suddenly felt very proud. Because when you're running about trying to control a fighting mob, using your baton, getting your horse into the thick of it, and knocking folk down, and with all kinds of missiles being thrown at you, you begin to think that everybody hates you. But here were folk showing their appreciation. It was very poignant.

Nobody was surprised that there were aftershocks. Plenty of them. The city of Glasgow reverberated for several hours later. One of the places where the conflict took on an almost bizarre aspect was in a hospital. The Victoria Infirmary was one of Glasgow's best known hospitals. The Vicky was where they were taking the injured from Hampden. It was crowded with both supporters and those police who had sustained injuries from being hit by bottles and a variety of missiles. PC Willie Allan, physically unscathed himself, witnessed the scene:

> At first we were told to get back into our car and patrol the streets looking for any repeats of the trouble. But we had just started to do that when we got an urgent call to go to the Vicky. We heard that rancour had broken out between the police, who had gone there to be treated for various injuries, and some of the fans who were there for treatment too, and it was getting serious.

When they arrived, the hospital authorities warned them that the aggro between the police and the fans was about to tip over. The obvious thing was to separate them into different rooms. They did this, eventually thinking the crisis was over. It was not. When they had returned to the fans area they discovered the rivals were starting to fight with each other again, right there in the antiseptic atmosphere of A&E. The scenes were frightening enough, but PC Allan cannot forget one of the incidents, which could have been a sketch from *Monty Python's Flying Circus*:

> I will always remember this guy. He was in a wheelchair. A Rangers fan. Quite badly injured. He wheeled himself across towards a Celtic supporter who was lying on a mobile stretcher. And he started to knock lumps out of him, before we realised what he was up to. We jumped in. Not that this ended it. Even though all the walking wounded were there, some in crutches, many of them still wrapped up in bandages, they were still arguing and pushing at one another and occasionally fists being thrown. It was bedlam. I suppose it was understandable. If they fought at the ground they might just as well fight here. There was no difference to these people, no consideration for the folk trying to help and so bad that the nurses were saying to us, 'Please! Do not leave this hospital! We're scared!'

It eventually dawned on the authorities that they were not coping with people who thought rationally about their behaviour. With a strong police force now present, order was eventually restored. This meant that PC Allan's patrol could go off on other duties. One of these was to head for Castlemilk, to the south of the city. Its many Old Firm supporters groups meant there was a potential for unrest – to say the least. However, on his way there he was presented with a cameo that could have acted, both as a postscript for the day and an ironic comment on the senselessness of the riot. He saw three injured supporters limping their way home. Two Rangers supporters were supporting a Celtic fan in the middle. You wouldn't have needed to interview them about this odd camaraderie. Clearly, they had been at opposite ends. They all looked to be hurt in some way, with the Celtic supporter the worst. They almost certainly would have been in the middle of the pitch, throwing things. Friends really? Clearly they were. It would be difficult to explain that to an alien. But PC Allan understood it, as I do, that when friends put on these different colours and enter that arena of bilious hatred then, apart from anything else, the Old Firm can be accused of identity theft. They are taken over by tribal loyalty. The lad who would help old ladies cross the street, the articulate lawyer dealing daily with the fine balance of legal judgement, the woman running the local Oxfam shop, the douce churchgoer who takes round the collection plate every Sunday, they can all become raving extremists in that setting. I have seen this transformation with my own eyes, just as distinctly as I watched Lon Chaney Jr. in the cinema of my youth, turning into a werewolf on the screen.

PC Allan's colleague, PC Jim Buchanan, was on the pitch at the end of the clearance awaiting further orders. He had left a prisoner handcuffed to a bed in the Vicky but by that stage was not concerned about that (even had the prisoner taken bed and all with him, in a dash for freedom), since other more urgent matters were to hand. His role now was to take the patrol car and roam around the various well-known flashpoints in the way back to the centre of the city. This ended at Central Station where the mixed crowds were arriving from Hampden. It astounded him:

You couldn't take it all in. There were people running everywhere. When you went to quell a skirmish it would break up and then another one would start just as soon as one had ended. I had never seen so many people wanting to fight with one another. I had been at games before but nothing as bad as what I was seeing. It was like something out of a movie.

Sporadic fights were continuing in several localities, one of which surprised Hugh Keevins, returning home from his stint for *The Scotsman*:

I came home by bus and the route took me past Bearsden Cross, the apotheosis of middle class life in Glasgow. Even so, there they were, rammying at the Cross. I was watching it from the top-deck of the bus and I could hardly believe it. When, in the history of these games, was there ever an Old Firm fight at Bearsden Cross? I always look upon that game as the time when the city of Glasgow lost its senses.

Eric Craig had been able to walk slowly out to the carpark, but conceded to Ian Torrance his colleague that he couldn't drive. But as his friend took over that role he made one stipulation:

'Don't take me to the Vicky, it'll be a madhouse there. That's where they'll be taking all the football idiots. Take me to the Western.' Well, Ian did and they attended me right away. But after that initial inspection, I decided to get up and make a phone call home, even though, by this stage, my speech was definitely slurred. I had just finished it when a doctor from casualty came looking for me. He wasn't pleased. He told me that I shouldn't be up on my feet and I needed to go back and lie down. That's when I realised how serious this was. Then, later, he told me I was to be sent to the Southern General for special treatment because I had a fractured skull. And the seriousness of it sunk in, even further, when they put me in an ambulance and it took off at speed with the blue light flashing.

When I eventually descended from my eyrie and reached the pitch I was witness to a group of stunned men in uniform. At that stage I wouldn't have known one from the other, but they conveyed a kind of hushed sense of bereavement in the now empty stadium where some seagulls, arriving from God-knows-where, were squawking irreverently, like a Greek chorus trying to mock some of the main actors. They made a stark contrast to the ganglia of gloom that the uniforms formed. Were they feeling some guilt? Hamish MacBean had watched all this unfold before his eyes with a mix of emotions, as I was only to learn decades later. He knew it had gone disastrously wrong. As he stood surveying the now deserted but desecrated stadium, there was one consolation for him, which he eventually put into words for me with a sense of relief:

> Thank God there were no fatalities. But I can only put that down to luck, pure luck. And, honestly, standing there, I didn't feel any sense of failure about it. We had obviously dealt with a major incident. But after dealing with it and eventually clearing the pitch and getting the factions back to their own terracings, you don't think about success or failure, you just think about how we completed our job.

He had good reason to talk in terms of exoneration, which would become much clearer when the investigations began. I said nothing to the police who were there at the time, since I suppose I was simply wondering how well the BBC had covered the whole rigmarole and if my words had been appropriate or not. You could never tell in any post-match scenario, and particularly on that day.

The annual end of season bash at Queen Margaret Drive for all the BBC staff who had worked on the long day of live broadcasting on the Scottish *Grandstand* was muted. It's not that we didn't try to enjoy this normally demob-happy occasion when we would feel a huge sense of relief that the league and cup season was now behind us. But the events of that afternoon had shaken us all. And on top of that, we had to face up to the challenge of broadcasting the Scotland–England game in two weeks' time, 24 May. What would it be like on the terracings, that day? English supporters had been demonstrating, in that era, that their strategy of dismantling their opponents came from a Visigoth's manual. Their conduct had been categorised around the world as 'The English Disease'. Chelsea and Tottenham Spurs fans battling on the pitch before the White Hart Lane side helped relegate their rivals in a game dubbed 'The Relegation Battle' in 1975. Leeds United and Manchester United were both banned from European football in 1975 and 1977 respectively because of rioting by their fans. All of which led to the Minister for Sport Colin Moynihan famously describing it in later years as 'cancer in an otherwise healthy body'. It was not till 1990 that UEFA lifted its ban on English clubs. So what kind of gifts were they going to bestow on the Strathclyde Police in exactly 14 days' time? The police force was now under great pressure, with bewilderment at their inability to handle Saturday's debacle turning into outright hostility.

This certainly was engaging our minds that evening and we were suffering another aggravation. For one of the ambitions of any broadcaster outside London and network productions is to get one of our programmes to a British-wide network audience. This was an exception. We had the excruciating experience of having to sit and watch scenes of our Hampden production hitting BBC's national news. We cringed with embarrassment. You can imagine what was going through the minds of the Scottish Tourist Board. All that drained me. And I had been sitting in some comfort all afternoon. I could only imagine the state that the very active police were in.

PC Tom McLeod was a satisfied but tired man as he trudged home. Singly, he had performed the most dramatic rescue act of the day at the foot of the terracing. Not that he attached much significance to it. He was a tall man, bulked up through exercising and weight-training. Not somebody you would mess around with. Even so, the sheer physical effort of chasing mobs from a football pitch and avoiding injury himself, had taken its toll. He was on the point of exhaustion by the time he got back home:

> I lived in a top flat in Dennistoun. I climbed up and ran a bath for myself and then sat on the edge of my bed to take off my uniform and boots. Would you believe, I fell asleep right there on the edge of the bed. I was wakened by the neighbours from downstairs coming up to complain that I had kept a tap running and the water was running down the walls and flooding them.

The other tap he had turned on, at Hampden that day, by opening a gate, allowing a flood of young supporters to escape the dangers of crushing, has never been officially or publicly acknowledged until now.

# The Aftermath
## 1980 to 2020

## CHAPTER 10

# The Blame Game

ON 15 MARCH 2018, the Scottish Parliament voted to repeal the Offensive Behaviour at Football and Threatening Communications Act which had been made law in 2012. The debates were fierce in and outside parliament and the vote was close, 62-60. Almost four decades on from that riot when we were all aghast at what had occurred, no consensus view had been reached on effectively stamping out the insidious nature of this particular football crowd, which when aroused could roar like a sectarian beast as loudly as it did on 10 May 1980, when, coincidentally, the Rubik's Cube first appeared in stores. Our legislators, since that year, had dealt clumsily with this chronic problem, like someone trying to solve that cube wearing boxing gloves.

At first, the moral indignation which swept through the land was like colonic irrigation. It was like we were talking about shit, publicly, like we never had before. It all looked so promising. Yes, it was a terrible day. So let's move on with renewed vigour, we thought, to tackle a serious social problem that had deep roots. But of course there was a naivety attached to that, simply because there were too many elements overlapping one another on the actual day itself: the players' conduct, the police strategy, the fence, the booze, the SFA's role in hosting the event in the way they did and the unending evidence of sectarianism that underpinned the entire day.

So who was going to venture forth first and wade into the morass? Not the Old Firm. They did not get their competitive teeth into this immediately. Their rancour was put on hold as the media went on the offensive. The bold print of headlines in the newspapers could have been seen from the surface of the moon. 'END THIS MADNESS' on the front page of the *Scottish Daily Express* on Monday 12 May was followed by its sister paper the *Sunday Express* with 'NEVER AGAIN!'. The column inches devoted to this, in both tabloid and broadsheet, could not have been knocked off the front pages, even had Russian tanks burst through Checkpoint Charlie in the festering situation in Berlin at the time. You felt they were reflecting a global catastrophe, with their headlines of dismay, anger and moral indignation There was unprecedented collusion between sports writers, news reporters and leader writers.

*The Scotsman's* editorial on Monday 12 May suggests that the writer had spent his afternoon scrutinising the scenes closely:

> And that was what was at the centre of Saturday's kicking, punching and butting – prejudice. Prejudice so mindless, blind and damaging that it prompted the commentator into making the simple but hopefully effective comment, over the scenes of violence, 'These supporters hate each other'.

*The Glasgow Herald* was almost guilt-ridden in its leader column:

> After decades of Scottish football rowdiness, after the trail of havoc created by Scottish supporters from Barcelona to Burnley, it seems ludicrous that this should apparently take us by surprise.

There was a kind of collective *mea culpa* about much of the reporting as if, for too long, we in the media had settled into a comfort zone about this abomination of sectarian theatrics, as if we were an audience in the grand circle, separated by the proscenium arch from the antics on the stage, and that we could hiss or boo, but never invade it. Never.

An article by one of the journalists close to the pulse of Scottish football, Hugh Taylor of the Glasgow *Evening Times*, under the headline 'WHY I CRY FOR SCOTTISH FOOTBALL', seemed to reflect a change of mood among the media:

> Scotland are the scum of soccer. I have been reporting Old Firm matches for 40 years. I have enjoyed most of them, enjoyed the conflict, the moments of brilliance. But now? After watching the mindless thugs, pseudo-religious fanatics, I would not complain if these matches were banned.

Hugh, whom I had known for years, had never previously suggested such positive intervention. We had listened to recommendations for the fixture to be banned before, but these were largely from the pulpit or from dignitaries aloof from the sport, whom we dismissed, too lightly, as football illiterates.

Entering into the fray came someone with much less experience, but with a keen eye, perceptive touch and exuding cosmopolitan confidence, ex-public-schoolboy journalist Ian Archer in the *Scottish Daily Express,* writing:

> I propose a ban, in sadness, because those clubs have given much fun at home and abroad. But I love my country as well and would have the rest of the world know it with affection, for its many good qualities rather than its much publicised twin curses of alcohol and intolerance.

Every publication was in screaming mode. Jimmy Reid, of Clydeside shipbuilding revolt fame, and then a political pundit, wrote an article for *The Herald* which used one of his statements as the headline, 'TOO MANY PROTESTANTS, TOO MANY CATHOLICS, NOT ENOUGH CHRISTIANS'. *The Sun* correspondent Graham MacLean, writing for a paper which at that stage had no Scottish base, echoed that idea:

> Shameful scenes at the end of the Scottish Cup Final between Rangers and Celtic may lead to a ban on their playing each other again.

He then went on to use language which was to appeal to an English audience, whose familiarity with this fixture was based on only one aspect, religion:

> Saturday's Hampden hatred began after the predominantly Catholic supporters scaled an 8ft fence and got on to the pitch. Hundreds of Protestant Rangers fans hurled bottles and beer cans at them, and then charged.

The Scottish newspapers had no need to specify it that way.

As many writers demanded the gallows for the fixture, I doubt if there was a single one of them who actually thought it would ever be outlawed. For instance *The Glasgow Herald* of 12 May reported:

> For two hours yesterday the Chief Constable and his top aides met to discuss the riot. Later it was stated that the possibility of a ban on all future Old Firm games has been discussed, but that would be up to the regional council.

There was as much chance of the city of Glasgow District Council in 1980, packed as it was with Old Firm supporters, proposing an abolition of the fixture, as they would rendering all Glasgow pubs non-alcoholic. These two clubs were interlocked with so many vested interests, and formed the keystone of a Scottish league system, which if pulled out would result in an unprecedented collapse. It was simply unthinkable. And everybody in the media knew that. But, they had to make the right kind of noises to a public who were just as sceptical as they were about the possibility of a banning but could hardly have expected writers not to have vented their feelings that way. Of course, there was only one way in which separation could have been achieved: one, or both, be banned from playing in their own land. In different degrees of intensity, and in different eras, both clubs, not entirely secretly, had coveted the idea of moving to England anyway. Leaving aside the multiple hurdles that would have to be faced to achieve that lingering inclination, on the basis of the images of the battle at Hampden being beamed around the world, they would not even have been accepted at the time by the Mongolian FA.

Who was to blame? A chasm was to open up between the two clubs, largely based on words spoken hundreds of miles away in London.

The government had demanded an immediate report for a statement to be made to the House of Commons at Westminster on the following Monday afternoon at 3pm. Match Commander MacBean, along with colleagues who had been present, spent the whole of Sunday going over the details from the police's view on the riot. This was provided in time for the Secretary of State for Scotland, George Younger, who, perhaps inadvertently, fuelled an already explosive atmosphere that encouraged the tectonic plates of Ibrox and Parkhead to shift and cause an unsurprising earthquake. It seemed just a simple, barebones account of the information passed on by the Chief Constable of Strathclyde Patrick Hamill. However Younger had some problems even before he rose to the dispatch box. Firstly, he was perceived as a Tory grandee, close to Margaret Thatcher, who had applied economic policies which hastened the deindustrialisation of the country, with thousands of job losses and damage to specific communities, most notably in mining areas. Mining had a special affinity with football having spawned many of its great figures. Stein, Busby, Shankly, all had been miners. However diligent he might have been in interpreting what had been laid before him, there was a feeling that he was commenting on a culture he little understood, one which was instinctively wary of anything such a patrician figure might utter about the sport. His highly successful family brewing company had sponsored the Scottish Cup Final, and it is a safe bet that their product had not cooled the passions that sun-drenched afternoon.

That alone made him vulnerable at the dispatch box. Wisely, he stuck to the script. But was the script itself accurate? He spelled out that 73 arrests had been made, before and during the game, adding, 'The number of arrests at that stage was not unusual for such an occasion'. That qualification alone drew astonishment in the House, especially from those who knew nothing of the history of this fixture. He then went on to say that 400 officers were on duty within the ground, which differed from the police figure of 289 given to the media; that a total of 179 arrests had been made, that 29 people had been treated by ambulance workers, and that although nobody could tally at that stage how many casualties there had been, only four police officers had been injured and none taken to hospital. That last assertion puzzled me. I had spoken to police witnesses who had watched colleagues being treated in the Vicky and as was noted by the *Daily Telegraph* two days later, reporting that the casualties 'included four policemen'. Nor did he seem to be particularly accurate with arrest figures which were eventually to be recorded as 210. When he went on to talk about the duration of the riot, he indulged in bureaucratic exactitude, which simply raises doubts:

By their prompt and vigorous action the police were successful in completely restoring order within 15 minutes from the start of the disturbance.

Hamish MacBean's response was one of incredulity:

Fifteen minutes? No, no way. I know of no officer who had a stopwatch on this anyway. Remember I had to get the mounted police around from the north-side of the stadium to get on to the pitch but they couldn't even do that easily because thousands were still pouring out of the stadium and blocking their path. Meanwhile, the fans were charging into each other on the pitch. Certainly when the horses appeared there was a rapid change in the whole atmosphere and they did get things in order very speedily. But 15 minutes, no I can't accept that.

It had seemed like treble that time to all of us. It felt like a chunk had been taken out of our lives, having to witness the worst elements in society in full throttle. To be sure, myth can surround these events. After all, through novels and film, the gunfight at the O.K. Corral between Wyatt Earp and friends and the Clanton gang was depicted as going on for about 20 minutes. In fact it was over in 30 seconds or so, according to contemporary eyewitnesses. I still retain the sensation that the riot seemed to go on for an eternity. It was the sudden ferocity of it all which perhaps distorted the passing of time for witnesses. But, it was the closing sentence of Younger's statement that took us into territory which would inevitably provoke another Old Firm jousting match:

> The main responsibility rests with the football clubs and authorities themselves, and I have no doubt they will be closely examining to what extent it was the actions of players at the end of the game that caused disorder.

The report endorsed the finding of the Chief Constable's team, that Celtic players were to blame for the whole episode. It reeks of incitement, although semantically camouflaged. That single sentence aroused the scepticism of the redoubtable Tam Dalyell, MP for West Lothian; parliament's great dissenter, Dalyell was the scourge of wafflers and the dogged pursuer of the shady purveyors of doublespeak, as his relentless criticism of the Gulf War exemplified. Nothing passed him by that he considered odd. And this, he felt, was on the shady side of odd. He was genuinely interested in sport, particularly on those occasions when it looked as if it would suffer through political interference.

He always made the justifiable claim, that had he not stood against Thatcher's attempt to stop athletes from competing in the Olympics in Moscow in 1980, and added support to the British Olympic Committee to encourage them to go, Alan Wells and Sebastian Coe would never have won gold medals. He was always proud of that, almost as if he had coached them himself. Dalyell's challenge to Younger led to a short but interesting exchange in the House of Commons.

> DALYELL: In terms of the last sentence of his statement, on what precise ground does the Secretary of State suggest the players were to blame.

> YOUNGER: It is not my view that that is the case.

> DALYELL: Why put it in the statement?

> Younger: As I said, it is not my view that that took place.

> DALYELL: It is in the statement.

> YOUNGER: The police view is quite clear, that had the Celtic players not acted as they did an invasion of the pitch might not have occurred. I am only recording the view of the police. The police might be right or wrong, but that appears to be the case.

And, in case the House was not getting his point, that we should all concentrate on the behaviour of the Celtic players, he added:

> I am sure the House will join with me in deploring the disgraceful scenes of violence that took place, and in congratulating Strathclyde police on their firm and effective response. Had it not been for such prompt action, a much uglier scene might have developed.

The blame game had started with a vengeance. The captain of the winning team runs innocently and harmlessly to their own supporters and a riot ensues? This was seized upon as the blindingly obvious reason for the influx. But that was too simplistic a response. What were the other factors which brought crowds on to the field? This leads me to think of the 'butterfly effect' concept. Edward Norton Lorenz, the American mathematician and meteorologist who introduced this notion to the world, instructed us that even a tiny, apparently insignificant event can spark off a chain reaction which can lead to a major catastrophe. A butterfly flaps its wings in the Amazonian jungle and a tornado is set off in Texas as a result. It's a belief that has attained a certain traction in chaos theory. And in politics. Hanging chads, the tiny pieces of paper still clinging to punched ballot papers which were not counted in Florida during a Presidential election, gave the world George W Bush, with subsequent disasters in the Middle East and the eventual downfall of Tony Blair. So to blame Danny McGrain carrying the cup to his supporters for the resultant chaos was to fail to go further back in time to see where the flapping of the wings really began. You have to go back to an event which seemingly had no connection with football in any shape or form. We find ourselves perhaps seeking the origin of that ultimate tornado at Hampden, in the election of Margaret Thatcher as Prime Minister in 1979.

\* \* \* \* \*

On the steps of Downing Street, on her first day in office, Margaret Thatcher uttered words from a misattributed prayer of St Francis, the first line of which was, 'Where there is discord, may we bring harmony'. A superbly appropriate sentiment to apply to any strife, including that historic one between two clubs north of the border. Whether it informed her political strategies is a matter of contention which historians still mull over. Shortly after taking office, since she had impressed the electorate, especially in England, with her emphasis on strict law and order policies, she presented the police with what many perceived to be a veritable bounty. They had suffered chronically low pay over many years and had seen their remuneration fall behind others in public service. Many police were moonlighting, some taxi-driving in their spare time to make ends meet, others working themselves into the ground with extra shifts to keep pace. In 1977 the previous Labour government had set up an inquiry, under the chairmanship of High Court Judge Baron Edmund-Davies, to investigate this increasing disparity. It came up with a recommendation that pay should be increased across the board by 45 per cent. The new Prime Minister endorsed this huge increase and so set in motion the knock-on effect of the cost of policing at football grounds.

It rose steeply. Many clubs complained about this, which led to a stringent rethink of how many uniforms actually needed to be in operation in and around grounds on match day. The clubs were driven into economising on policing for matches, which prompted a rethink by the police themselves on the matter of the most effective use of manpower. Hence the strategy employed at Hampden by the Chief Constable and his team. They were short of numbers. They were saving money. Had there been a bigger presence of uniforms all round then barely a soul would have got on to the pitch. You could say the butterfly's wings fluttered that night on the steps of 10 Downing Street when Maggie came to power, resulting in economies imposed around football grounds. It meant that both Rangers and Celtic, in a spurious and temporary show of unity, heaped much responsibility on the shoulders of the Chief Constable of Strathclyde. And the media were quick to remind us that he was the first Catholic to have attained that post. He was also a major casualty of the day.

# CHAPTER 11

# In the Firing Line

PATRICK HAMILL, HEADING one of the biggest police authorities in the UK, must have known then he was about to face public scrutiny on an unprecedented scale. PC Kenny Malgrin had already observed a man in the first stages of panic, a far cry from the cool, not to say remote and austere persona he presented to most of his officers.

Our own eyes had told us that the overall strategy of policing the Old Firm match on 10 May 1980 had badly misfired. It was so obvious that John Hamilton, Secretary of the Police Federation in Strathclyde, was provoked to voice his strong concerns immediately after the event:

> In the past we have had a record second to none in relation to disturbances of this nature. We in the Federation have been in no doubt how we sustained that record. It wasn't by building fences to keep the hordes on the terracings. It was by presenting to the would-be invaders a show of police strength.

The eventual SFA report on the matter was quite unambiguous. It states that:

> In the opinion of the committee the whole incident could have been nipped in the bud had there been an adequate number of policemen on the track when the match ended. The few who were there were hopelessly outnumbered and quite powerless to influence events.

That specific accusation was not countered at the point where the buck stops. For Chief Constable Patrick Hamill had now become as prominent as a garden mole.

He put someone else in the firing line. Someone who was besieged by the media from around the world in an affair which had now attracted global interest. Chief Inspector Ian McKie, the press officer for Strathclyde Police was at Hampden that day and had himself been involved on the pitch, trying to arrest individuals attacking his colleagues. That was the easy bit. Now he had to face the world, but inadequately briefed, as he later told me:

> I thought immediately after the riot there would be a meeting with all the people involved, including the Chief, so that we could provide everybody with answers and explanations. You felt all that would have been done right away. Not a bit of it. I was left to face the world's press with little information, no great details of the planning and what had gone wrong. All Hamill had said to me was, 'We'll have to say something I suppose'. And then I didn't see or hear from him for another two days. So I was on my tod, trying to defend the Strathclyde Police against a tidal wave of criticism. It was not easy. It was a very invidious position to be in. And I was making statements on behalf of the Chief Constable that he hadn't actually made. I remember one clearly. I told the press, 'This will never happen again'. That was prominently reported. So, in a debrief about four days later Patrick Hamill asked me why I had said that. When I told him I thought it was a sensible thing to say, given I was upholding the reputation of Strathclyde Police, he just retorted, 'How do you know it will never happen again?', being the kind of man he was. I have to tell you I was no great admirer of his.

Others were, though. He classically portrayed how being shaped by the hazards and pressures of office inevitably leads to a public face that is in direct contrast to the private persona.

Sir Patrick Hamill was appointed to his post in 1977, having joined the force in 1950 straight from school. *The Herald* obituary following his death on 24 February 2000 painted a picture painted of a thoroughly decent family man, which undoubtedly he was. It said that his name was 'synonymous with integrity, goodness and service'. Professor Leo Martin chairman of the magnificent St Margaret of Scotland Hospice in Clydebank talks of his wonderful charity work, a man of strong religious beliefs so dedicated to the cause that a section of the hospice is named after him.

Most serving officers saw a wholly different person. They saw him as an apparatchik who had never worked on the beat but had risen to the top through bureaucratic channels. He brought with him to headquarters in Pitt Street, Glasgow, a strong will which could be imposed with breathtaking severity. From several officers I learned he could actually reduce men to tears. As Ian McKie put it, 'He could bully people he knew could be bullied'. On one occasion, in addressing his officers over some issue, he picked out one in particular for criticism. The withering attack was so severe the officer collapsed in a faint at his feet. Hamill, as if nothing had happened, and without losing stride, continued his diatribe. PC Tom McKay said of him, 'When he entered a room a chill descended'. This is not the man others would see devoting himself passionately to the invaluable work of a hospice.

After the Hampden riot, he undoubtedly went to ground. In a grilling by *The Glasgow Herald,* the week after, it can be seen clearly that McKie was manfully doing his best to defend the force, but minus the real facts. The first question he was asked certainly showed that:

QUESTION: Of the 298 policemen on duty, how were they deployed during and after the match?

ANSWER: The number of police deployed both inside and outside the ground was the same as the numbers which have been used at major matches over the years.

Not so. McKie had simply no knowledge of the wrangle the Match Commander had with headquarters about numbers. He also made something else clear:

To this day, until you informed me, I had no idea that any gate had been opened on the fence by any policeman. I never saw that in any report on the matter anywhere. And may I add, I commend him for his sheer common sense.

That in itself shows how vulnerable McKie was in trying to answer questions without a proper matrix of information. At that juncture he had no information from headquarters about MacBean's own vulnerability, something of which the Match Commander was wholly adamant:

The track detail was too light. Not enough bodies around the track. I had put in a request to headquarters for the usual number. They turned it down. I put in another request, they turned it down. It was the Assistant Chief Constable of Operations that I dealt with but he was taking his instructions from the Chief. So I was left with numbers that I knew could be too light at the end of the game. That was because the conventional procedure was to deploy resources to the hotspots just outside the stadium, about ten minutes from the end of the game. And that is what we did, following ordinary procedure. But it left us with a skeleton force around the track. We were caught out.

The double rejection meant that the 'normal numbers' simply were not at Hampden that day. That was a major defect. So both McKie and MacBean in different situations had been let down. Minimalism had come into play and the public were not to be made aware of that. It is that which lay at the heart of Hamill's invisibility. Why would he want a dispute between his Match Commander and himself to enter the public domain? MacBean had been denied the numbers that would perhaps have prevented the scale of the invasion, if not stemmed it entirely. No wonder he emerged from that day unscathed:

I had absolutely no criticism made of me by anybody. I was not taken to task for it. I was never questioned about it. Nobody queried me on anything. Nothing. They knew the track detail was too light. It was as simple as that.

MacBean's exemplary supervision of an inadequate force was praised by Detective Superintendent Joe Jackson. His excellent book *Chasing Killers*, relates his experiences in the force, particularly as a leading light in the Strathclyde Crime Squad, which had been created only a couple of years previously. He was in the stadium at the tunnel mouth at the end, as he put it, 'In my detective clothing of a blue lounge suit', watching the fray. But he could not restrain himself for long. He noticed a Constable being attacked by an individual, who had obviously seen too many kung-fu films and was laying into this officer, who was struggling with another figure on the ground. He strode on to the pitch, with a colleague to arrest the imbecile, despite the bottles raining down.

Sammy Cox (above)
Charlie Tully (right).

Their collision at an Old
Firm clash at Ibrox in
1949 sparked a riot and
ensnared me for life.

The Greatest Ever Ranger, John Grieg, led his side into the 1980 final as favourites, after a disappointing season in the league.

At the 1980 Scottish Cup presentation, Billy McNeill could not rid himself of tension as he could not yet forget the disappointment of losing the league title. And at his back a storm was brewing around Hampden.

The Hampden riot on 10 May 1980 was the first charge of mounted police in Glasgow since 'The Battle of George Square' on 31 January 1919, against striking workers.

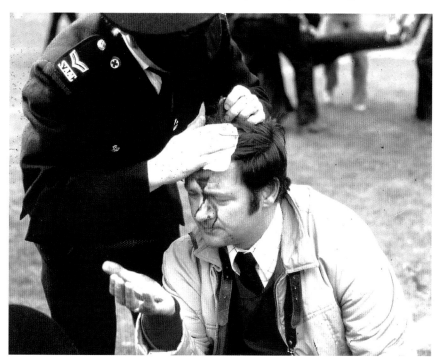

Eric Craig, photographer, struck by a bottle during the riot. The serious injury required surgery and he was left with a hearing deficit that was to change his life dramatically. Photo courtesy Eric Craig.

'At the end of the day, let's not kid ourselves. These supporters hate each other.'
From Archie Macpherson's match commentary, 10 May 1980.

Seated on her white horse, Ballantrae, PC Elaine Mudie's upright stance in the middle of the turmoil was an inspiration to others.

Two of the wounded on the pitch in the aftermath of the 1980 riot. There were no deaths but many lucky escapes.

Jock Stein, who had only five more years of his life left, watched the 1980 final from the stand knowing his legacy was at stake, as well as a cup.

Above:
Sir Partick Hamill, honoured but also criticised for operational mishaps at the 1980 final.

Right:
Urbane but authoritative, SFA secretary Ernie Walker regarded Hampden as his personal fiefdom.

David Murray with a model of the new Ibrox that mirrored his self-confidence as chairman of Rangers FC. The capacity of Ibrox was increased to 44,500.

Without Fergus McCann's involvement as majority stakeholder between 1994 and 1999, the redeveloped Celtic Park stadium would never have risen.

Tired but triumphant, Celtic team captain Billy McNeill amidst the crowd on the Lisbon pitch in 1967, shortly before becoming the first British player to lift the European Cup.

The 'Lisbon Lions' express their jubilation in the showers after winning the European Cup in 1967.

Captain John Greig with the European Cup Winners' Cup on Rangers' return from Barcelona 1972 after beating Moscow Dynamo 3-2 on a night that shook observers. Because of the pitch invasion that European Cup Winners' Cup was presented inside a dressing room.

John Greig's strength of character led Rangers to many moments of celebration.

Fergus McCann and Brian Dempsey bonded to save Celtic then fell out.

David Murray relinquished Rangers for a song and plunged a whole community into crisis.

Anti-sectarianism crusader Cara Henderson in 2001, about to sample an Old Firm game for the first time. With courage and tenacity she gave birth to the charity Nil by Mouth, which she set up as a teenager in response to the sectarian murder of her friend Mark Scott in 1995.

Lord Jack McConnell as Education Minister was the architect of change in schooling. His speech on sectarianism in 2002, entitled 'Scotland's Shame', jolted society and led eventually to new legislation on the issue.

COVID-19 forced the duel of Neil Lennon (above) and Steven Gerrard (right) into a contentious pause over the termination of the Scottish Premier League in 2020, which echoed old feuds.

The end of the affair: mounted police clear brawling fans from the pitch at Hampden on 10 May 1980.

When the man tried to fight him off Jackson admits he floored him with a left hook, and in eventually arresting him with a mate, received a standing ovation from the spectators ogling all of this in the safety of the stand seats. These customers were getting more than they had paid for. Heaven forfend that anyone would suggest the struggle on the field was a social class thing, with the better-off in the seated area made to feel like well-heeled tourists in a safari park, watching some primeval struggle for survival. The thought is inescapable though. However, as Hamish MacBean had already pointed out, the fighting actually started in the centre stand. So there was a division there as well. But, such summary justice, as performed by Jackson, in these circumstances would, I think, still arouse acclamation in a contemporary setting.

Jackson's overall assessment seemed to chime with much of what I heard from other officers. He wrote of his bosses:

> The Chief Constable and the Deputy Chief were both, to use a football term, as sick as parrots after what had occurred. They were obliged to rethink the new strategy, which had obviously been presented to them by some academic or office-bound police officers.

In these words you can almost feel a sense of betrayal of the men on the ground, of the officers who had to go out and forge the practicalities of any policy. That Hampden day was evidence of the gulf which existed between planners and operators, of the frailty that ensued from the remoteness and intransigence of superiors. But there was an immediate rethink.

Hamish MacBean verifies that never again was a request turned down by a Match Commander for an appropriate detail to manage any ground. They could not afford to make another mistake when it came to manpower. But since all these scenes had been transmitted throughout Europe, and particularly grabbed attention in England, Patrick Hamill wisely decided to initiate an analysis of the occurrences at Hampden, but set against an examination of police strategies at grounds in England, so that a productive conclusion could be reached as to the best way forward throughout the UK. The man he chose to report on this was Superintendent Ken Stewart, who at that time was officiating in the Hamilton area in Lanarkshire.

For two months he went up and down England visiting some of the more prominent stadiums and came back with a wealth of material that reminded us that we were not alone in having potential stadium problems. One visit intrigued him, and would again make interesting reading to those fascinated by the issue of strict liability. It was at an Aston Villa–Arsenal match. On paper, that would seem to lovers of the game as a perfect Corinthian sort of occasion, a kind of Middle England affair that would cause no more hullabaloo than that of the clapping of a boundary at Lords. But it had another side to it which, student of the game as I thought myself to be, took me unawares. Stewart himself was surprised to learn that there had been deep hostility between these two sets of supporters then but went to the game with an open mind:

> I had heard in the previous game between them, some Arsenal supporters had dressed up as Villa fans and got into their end of the ground. They started a mini-riot there which the police had to sort out. So I went round to speak to the sergeant who was given responsibility to steward that particular end of the ground. I asked him if anything special had been set up for this repeat fixture. But all he said to me was, 'We won't need any. We sorted it out the last time'. Well, would you believe it happened again. Exactly the same trouble, supporters dressed in the wrong gear getting in amongst the opposing fans and causing mayhem.

Quite apart from learning, for the first time, that elements of the Arsenal support had departed the traditions of their great iconic manager Herbert Chapman and had adopted the infiltration methods of the Viet Cong, his recollections displayed to me the problem of attaching blame. Could Villa not have their own premises properly policed? As stakeholders, were they responsible for anything that occurred within their property, even from the invading impostors? Questions we simply dangle here at the moment, but which nevertheless indicate the complexity of stadium control anywhere, with strict liability of a club's responsibility to carry any penalty for trouble, a recurring political theme in football around Europe. In this case even the Birmingham police, to whom he talked, couldn't adequately explain why there was such enmity between these two clubs. It certainly was a warning about complacency. This is something that clearly did not exist in Merseyside, his next stop. The Everton–Liverpool derby is one of the most intense in British football. Stewart stopped off at Goodison Park for the FA Cup game on 24 January 1981. It was hectic, lively, with the normal intensity of that fixture. Emotions were high. Everton were to go on and win 2-1, played out on a mud heap. On the final whistle, in a surge of euphoria, about a couple of thousand Everton supporters suddenly invaded the field and ran down to the opposite end of the pitch, where they assembled in front of the red throngs and noisily rubbed their superiority right into their faces. This is how Stewart described the scene to me:

> There they were, thousands of Everton supporters on the pitch right down at the Liverpool end and clearly enjoying themselves. And would you believe not a single Liverpool fan tried to get on the pitch in response. It was very surprising. They just all stood there taking it all. Mark you, there was a strong line of police in front of them guarding the pitch. To me it was strange because I was waiting for the fuse to blow.

Whether intended or not, he was offering a direct comparison with the response of the Rangers supporters at Hampden, culminating in the riot. But there is another way to look at it. However fervid the Merseyside derby was in those days it could never be bracketed along with the same kind of venom that pervades the air of an Old Firm game. Although, admittedly in more recent times, you find the likes of Gregg Roughley writing in *The Guardian*:

> If there is one myth that has lingered even longer than the mist over the river Mersey, it's the notion that Liverpool versus Everton is a friendly derby... the reality is a little different; the modern derby is a hate-ridden, noxious affair that should come with a health warning, lest one inhales the fumes rising off Gwladys Street or Spion Kop.

In the '80s it did command respect for its comparatively neighbourly atmosphere, which might go some way to explaining the surprising passivity of the Liverpool support. The other factor for the non-invasion was the show of police strength in front of them. That simple tactic, which was absent at Hampden, perhaps better accounts for the reluctance to counter-attack.

Stewart slaved over his 40-page report, which made proposals on the desirable methods of policing in stadiums, relating above all to the safety of the public. But, at a meeting in the Grosvenor House Hotel in London, where he presented his views to the meeting of UK officers and other interested parties, he was met with palpable disdain:

> As soon as I mentioned I was with Strathclyde Police I could feel they were not going to take me all that seriously. I remember when I talked about the special problems with Rangers and Celtic, Jimmy Hill, as if in his former Players' Union role, just smirked at me as if I was talking about a minor league somewhere.

I sympathise, since I have experienced that Metropolitan conceit on other occasions in broadcasting. However, there is little doubt that the scenes of uncontrolled madness, which the world had witnessed at our Cup Final, could not have encouraged empathy with an officer from a force which had seemed to have suffered dereliction of duty.

That report of his, which he had slaved over, has simply disappeared. He certainly hopes it played a part in the deliberations which then ensued. You gain the impression that the intensity of press comment about the role of the police was not matched by the pursuit of the relevant facts by any of the authorities. And the emphasis on the culpability of the police was seized upon by one side of the Old Firm. Almost as if they were clinging to the wreckage.

# CHAPTER 12

# No Excuses

CAMPBELL OGILVIE, SECRETARY of Rangers, one of the most agreeable and approachable figures in the game, was the first to put his head above the parapet, on 14 May, before anything was heard from the east end of Glasgow. He did so because of the incidental encouragement of the statements made at Westminster by Younger and by Willie Harkness, the President of the SFA. Harkness, a very amiable man whose hospitality down at Palmerston Park as chairman of Queen of the South FC was second to none, established conviviality as a cornerstone of his SFA Presidency. He clearly loved the social life, which came as regular feature of his period in office, and since many of us in the media were not averse to the kinds of pleasures that he himself enjoyed, his popularity was unbounded. Always approachable, always with the best of intentions, he nevertheless had a pleasant naivety to him, that at times incurred the occasional clanger. Sometimes he was kept in check by the much more sophisticated secretary of the Association, Ernie Walker, sometimes not. Such an occasion was when we went out to the World Cup draw in Spain two years later. And, on a more flippant tone, I recall Harkness advising me he always drank the wine of the country he was visiting. At the dinner table with him at the time, I felt that was an entirely appropriate way to incur the favour of the locals until I heard him ordering from the waiter 'a carafe of lasagne'. It was the kind of harmless gaffe that endeared him to the Scottish media. But his first words on the Hampden riot gave the immediate impression that he was out of his depth when it came to assessing a major event like this, and that what he provoked in his initial statement, carried a more serious consequence than simply amusing a Spanish waiter.

On the Monday morning following the match, he dipped his oars into what he must have known would be stormy waters by issuing a statement to *The Glasgow Herald*:

What helped spark off the invasion was some Celtic players going up to the Celtic end to acknowledge their supporters. They should never have been allowed. This was followed by them invading the pitch. If Celtic players had just come off there might not have been any problem, but this doesn't excuse the disgraceful scenes that followed.

This was even before George Younger had arrived at the dispatch box, and totally ignorant of the reply given by the Shadow Secretary of State Bruce Millan. The Labour MP had replied to Younger suggesting that the government was over-simplifying the matter to the point of naivety:

The scenes at the end of the match on Saturday were utterly appalling – worse than I have ever seen. If anything they were understated in the Secretary of State's statement. He attributed the blame to one incident. I think that is rather unfortunate, because I believe that what happened on Saturday was rather more complicated than the Secretary of State indicated in his statement.

To those of us who were there, even those words of Millan's seem an understatement. Of course it was complex. Much more so than Harkness's initial statement had been. I was not present when he talked to the journalist who wrote this up, but I would bet my life on it that Ernie Walker was nowhere to be seen at the time. He would have stifled that central comment, 'They should never have been allowed', since that was a blunder in a different league from thinking lasagne had the properties of a Rioja. The following day, this was pointed out to him by Alex Cameron in the *Daily Record*:

Blaming Celtic is the easy way – especially as no one had researched the fact that the Parkhead club was entitled under SFA rules to go to greet their fans with the cup.

However, a neon-signed path had been laid for Rangers to follow. From Ibrox came this:

Rangers FC strongly deplore the incidents at the conclusion of the Scottish Cup Final at Hampden on Saturday. The Secretary of State and the SFA president have already made statements about the cause of the incident, and we do not disagree with these. Rangers are of the opinion that to alleviate problems such as were witnessed on Saturday, seated stadia would prove to be a major deterrent against such behaviour, and we have already implemented this policy with encouraging results. We trust there will be an early inquiry into this matter, and will co-operate fully.

Four sentences, neat, concise, clinical, but ultimately evasive. No press conference, just an echoing of what the other authorities had proclaimed. They certainly wanted to emphasise the seated stadium factor, as they were in the first throes of completing three new stands at Ibrox, which was way ahead of modern developments anywhere else in the UK. All this was about the logistics of the day. There was nothing about the behaviour of the respective supporters, other than endorsing the view, without actually mentioning them by name, that the Celtic players had started it all.

Indeed, the first two opening sentences of the statement wear a kind of blandness that reminds me of how a London editor of *The Times* once ran a competition to see who could come up with the dullest headline for a disaster. It was eventually won with 'EARTHQUAKE IN CHILE. FEW DEAD'. That brief opening Rangers statement carried the same sense of dampening any further suggestion of looking deeper into a more complex situation, whose consequences demanded increased detail and further questioning. Ibrox was obviously happy to be in tandem with the authorities who presided over the whole event. However, I am absolutely convinced there was no collusion over this. There didn't need to be. If the police, the government and the SFA had all come to the same conclusion, then all Rangers needed to say was, 'Hear! Hear!' But, knowing the pleasant and astute Campbell Ogilvie as I did, I am sure that he must have realised that although it was patently true that Celtic players had indeed run down the pitch with the cup to start with, linking it directly to a riot was going to be interpreted at Parkhead as both evasive and provocative. Celtic's response came a few hours later.

Desmond White, the Celtic chairman, according to those who were present at a prearranged press conference in his chartered accountant's office in Glasgow, was livid. This is despite the fact that a much more cordial relationship had been developing between the two boards. Hugh Keevins of *The Scotsman* wrote:

> The news of Rangers' reaction given to White, literally minutes before he read out Celtic's official version of the ugly scenes at Hampden, caused him visible upset.

White was a tall, straight-backed man with a booming voice that seemed to fit naturally with the imperious stance he sometimes adopted to face the world. He had a charming American wife who spoke pleasantly to me on the phone once, when I was following up a report that nobody from the BBC was to be allowed on a Celtic charter flight to one of the club's European games, because of a dispute we were having with Jock Stein at the time. She handled this coolly and effectively and I recall her saying, 'Oh, not to worry. I'll sort this out with Desmond'. When White did phone me back the matter was swiftly resolved, leaving me with the feeling that despite Stein's apparent omnipotence within Celtic Park, the chairman and his wife did have influence.

At the press conference, White opened by pouncing on the inaccurate statement from Willie Harkness about cup-presentation protocol. The Celtic players were absolutely entitled to go back on the field with the trophy and show it to their fans. This was something the press already knew, although by that time the SFA chairman was not easy to track down for a retraction. White was right to emphasise that point, but he suddenly changed tack altogether. He turned on Rangers. He was incensed that they had endorsed the suggested connection between his players coming back on to the field and the battle royal later. According to him the reactions of the Rangers fans had to be put into historical context. Whether appropriate or not for that occasion, he hit Rangers where he knew they would be vulnerable; their unwritten, unspoken, but demonstrably sectarian stance. This was the real nub of the matter, he insisted, clearly implying that this is what drove the reaction of the Rangers crowds. He was attempting to raise the discussion to a new level that would engage a wider audience. To back up the line he was now adopting, he dipped into statistics:

> Although I only checked on the details later I can tell you that Celtic's Cup Final side featured six Catholic players and five Protestants who included our captain Danny McGrain.

The inference was that the composition of the Rangers team had no such diversity, that they were uniformly Protestant, and that our focus should be, not on who got over the fence first, but on the basic hostility that arose from an obvious sectarian stimulus, perpetuated by Rangers' signing policy. He also knew that Rangers had no grounds for rebutting his overall assertions, and that in dabbing some moral overtones on to the discussion, he would win favour from a more discerning public. It was an astute way to defend Celtic's players from the straightforward accusation that they caused it all. What he did not refer to was the growing suggestion among the media that some Celtic fans had deliberately provoked a response by goading the Rangers support. There was undeniably a strong element of that in their encroachment into the Rangers end. Of course, a Celtic supporter kicking a ball into the empty net as a trumpeting of triumphalism might not constitute a crime against humanity. The average person of liberal instinct might even applaud such hilarious audacity. But we were not dealing with such bland normality. Nor do we believe that many on that terracing had signed up to Quaker principles. These were people honed in the antagonistic culture of this event and saw it as a challenge. However deplorable it was, the response was inevitable.

The Match Commander Hamish MacBean viewed their turnaround:

It was an amazing sight. A huge gap had appeared on the terracing at the Rangers end between top and bottom. There were still a few down at the foot near the fence, but the majority were massed up at the top trying to get out. Then all of a sudden they turned round. The Celtic supporters had come down to the other end and that was that. That seemed to change the whole scene. The Rangers fans simply turned on their heels, and back down the terracing they poured and over the fence. Of course they were out of order. But I was not in the least surprised at their reaction.

All-consuming hatred had turned them back towards the pitch. They were welcoming what they now saw as an invite. But White had astutely launched the right kind of counter-attack himself, and succeeded in defending his players, and diverting attention away from the perception of provocation by his own supporters. In referring to the recent détente which had been established between the clubs and which seemed to herald an extended pause in the mutual carping at each other, White told the *Daily Record*:

> They blame us. This annoys me. In fact it appals me. We had not drifted apart until the Rangers statement today. It's not our doing. Don't blame us for drifting apart.

This was a full-blooded question and answer press conference, in contrast to Rangers issuing a bare statement, then batting away any other press requests. So much for a mutual peace pact as a going concern. It was now back to the old warring instincts again, producing boardroom acrimony across the city, with White's words attempting to be as lethal as a Pomagne bottle flying through the air.

Rangers, though, just ducked. That sort of invective had been railed against them since the First World War. They knew that without some full-blooded debate in public, within a kind of jurisprudence context, which was highly unlikely, all they needed to do was hunker down until the first flush of passionate attacks on their inflexibility abated and it would all become part of Scottish football's background wallpaper again. But, they could not hold out forever. Although I doubt if the respective chairmen of the clubs would have been holding their breath waiting to see how their governing body would act. It did. Disappointingly in a way, that did not shake the football establishment to the core.

The Executive and General Purposes Committee of the SFA met on 1 July 1980 and distinguished itself by demonstrating how inept they were in being unable to grasp the realities of the Old Firm entrenchments. They had interviewed the respective club chairmen, who as I recall, immediately after, in some of the interviews I attended, did not appear to be traumatised by the experience. They were both fined £20,000 for the misdemeanours of their respective supporters. In the values of recent years that would be about £80,000. Even had that latter figure been the actual sum, do you imagine that either club would have been scurrying around the banks to raise that sum? It was not only a pitiful gesture, it was reinforcing the view that these two institutions were virtually untouchable and that the SFA were only masters of impotent outrage. They could deliver fine words like this in their official report:

> The brutal and disgusting scenes which followed as bottles flew and drunken supporters charged and counter-charged from one end of the field to the other, brought disgrace upon the two clubs concerned, upon Scottish football generally, and were an affront to Scotland as a nation. It is pointless to speculate that the supporters of one club were any worse than those of the other. Jack was as good as his master when the brutality started.

It is a safe bet that the last sentence was not concocted by Willie Harkness, the chairman of that committee. It bore the imprint of the SFA secretary Ernie Walker, who liked to colour his reports as if he were a columnist on a newspaper. But he added little colour to the paragraph which referred to the basis of the traditional bitterness which had surfaced so violently. It just limps across the page:

> The committee sought assurances from both clubs that they would, by their actions and policies, renounce all forms of sectarianism. The Celtic club is willing to co-operate. The Rangers club insists that its present policies are in keeping with the Association's wishes. The committee is not satisfied with the latter's assertion.

The last sentence is hardly like throwing the kitchen sink at an institution. Indeed, the toilet roll which struck Ballantrae on the rump and caused it to bolt was more lethal than the SFA's so-called indictment. There is certainly no thrust of ultimatum in their overall summation, as there ought to have been, over such a violent episode. But the White strategy of focusing on his opponents' vulnerability, had at least caused it to be discussed as a problem staring everyone in the face. Airing it alone. though, which had been done on several occasions in the past, meant nothing in itself, especially as the SFA committee had an escape route out of the issue, which they were at pains to make clear:

> having sought the advice of the Association's legal agents, it regrets it has no authority to insist that the clubs should renounce

any act of policy which could be said to encourage political or religious bigotry.

The word 'morality' appears nowhere, not even as an addendum to their considerations. It could have been, if there had been any bolder minds on the committee appreciating that one club clearly, although unofficially, was regarding some of its fellow citizens as inferior beings. Knowing Ernie Walker as I did, I was equally convinced that he was the very man to broach the subject with little compunction. I know that throughout his career he did ask awkward questions of Rangers without, of course, denting their stance. However, although he was the instigator of many changes about to appear on the horizon for the SFA, there was little chance of him nudging his members towards a full-blown debate on what many outside the inner sanctum of the game saw as a prime social issue. Within just a week you could sense a lowering of the temperature around the issue, even at a time when the country was sweltering so much in the fierce heat that the Forestry Commission was closing 100,000 acres of their woodlands for fear of accidental fires being ignited. The money markets were similarly incendiary, with the UK suffering a stratospheric 21 per cent inflation rate, the highest in the developed world at the time. In short, people were now being distracted by events that were hurting them in other ways, perhaps daily life becoming more expensive, or alternatively, offering unexpected pleasures, like 'doon the watter' now being as attractive as a sojourn in Benidorm. So even a short passage of time was beginning to minimise the effect of 10 May 1980. This was especially so when England came to Hampden two weeks later and we all felt a sense of relief in turning our backs on the choking parochialism of the Old Firm final.

The result did not help though. Scotland lost 2-0. I doubt if I had ever witnessed such a numbed ending to this fixture. It was a cruelly sobering experience. Only the police could gain satisfaction from the funereal ending. Their presence had been doubled to manage a similar-sized crowd. But there was still a hangover among the public from the Cup Final.

Superintendent Ken Stewart was on duty at Hampden that day. He recalled the police shift change during the game, with the early-duty officers being replaced by the later shift:

They came on duty around the track indicating their strength of numbers. But the crowd suddenly intervened. They started to chant, 'Too late! Too late!'

Their minds were still etched by the Cup Final miscalculation.

Ken Stewart reminded me there was no strict separation of Scottish and English supporters in that period. Strathclyde police were definitely conscious of that, after the catastrophe of the final. And yet, there were only 20 arrests at the Scotland–England match, partly due to the negative publicity attached to the Old Firm match and the serious warnings about conduct which were megaphoned to the public. The spectators were acutely aware of a higher visibility of police in and around the stadium, but you could hardly claim the disaster of the Scottish Cup Final had driven home a lesson on abstinence at a football match. For if you were to read the press afterwards, the police had been successful in preventing booze going through the turnstiles, with more bins having been provided at entry points. However, after the game, when Hampden had been cleared and cleaned up, the authorities were left with three large skips loaded with bottles and cans of booze. It was evidence of smuggling artifice on the scale of a Colombian drug cartel. Indeed, Hamish MacBean witnessed a sight as Hampden drained of spectators which might have made a case for alcohol as a force for breaking down cultural barriers. To his great amusement he noted two Scottish fans and two from England, who had their arms wrapped around each other. They were, 'roarin fou', obviously having guzzled much throughout the game. The merry carousing went on until they released their grip on one another. At which point, with no other visible means of support available, they collapsed, laughing, onto the terracing, hopeless but harmless wrecks. There were four empty spirit bottles lying at their feet. Scotland had lost to the Auld Enemy 2-0, and yet neither antagonism nor triumphalism was present in that foursome.

WPC Mudie was at that game on her horse. Eric Craig was not. He had photographed the policewoman in all her majesty in the Cup Final but now the massive publicity they both received portrayed them as a Winner and Loser, even more so than Billy McNeill and John Greig.

# CHAPTER 13

# Heroes of the Hour

WHEN HE ARRIVED at the Southern General Hospital by ambulance after the 1980 Scottish Cup Final, Eric Craig was still fully conscious, although his hearing remained dulled. They had brought him to a hospital which was an institution renowned throughout Europe for brain surgery of all kinds. Being fully aware of that reputation, he felt a degree of comfort in knowing that he would be receiving the best of treatment. He was still trying to comprehend just how serious all this was. The x-rays and scans were completed quickly and the gravity of his condition was spelled out by a young Australian surgeon, who told him, 'You have a depressed fracture of the skull'.

To anybody, not least the man having to lie there and hear that pronouncement, it would sound scary. Craig, though, simply wanted them to get on with it. They had to caution him to be patient. The surgeon told him the operation would not take place that night because he would have to receive various medications. It would take place the following day. The memory of that night awaiting his fate in the operating theatre is not one he treasures:

> I was put into a small ward with three other people, which sounds cosy enough. We were all curtained off. But in the middle of the night two of the folk there were carted out. Dead. I suddenly realised that this was a bloody serious place to be in and bloody hell I hope I'm not next.

They prepared him for his op. As many of us know, lying on a trolley awaiting the ultimate push into the operating theatre, it's difficult to resist the feeling that something might go wrong. The outside world can seem remote in that antiseptic, lulled atmosphere, as you place trust in total strangers, no matter their recognised expertise. One nurse, however, boosted his confidence with a special request that although seeming so utterly detached and inappropriate in this perilous context, nevertheless encouraged him to believe that he was going to battle through this successfully. For her sake, he had to.

His face, and the news of his injury, had been spread all over the Sunday morning newspapers. This nurse thought she recognised him and was clearly keen on verification. Yes, he was the man everyone had seen at Hampden being struck by a bottle. Yes, he had been the most serious of all the injuries. Yes, he worked for the *Daily Record*. Yes, he was a photographer. Then, with that confirmation, she asked the question that suddenly gave him a sense of purpose:

Do you think you could get my husband two tickets for the Scotland–England game coming up?

Ordinarily, he, like many of us in the media, would have thrown himself out of a window to avoid being pestered for tickets for this fixture, which were as hard to get, even for us in the business, as gold nuggets in Sauchiehall Street. But lying in a bed with the thought of people about to poke around in his skull to mend him, he still retained a composure and struck a bargain:

You get me out of here in one piece and I'll get you two tickets for that game.

The surgeon, thankfully for Craig, was an Australian who obviously had no interest in football because all he talked about was what they were going to do with his skull. They were going to lift it. Craig was warned they would possibly have to insert a metal plate in the specific area of the fracture, depending on the depth of the depression. They would only know that after they had gone into the area. Initially, the medical team had to be concerned with a subdural haematoma, that is a bursting of a blood vessel under the skull, which could cause the formation of a clot that could enlarge and cause irreparable damage to the brain. They examined the optic disc in the retina to give them an indication of the extent of the clot. Its size would have determined the nature of the procedure. But, the brain, in any case, was under pressure from the depression on his skull. The fact that operations of that kind were hardly ever performed on a Sunday at that hospital underlined how serious a state he was in. The medical team started their task around 7am in the morning.

Craig cannot say how long the operation itself lasted, but he did not recover full consciousness until early in the afternoon. He learned that they had decided not to insert a plate, and that they had successfully lifted his skull to their satisfaction, to eliminate any immediate danger. The lengthy process was successful, in as much as it saved him from major consequences, but it certainly did not leave him unscathed:

> Even to this day, if you took your finger and pressed down on my skull, even with a full head of hair that I have, you would feel a depression of about half-an-inch. That was the actual point of impact of the Pomagne bottle. It's still there.

As he lay in hospital recuperating from this serious operation, he was at least immune from the debate raging in the outside world. Though he was not being ignored by his own colleagues in the media, who began to portray him as a symbol of the degradation of a major sporting event. He was gratified by the quick response of those who knew him well, the Rangers and Celtic players who were prominent visitors for this man who had been an essential conduit to their own public. He was seen as a downed image-maker, a pal and possibly an underrated asset for the promotion of the game in general. Significantly, he had no visitors from either the police or the SFA, in all the time he was in the Southern and General. Decades later he is still conscious of that. As Craig himself put it:

> I learned later that the SFA and the cops were expecting me to sue the pants off them for gross negligence.

In fact he had no intention of doing so. He was a professional who intended to keep working at his trade, and consequently he felt he had to keep a trustful relationship with these authorities.

In any case, as Craig himself points out, in those years, society was probably less litigious-minded than in the 21st century. More importantly, he was simply glad to be alive and recovering, albeit with a defect that was to plague him for the rest of his life. For all the marvellous work they had performed on his skull, his hearing had been affected by the blow. Nothing was sharp and distinct any longer. He was weeks in hospital, but they could do nothing to change the dullness in the ears. But, if you have been saved from a truly life-threatening injury, then an ear problem might seem trivial. It was to prove anything but. It is ironic that, in pursuing a solution to this, it took him to a place that through the years has sadly inspired many of the sectarian hatreds of the Old Firm, and of which, effectively, he was a victim. He was to go to Belfast.

*****

WPC Elaine Mudie was having drinks in a bar in Glasgow with her fiancé at the time Eric Craig was being whipped to the Southern and General. Her partner was a policeman as well and they would have completely relaxed had a news bulletin not been flashed up on the television screen. Her fiancé watched with a mix of pride and apprehension as Elaine galloped into the throng on her white horse. Her liberal use of the baton might also have been a cautionary sight to a man about to wed this warrior. Although he would have known, unlike the others in the pub, that the scene did not reflect her natural charm. In that pub they were cheering her on. We never came anywhere near putting a name to her before our broadcast went off the air, but we realised there would be an almighty rush, by the press, to identify and praise her. She was blissfully unaware of this interest as she left the stadium, her work a triumph. Much of her life, immediately after that day, would be in the same bracket. As they sat in the crowded pub that night, she was experiencing for the first time, the peculiar sensation of being talked about as a television personality, however briefly. She didn't yet realise it, but this was merely the start of fitting into Andy Warhol's thesis, 'In the future everybody will be world famous for 15 minutes'. She was to outlast that prognosis. She got another early warning of being propelled to fame when they travelled back on a late night bus and were able to see the early editions of the newspapers for sale on the streets. Her name and face were splashed all over the pages. She decided to make a comment to one newspaper, after she had been told that her horse Ballantrae had been seen foaming at the mouth near the end of the mess. She retorted, 'So would you be, if you'd been between my legs for four hours!' Cute. But like Neil Armstrong's first quotes on the moon, it was not spontaneous, but had been a standing joke in the police community, which she had then used with impeccable timing.

More importantly she was now a local favourite, a Glasgow girl who had 'done good'. This voiced itself at Hampden when she went two weeks later to patrol the Scotland–England match. She had a female colleague with her this time. So now there were two blonde women on white horses and on her admission, they 'gabbed' together like they were on a hens' night out, to the annoyance of their superintendent, until the shouts of acclamation greeted them. And above all she was hailed as a hero by many shouts of 'Haw, hen. Widyae gie us your autograph?' No greater honour could be bestowed on her than being afforded Glasgow celebrity status. But of course this had been a global affair, given that the riot interest had spread like a plague. So fan mail came in. That was inevitable. It came from all over. But one day she opened a letter and discovered it had come from Hollywood.

*****

The nurse at the Southern and General did get her two tickets for the Auld Enemy game. An appeal by Eric Craig to Ernie Walker of the SFA accomplished that. He was deeply indebted to the hospital staff, from surgeon to nurses. They had saved his life, but he was still unsure about his future. He could not hear properly. Sound was thick and fuzzy, although discernible. His morale was boosted by the attitude of his employers at the *Daily Record* who made it clear to him that he could stay off work for as long as necessary, and, perhaps more importantly, that he would have a job at the newspaper for as long as he wished. Although he did baulk at one suggestion from within his trade that all photographers should wear a helmet, or a hard hat of some sort, when covering football matches from then on. He dismissed that like the hardy, fundamentalist photographer he was:

It would just make you a bloody target, not the opposite. I was the first to say 'No!' to that.

He was equally adamant to everybody he met that he was suffering no mental traumas about the incident, although you might have

HEROES OF THE HOUR

expected such. Then, shortly after his hospitalisation, he learned that Detective Inspector Joe Jackson was making major efforts to identify the person who had thrown that brutal Pomagne bottle. In his book, *Chasing Killers* Jackson recalls the search and how he categorised this specific incident:

> It was, in actual fact, an attempted murder. The only way I could perhaps identify the proverbial needle in the haystack was to approach the various news agencies and request that they supply me with all the footage and photographs. The media responded quite readily and soon my small office in the Gorbals was festooned with photos of the riot in its various stages.

This was to no avail. But he felt the video footage from the BBC would solve the search for the culprit.

> This was extremely helpful, as at one point the camera was focused on the mounted policewoman and her male colleague as they galloped around the track near the Rangers end where Eric Craig was standing and I managed to get a clear view of him seconds before he was struck. Unfortunately, I could not spot the bottle hurler, and he was never caught.

It does show, nevertheless, how seriously the police were taking this. Naturally, Craig was disappointed that they could not conclude the investigation, but he had other matters to be concerned with. In the four months before he could take up regular duties again, his worries about the muted world around him increased. His hearing was getting no better. This was becoming more evident in his daily work at the newspaper. So his employers stepped in.

Craig had learned of the work in the Royal Victoria Hospital in Belfast, especially that of a Professor Gordon Smyth. By 1980 that hospital had become distinguished in its work on injuries, from explosions of all kinds, at the height of The Troubles. Smyth headed a specialist unit which dealt with hearing problems emanating, un-surprisingly, from bomb-blasts. The *Daily Record* decided to send their chief photographer over there for treatment, to the very city that spawned many of the Old Firm hatreds which had taken their toll on him at Hampden that day. He saw the irony of it. And, despite the fact that this was still at the height of The Troubles, he took it upon himself to walk through the tribal landmarks that were part of the street jargon in his own city of Glasgow, even though lines of soldiers were patrolling these areas, the Shankill Road, and the Falls Road in particular. He was compelled to visit places he knew were held in some odd reverence by the fans, who used to flock from there to Celtic Park and Ibrox every week. What did surprise him was that soldiers were sometimes to be seen actively on duty in the corridors of the hospital itself. This was simply because it was sited in a continuing war zone and some of it had inevitably spilled over into the building.

Dr Denis Coppell, a consultant who worked there during The Troubles, recalled it well:

> You had to protect patients from the gunmen. You had an IRA man who was strapped up with fractures. The IRA came in one night, cut him down, and took him away.

As a consequence he was forced to contact the Prime Minister.

> I wrote to Margaret Thatcher and explained the problems of security in the hospital. She replied, 'Whatever needs to be done, will be done'. Very quickly we got a secure unit – bulletproof windows, doors and guards.

Secure or not, Craig, lying in bed awaiting treatment, found it all scary. In fact he refused to allow his family to come anywhere near the city because of his own anxieties. With soldiers running along the corridors from time to time, he was in wonderment at how the medical staff could still practise at the highest levels. Equally, he was still trying to come to terms with the fact that he had emerged as a victim of Hampden's sectarian battleground, only to find himself in a worse reality that made the riot seem like a game of Trivial Pursuit.

The medics diagnosed severe nerve damage in the ear. They stripped it down, rebuilt the inside of it, and inserted a couple of bits of plastic. This took time. During his residence at the hospital, Craig became acquainted with the strange hierarchical culture of the urban warzone, right there in the middle of his ward of four. There was a patient opposite him whom he began to believe must have been high up in the IRA. He seemed to have a hold over the staff and did what he liked. People respected him in a way that seemed to suggest he was of great significance and that offending him would not be the wisest option. He had a locker full of cigarettes and booze, which was against hospital rules. The day before Craig was due to be discharged he offered him a glass of lager. Although the photographer did feel like it, he had been warned off alcohol as it might have affected a urine test which he was to take before being allowed to leave. However, the nameless man told him there was nothing to worry about and that he really would like a farewell drink with him. He would take care of everything. Even the urine test. Craig, aware of this individual's uncanny authority, relented. The drink was taken, the blood test wasn't. So Craig left Belfast much the wiser about the ways of a troubled island and the power of its godfathers.

\* \* \* \* \*

Elaine's letter from Hollywood was signed by a Gregor Roy. It was the first of several from a man who was a writer, an academic, winner of major American poetry awards and of the 1974 American Heritage Award, which was connected culturally with the Kennedy Centre, Washington. He wrote to her not from the capital but from Hollywood, because he was also an actor. Not in the same league as say Paul Newman, but he did appear in the same film as the renowned actor, in *The Verdict* where he played the role of the foreman of the jury. Not a part as challenging as King Lear exactly, but it was one of several movies where he played small parts and seemed to be firmly in the actor's community out there. Why did he become fascinated by a Glaswegian policewoman? For a start he had been born in Bonnybridge near Falkirk in 1929, and obviously yearned for reminders of his homeland. Then he made it clear in his letters that he admired her spirit. Being a poet, and also someone who had served in The Black Watch, he clearly saw something romantic in her role. A blonde, a white horse, a crowd of hostiles throwing things, the stuff that scripts are made of. Boudicca? Joan of Arc? Guinevere even? Being in the creative arts I suppose he could imagine Elaine in a more exalted situation than dealing with Old Firm thugs. To give her a taste of what he was immersed in himself, he even sent her the script for *The Verdict*. They corresponded over several years which suggests her appearance had stirred some inexplicable emotion in this man. She cannot recall now if she ever replied that her thrilling charge had initially been caused by a toilet roll striking Ballantrae's rump. That might not have matched his Arthurian take on her role.

The impact Elaine had made on people was one positive to have come out of the global exposure of the game. But this pleasant woman with a hearty laugh and sense of humour that sends you away with a lilt in your step was never blown away by the kind of exposure that could lead a man on the other side of the world to place her on a pedestal. Nor did it upset her lifestyle. She went on to have two daughters, never stopped being a breadwinner and seems immensely content with life. Although she was at pains to boil it all down to her own, almost dismissive, summary:

> Look, it was just because I was a blonde on a white horse. That was all.

However there was another more lasting impact she made by her actions at Hampden. Something that struck a cause for her gender, despite her own modesty on the matter. To put it in a historical context, consider this exchange in the House of Lords, several days after the final.

> KILMANY: My lords, while many people admired very much the courage of the mounted policewoman, riding a white horse, who joined in the police charge at Hampden Park in very disagreeable circumstances, may I ask if this is not really the most suitable way to deploy female labour, however courageous?

> PAGET: My Lords, is the noble Lord aware that, speaking from long and personal experience, once you put 'em on a horse, the female sex are far more deadly than the male?

That was parliament in the '80s, not Simla at the time of the Raj. Nowadays such chat would put even a couple of Lords into the Tower of London. It reeks of male arrogance. But it was worthy of ridicule even then, as it hinted of a claustrophobic parliamentary clique, unable to sense the changes, albeit tiny, that were advancing women in society.

But it would be wrong to think that such thinking was confined to well-fed Neanderthals in the Lords.

Elaine, with almost disarming modesty, made it abundantly clear to me that at no stage before, during, and after the riot, did she identify herself as an isolated pioneer. It never occurred to her, even after the first wave of enthusiasm for her performance swept over her, that she would be seen as an inspirational figure to other women. But that is exactly how Jenny Shanks, West Area Chair of the Scottish Police Federation saw it back in 2019:

> What Elaine did was great for the police and women like me. What an iconic picture it was that day. Remember, it was fairly unique for a woman to be in the police at all, at that time, let alone being in the mounted branch. When I joined in 1991 there was only about ten per cent of women in the force. And let's be frank there was cultural and open sexism in operation. Some of the names women were called were appalling and that was by their own colleagues. Indeed there was a male officer in my shift who refused to work with me because I was a woman. And that wasn't uncommon. But I have to say other men on the shift did actually help us. They were the younger ones who began to realise that women were going to be part of them from now on. Although attitudes were stubbornly sexist. For example when a woman got promotion one of the first questions anybody would ask was, 'Who was she sleeping with?'

Jenny also recalled a practice within the ranks which might be reminiscent of what Caligula got up to:

> It was called the Office Stamp. When a female was new to a shift, part of the initiation was to take her upstairs then her tights and her drawers would be taken down, and she would be stamped with the office stamp on her backside. She now belonged to the office. She belonged to the shift.

In one single afternoon in the middle of a football pitch, whilst the majority looking on were concerned about a football result and its consequences, Elaine popularised the fight for an appreciation for women's status in society, unwittingly perhaps, by putting put her own stamp on sexism's backside. Everybody I spoke to agreed that she had done more to encourage female recruitment than several promotional campaigns, especially seated on her white horse, Ballantrae, who, for the record, passed away in retirement on a farm in the Highlands years later. It's a story Disney could still work wonders on.

\* \* \* \* \*

On the other hand Eric Craig's experience in the Royal Victoria in Belfast might have attracted the script writers of *Line of Duty*. It opened his eyes to how sectarian issues can permeate even a valuable institution which was neutrally coping with the outcome of violence. Alas, they did not solve his hearing problem which deteriorated over the years to the stage that, without two hearing aids, he would be completely deaf. You can take it he still has a distaste of Pomagne. But, long before that gradual deterioration had reached a critical stage, and not long after he had finished his recuperation, he went straight back to work at football matches. Indeed, one year after the riot, on 9 May 1981, he returned to Hampden to work on the Rangers–Dundee United Scottish Cup Final. He found the old place had changed.

# CHAPTER 14

# Sober Times

HAMPDEN PARK HAD been dried out. The McElhone Report on Scottish football crowd behaviour, produced by the Glaswegian MP Frank McElhone in 1978, had lain collecting dust. It needed the kiss of life. Paradoxically it received just that on the day of that Scottish Cup Final in 1980: emerging from the aftermath came the proposal to ban alcohol from all Scottish football grounds. Thus, it was given legislative force by the Criminal Justice (Scotland) Act 1980, which went even further, enforcing a ban on alcohol from trains and coaches carrying spectators to grounds for games. For some this was hard to take, considering the culture of indiscriminate drinking which surrounded football, and many supporters told me that they felt they were being treated like cattle by the police, being herded on and off buses and searched for booze. I saw this with my own eyes travelling to games, and had a stranger from our society witnessed this, they might have concluded we lived in a totalitarian state. Some occasions brought to mind the way people were treated around grounds during the World Cup in Argentina in 1978, at the height of the Videla military junta dictatorship. Of course to offer any sympathy to fans in that matter was to bring loud protests from those who could easily cry 'They brought it upon their own heads!'. Without question it brought sobriety in general to stadia.

Those who were allowed to drink behind curtains or venetian blinds in their executive boxes could also let their passions get the better of them, as I know only too well. For alcohol was hardly diluted because of your status in life. There is the example of the man I have already identified, Ken Stewart. The effort involved in completing his report on the Hampden riot, and the task he was charged with when appointed as security officer for the SFA in 1984, took a heavy toll. As he put it himself, 'I hit the bottle big time'. This resulted in him having to leave his SFA position because of a drink-driving offence. That very factor of alcohol, which lay at the heart of the Hampden riot among the less reputable in society and over which Stewart and his colleagues were then anguishing, had ironically snared him. Set against the serious issues of public conduct, often associated with alcohol, which he was pursuing diligently, this was no longer an abstract issue, but a cripplingly personal demonstration that the problems of drinking should not be viewed in any narrow context, as say, in a football stadium, but as a wider social problem. To his great credit, Ken Stewart showed great resilience in fighting back to normality. With the help of the Priory Hospital Glasgow, he went on to gain a degree in Psychology at Glasgow University and became a full-time advisor at that same clinic.

Although some clear-headed, and immaculately behaved supporters were dragged into the consequences of these changes, I did accept that this legislation fulfilled the social need to move football on from the age in which the recreational pleasures of the least advantaged in society were alcohol-dependent. The working-man's sport had been mired in the habitual practise of stoking the senses to make football more meaningful. The 'cairy-oot' from the pub was as vital to many supporters as an oxygen mask was to a space-walker. Prohibition was to breed a different kind of supporter through the years, although with glaring exceptions. But, in an immediate sense, photographer Eric Craig, on his return to the scene of his mishap, was working in a different Hampden. Shortly after the 1981 final I recorded an interview with the secretary of the SFA, Ernie Walker, who always talked about the stadium as if it were a shrine, and which he felt had been desecrated the year before. He was in a much better frame of mind the day I spoke to him. He recalled:

It was a quiet Sunday morning. I took my two girls to Hampden to have a look around. It was the day after the Rangers–Dundee United Scottish Cup Final, which I had attended. The place, of course, was deserted. We went firstly down to the end where the United supporters would have been and climbed into the terracing. Now, usually on a Sunday morning after a game like that you wouldn't have been able to walk anywhere for thousands of bottles lying about. It was devoid of them. So I told my girls, 'I'll give you a pound for every bottle you can find'. About 20 minutes later one of them came back with a single

Coca-Cola can which had been flattened underfoot. That was all. Then we went down to the Rangers end where the bulk of the crowd would have been. We could not fill a single shopping bag with what had been left. In all the previous years we would come and see ten huge industrial skips being filled with bottles. Now I had been cynical about this legislation and felt the habits were so ingrained in the fans that they would still bring the bevvy to the game regardless. But I was astonished. It worked. It was the most spectacularly successful piece of legislation I have ever known. This was an historic watershed in our game. I'll always remember that squashed Coca-Cola can. It told the whole story.

It is clear that politicians were heavily banking on the new legislation solving all the problems of football. In one sense it has not. We now know, almost 40 years on, that clubs are facing a new problem. In their searches of the stands after games they are finding evidence of drug use during matches. That is obviously more difficult to police. Sound bites from politicians promised much, but essentially they were ducking issues. Such was Alex Fletcher's posture. The Scottish Office Minister simply went off at a tangent in his first utterings:

> Crowds at such matches may have to be limited to much smaller numbers, to a size the police know they can handle with the manpower available.

A grannie from Grangemouth, watching all this from afar could have come up with that. Malcolm Rifkind, the Scottish Office Minister with responsibility for Home Affairs jumped on the effect new legislation would enact:

> The events at Hampden prove how right the Government is to be legislating in the Criminal Justice Bill to prevent alcohol into designated football grounds. The banning of alcohol from the terracings would be a major step towards a return to more civilised behaviour at events like this.

It certainly would, if you were to discount the obscene bigoted chants and songs that would continue to assail the air in Old Firm matches

in an atmosphere of supposed sobriety. Bigotry carries its own
intoxication. Councillor Jeanette Mason, regional member for the
King's Park area, absolutely wanted closed doors at Old Firm games
at Hampden:

> The people of the area have suffered enough animal behaviour of
> the hooligans of the supporters of both clubs. It is time they got
> rid of the religious element that surrounds these games – but how
> they go about it I don't know.

Certainly John Maxton, the Labour MP for the Hampden area, had
touched on it when he said religious bigotry was a major factor in the
violence. He told Gordon Campbell of the *Scottish Daily Express* that
'strong pressure has to be put on both clubs to end this bigotry'. But
like the councillor's plaintive bemusement at the end of her sentiments
these comments carried little weight, since they offered nothing
practical in the way of solution. Which is why they concentrated on
other physical aspects. There was the focus on the fence. Bigger fences?
Simple solution? Frank Campbell secretary of Queen's Park told the
Glasgow *Evening Times,* a few days after:

> The value of the Hampden fence is that it slows people up. No
> one is going to tell me that if you put a 40-foot high fence up
> people are not going to get over it. The Hampden fence was put
> up to assist in preventing fans from invading the field, and to a
> degree it does.

And as we have seen, paradoxically it might also have produced
a catastrophe, had not the alert police officer taken the initiative to
alleviate pressure against it at the Celtic end. But in all this outpouring
from various sources, everybody seemed to be skirting the real problem
of sectarianism. And of all the public correspondence to the press
at the time, ranging from outright denunciations of both clubs but
particularly Rangers for their enduring sectarian stance, one did catch
the eye. Not because it fulminated against the weak response from the
SFA but because the letter, published in *The Glasgow Herald* on 15
May 1980, adopted a wry, mocking tone which was just as effective in
pointing out the weak hypocrisy of those in office there:

Sir, – In light of the fact that a Highland League club almost faced extinction when the SFA banned them from playing at home for a considerable period following the pitch invasion by ONE spectator I trust that the same organisation will now impose a temporary ban on the Old Firm from the Scottish Cup. If not, people will ask if there is one law for the rich, and one law for the poor.

> Alan J Reid,
> 58 Dalry Road,
> Ardrossan

What really was occurring was the developing attitude that it won't happen again because with efficient, adequately resourced policing, trouble would be contained. This essentially diverted attention away from the root cause of sectarian division and all that flowed naturally from it. We could not have anticipated then that it would take another era for conditions to change that would, at least, lay the foundations for more radical approaches to the problem, and which would shake the footballing community to the core, in many ways. For I believe the outcome of 10 May 1980 influenced events enough to bring to the fore two men who would eventually reconfigure the Old Firm landscape with the elemental force of a hurricane. If the pair of them had a liking for an anthem that would have reflected their interests, it would not have been derived from Irish history, as was the culture of the legions, but from a Swedish ditty, 'Money! Money! Money!'

# CHAPTER 15

# The Dawn of a New Era

DAVID MURRAY, SUCCESSFULLY developing his wide business interests at the time, and Fergus McCann, exiled in Canada, viewed that day at Hampden in 1980 from different angles. The first-named would have been mildly aware of the result, but indifferent to that outcome. The other well-pleased. But, both of them were to emerge as two of the most significant figures in Scottish football over the period of the millennium. This was a result of one largely overlooked factor – the beginning of the downfall of one man, the Rangers manager John Greig. In the notoriety attached to that fixture for its pitched battle we tend to forget the effect of the game itself, and of what part it played for the losers. Greig's team should have won that final given the depletion of Celtic's resources in crucial areas. Had they won, the future of his club and even of its rivals might have been entirely different. The long-term history of Rangers would have been radically altered. For that day saw the early stages of disenchantment setting in around a man whom the Rangers support had revered for his valiant efforts, as a player for the club, in adverse times for them. As his opposite number Billy McNeill once said to me, in admiration of the man:

> You felt at times that Greggy single-handedly kept Rangers going when he was on the park. He was a great inspiration.

In 1999 the supporters were to elect him as Rangers greatest ever player. But, as manager, if you could complete a season without winning anything, and, crucially, aggravating that with a defeat in a Cup Final against bitter rivals, then, at the very least, doubts would inevitably arise about your suitability. These doubts grew in geometric progression. He would leave Rangers in October 1983 with a decent record in cup competitions but never having won the league. And having average attendances of around a paltry 16,000 at Ibrox at the time of his departure, it set off a chain reaction that would eventually put Murray centre stage and which Celtic, eventually, were compelled to respond to 13 years later as the club, unable to compete with Rangers at that time, also faced the possibility of extinction.

Thus, I have always identified Murray and McCann as products of that riot day. They were bequeathed the ultimate consequences of an iconic Rangers figure beginning to lose respect as a manager. What we were witnessing that day in 1980, in fact, was also the beginning of the end of traditional club governance. Everything about the two clubs had seemed set in granite under the dynastic control of two families – the Kellys and the Marlboroughs. But they were failing in different ways. Murray was the first to crash into the sacred domain with an entrepreneurish gleam in his eye. McCann would follow, much later, riding on a bulldozer, targeting the old ways and the people cosseting them. Murray was the classic business opportunist with little interest in Rangers previously, but buying them for a song at £6 million, and, at least in the initial stage, little interest in learning the words of 'The Sash My Father Wore'. McCann was not just a saviour of a club in distress but an iconoclast whose views on reformation were not limited to his views on Celtic. Nothing in the Scottish game was sacred to him. But, successful though they both had been in business, they were not out of the same mould.

Murray was loud and bombastic; McCann, quieter, but with the ability to say something that pricked the conscience of the listener. I recall Murray once saying to me, at a time when there was some rumpus going on about possible league reconstruction of which he did not approve, 'I'll buy the league'. A flatulent 'Trumpism', before we knew what that expression meant. McCann, on the other hand, could wither you with a studied silence – which he once levelled at me, almost with contempt, when I stood beside him in an airport, about to board a plane. My bland salutation was met with a grim-reaper expression that I felt as a rebuke which could have been translated into 'You are enemy!' A different breed had taken over. As you could tell from how they emerged from the maelstrom of the business world.

Four years after that Hampden final, Murray won the Scottish Young Businessman of the Year Award through his successful running of a massive steel group at the age of 33. McCann had instigated and was running a flourishing travel business in Canada and the USA, particularly connected with golf. Murray was from Ayr and had made a bid to buy Ayr United FC in the '80s, which had been rejected, but seemed to indicate that his interest in football was purely parochial. McCann, by contrast, was a devoted Celtic supporter who had been social convenor of the Croy Celtic supporters club in his earlier days, and who helped expatriates keep their interest in the old ways by beaming in special games through satellite for them. Sadly, one of those went slightly awry in 1972 when, against serious competition, he won the satellite rights to transmit the Celtic–Milan European Cup Semi-Final second leg from Celtic Park to Toronto's Maple Leaf ice rink. It was a game which saw the first ever penalty shoot-out in this competition. Alas, this game had gone to extra time and the satellite time had been booked for only 90 minutes, given the supreme faith the expats had in their team disposing of the Italians. The transmission had come to a premature end. So the patrons never saw the shoot-out and perhaps thankfully for them, Celtic's exit from the cup. It was a mere hiccup in his vastly successful business career.

For Murray, getting to the top in industry, was an early motivation, augmented by the deeply personal desire to show the world that he could overcome the tragic loss of both legs through a serious crash after a rugby match in 1976. Unlike McCann with Celtic, Murray did not look avidly for Rangers' results every Saturday. The first time I met him was in Livingston, where he owned a basketball team called Murray International. I had been invited to take part in a basketball shoot during the interval of a game the local side were playing, to aid the charity which helped Murray's fellow amputees and to publicise his sponsorship of the town's basketball team. As an early indication of his stellar ambitions and his attraction to big names, he had imported a marvellous American star called Alton Byrd to the team. He continued to rave about Byrd, with obvious justification, as we watched this great player dominate that game. I doubt if he knew the ins and outs of basketball, but he did know what could attract the public even to a minority sport. Little did I realise then that it was a foretaste of what was to come in a totally different sphere. His friendship with Graeme Souness is well enough documented. Together they simply towered menacingly over the stewardship of David Holmes who was running Rangers for Lawrence Marlborough, grandson of former chairman John Lawrence.

Many people did not take Holmes seriously. Indeed there is no evidence of anything within Ibrox now that reflects his time there. He has been airbrushed out of any historical presence in the stadium. A man who had worked up the ladder for the Marlborough building empire, from the tools to the boardroom, and then handed the task of taking a major institution with worldwide support to a higher realm, did not square with certain people. Jim Blair, a journalist for the *Daily Record*, belittled him with this line: 'The *Joiner* from Falkirk who would be the *Carpenter* from Nazareth'. In fact Holmes had shown remarkable fortitude and originality of thinking in the face of mounting scepticism about where his leadership would lead the club. I met him several times in interviews which were all fairly bland, nothing said that would hurt a fly, but off-screen he was more forthcoming. He went into detail with me about how he had earned his position. It was after a drawn 4-4 game at Ibrox on 22 March 1986 against Celtic, who for most of the match were down to ten men. In the boardroom afterwards, Holmes witnessed a scene that convinced him the directors around him were delusional and not fit for purpose. The manager gave them a burst of *The Sash* as he entered the room. They were celebrating the fact that they had achieved a late draw against ten men. On their own pitch. To them it had been a triumph. Having been at the game, it was no triumph. Rangers were at best lucky to get that score. Holmes went home, phoned the owner Lawrence Marlborough in Lake Tahoe in the States and told him he would only stay on if he was given the power to run the club. Arrogant? Above his station? You could say so, if it weren't for the fact that it was, above all, timely. For Marlborough, disenchanted with what was happening back home, agreed and that single telephone call transformed Rangers.

But bigger beasts surrounded Holmes, with Rangers in debt between £4 million and £7 million. Coppers, compared to what they would be lumbered with in future. In talking to him in those days he did give the impression that he was living on borrowed time. So Murray made his offer to acquire a 76 per cent share, with Souness becoming a director and taking 7 per cent. It all seemed cut and dried until there was an intervention. Suddenly, with the temerity of a Caribbean pirate attacking a goal-laden galleon, Robert Maxwell, newspaper magnate and general all-round con man, swept onto the scene with an outrageous bid to upstage Murray. Holmes, still in position as Chief Executive but knowing that his time would soon be up, was lunching with the editor of the *Sunday Mail*, Endell Laird, in the newspaper's offices, when in walked the abrasive Maxwell. The lunch had been arranged merely to soothe some of the conflicts Laird's newspaper had created with Ibrox, so Holmes was not prepared for the entry of the proprietor of the paper, who came to the table all guns blazing on the subject of buying Rangers. He was there to make an offer. Maxwell was an unrepentant bully. I bumped into him in a corridor of BBC Television Centre in London once, sweeping along with half-a-dozen flunkeys looking like subservient rickshaw wallahs trotting at his back, including, incredibly, the former British Ambassador to the USA, the Honourable Peter Jay, who had been beguiled by the man. This extraordinary force penetrated the office that day in Glasgow but was repelled. Rangers' Chief Executive might have given the impression, with his white hair swept nobly back from his brow, that he was of angelic stock. He was far from that. He was from Falkirk and knew how to handle himself. The evidence is that foul language bounced off the walls. Holmes made it clear he would not be intimidated by Maxwell's bombast and sent him packing. As he himself was, by a much bigger animal that toreadors wouldn't have slain. And so started the Murray era.

Not that their sectarian signing tradition became enlightened overnight. I recall Murray saying to me adamantly in the early days of his tenure that they would not buckle to outside critics of the club and that nothing would change in that respect. It was their institution and they would run it the way they wanted. Celtic, on the other hand, free of that kind of myopic handicap, nevertheless seemed to portray an institution that was set against modernity. Rangers were steaming ahead constructing their new stadium, which would eventually become all-seated and admired throughout the footballing world. While Celtic chairman and secretary Desmond White told *The Sunday Post* on 28 October 1984, in response to what was happening elsewhere in stadia development, 'But our supporters have illustrated they don't want our stadium to be all seated'. This was either a noble endorsement of people power, or, as even Celtic supporters would tell me at the time, just a convenient excuse not to spend money. The man who would boast often of having climbed the Eiger could be slightly disoriented at sea level. Rangers, for all the problems related to their hypocritical stance, denying a sectarian attitude that was clearly in evidence to all, were nevertheless now making Celtic look like paupers, housed in a stadium not fit for a modern era and unable to match the spending power of Ibrox, however much that spending became a matter of great contention in later years.

Enter McCann, six years after the Murray spending spree began, with the glittering prizes it brought, particularly league trophies. Rangers' strength was such that it began to look like they would eventually equal or even exceed Jock Stein's record of nine-in-a-row. Poverty, bankruptcy and the humiliation of a proud record being vanquished compelled this little man from Croy to return to Scotland.

By sheer coincidence, at the height of the Celtic crisis I was asked to present and chair *Sport in Question*, a panel discussion programme on Scottish Television. Our ratings blossomed as Celtic folk were sucked into watching the battlefield, which the studio began to resemble, augmented by Rangers viewers clearly enjoying the spectacle of Parkhead fratricide. The Celtic-slanted and potentially hostile studio audience sat there like a phalanx of sprinters on their blocks, tensely awaiting the starter pistol to attack. Loyalty to the owners was absent. This was especially so on one particular night's show. We had invited two cousins to come into this lion's den. As Celtic directors Kevin and Michael Kelly walked in, I could sense the tension developing. Even as I read the introduction on the autocue, I recalled Bette Davis in *All About Eve*, when she crisply anticipates some acrimony at a cocktail party with the comment, 'Fasten your safety belts, we're in for a bumpy night'. The turbulence was not slow in coming, for the invited audience turned this programme into an inquisitorial roughing-up of these cousins in a manner Torquemada would have envied.

It was common knowledge that Celtic were in dire financial straits and yet in the recurring hostility of the audience that night the two men talked as if they, and their handling of Celtic, was being grossly misunderstood. The Kelly dynasty was the problem. That was the loud and clear verdict coming from the audience. I then asked Kevin Kelly, the chairman of the club, outright, if he would ever sell his shares and relinquish ownership of the club. His reply was specific and significant:

I would need to know the person and need to know if his motives were right for the club.

Michael Kelly, who had resolutely defended the existing structure, supplemented his cousin's apparent change of heart by stating clearly that he would be prepared 'to listen to any decent offer'. I remember that line well. The audience took a moment to realise the implication of what had just been uttered, then burst into applause, an acclamation that suggested strongly, 'Well, you've said it and we'll hold you to it. OR ELSE!' It was the first sighting of a chink in their armour. They were admitting for the first time in public that selling up was an option after all. I wondered if this was a smokescreen to get them out of the studio that night alive.

Without doubt the most articulate of all the Celtic-orientated people we had on the show was Brian Dempsey. As a young teacher I had helped his father, Jimmy Dempsey, when he stood as the Labour MP for Airdrie and Coatbridge. His son was a director of the club, a successful businessman and in my view would have enhanced Westminster had he chosen that destination. This was the man who stood on the steps of Celtic Park's front door to make inspirational speeches to the crowds of supporters who would turn up faithfully to hear his bulletins on progress. This articulate voice for Celtic, during their troubles, was to inform me that that the two directors knew full well that the club was hanging by a thread. 'I was watching football until very late one night when I got a phone call', Dempsey told me:

> It was just before midnight. It was from Kevin Kelly, who is a nice man without an ounce of malice in him. He said, 'We've got a wee problem. Could I see you tomorrow morning, but strictly in private'. I asked him to tell me what the problem was. His reply silenced me for a moment: 'If we don't have a million pounds in the banks tomorrow, the club will be put into receivership. And I have already spoken to Noble Grossart [a prominent merchant banking firm] about who would be the best receiver'. I remember replying to Kevin, 'That's a *wee* problem?'

At about the time that was happening, one of our guests on the programme was Liam Brady, the former Arsenal and Republic of Ireland player who had been appointed as Celtic manager in 1991. I sensed his unease. Usually articulate and with valuable insight into the game in general, it was clear he was struggling. All around him in the studio were Celtic people looking for blood. He still retained respect among them for his overall status in the game, even though his results in Scotland were not inspirational. His dilemma, that evening, was that his employers were being pummelled in front of his very eyes. He could neither defend nor join in the chorus of despair. It was one of the few occasions when I felt that we had made a gross mistake putting him in the line of fire. And then I learned of how just much of a dilemma it had been for him. As he lived near me I drove him home and just before he left the car he turned to me and said:

How do you think all this is going to end up? What's going to happen to Celtic?'

Brady, to my surprise, was attributing to me the wisdom of a Solomon. Worse, here was a man charged with the responsibility of stopping the rampant winning form of Rangers but making hardly a dent in their supremacy, completely in the dark about what was happening. He knew no more than the average punter going through the turnstile at Celtic Park. That was one of the most telling revelations of ongoing chaos.

Dempsey wanted the Kellys out, emphatically. And his announcement, 'The battle is over. The rebels have won!' when the dynasty eventually caved in, carried historical political echoes. It also hinted at a disjunction between himself and McCann. Because, inside the stadium in the restaurant McCann had told him exactly what to say. 'The game is over...' was to be its start. Being something of an effective public speaker, I think he was entitled to substitute the word 'battle', for oratorical effect. Their relationship was to deteriorate in a manner that had nothing to do with choice of words and had much more to do with a clash of personality. On one occasion, when Dempsey invited McCann to his home for dinner, an extraordinary scene developed. The host had left the room to collect something and when he came back into the study found the new Celtic owner lying on his back doing exercises that he concluded were of some yoga character. The exercises did not stem McCann's flow of words, because without getting up, he suddenly reprimanded his host by bringing up a malicious rumour that had been circulating about Dempsey. The host was enraged. He asked McCann to leave the house immediately. The relationship was never the same again. Dempsey resigned as a director just as the new owner set out his plans for the future of the club.

For all his lifetime devotion to Celtic, McCann was bringing a fresh mind to running this huge club, with an obvious distaste for the former owners. He must have known he would meet resistance from those of a conventional mindset, like Lou Macari, who lasted only three months as manager after McCann had installed himself in 1994. He detested the new owner:

> We didn't talk for weeks. The first real contact was by memo. He was only a few yards away from me in his office, but he kept sending memos to me, and this first one was to ask me to attend eight o'clock management meetings every Monday morning, with the catering manager, the groundsman and others. I'm not being big headed, but the Celtic manager sitting in at what he called a departmental heads meeting with all these others was just plain daft. I can understand now he was bringing his North American business practises to the job. But it wasn't for me, nor should it have been for any Celtic manager. So I just sent a deputy.

The contrast between the Murray and McCann acquisitions could not be more stark, even in the most basic ways. Murray with his original interest in sport certainly became fascinated with football and could be seen at times standing in the tunnel towards the ends of games, perfectly capable of making comments about players. After all, this was his baby now, this was the best way to publicise him and his other businesses and the games did seem to contain an intrinsic interest for him. This contrasted with McCann. His mission had been to save Celtic for the wide and faithful community of theirs. Once that had been secured, the football seemed to be almost a fringe activity. One of Glasgow's prominent publicans, who ran a renowned howff opposite the Theatre Royal and who was a close friend of McCann and was invited to many of the games, relates this perfectly. He said that after they had partaken refreshments at half-time in the boardroom, the announcement would be made to take their seats as the second-half was about start. McCann's lack of enthusiasm for a response was made obvious on one occasion, in pleading with his friend, 'Must we?'

Murray and Souness together saw amazing commercial opportunities in harnessing the global Rangers support. These two outsiders to the Ibrox community plied their respective trades to revive their fortunes and maximise the profit, on and off the field. To visit Ibrox in these early days of their tenure, after moribund years of stagnation within the club, was like being in an institution which had just given up the paraffin lamp for the electric bulb. They hadn't come in to save a club from the brink but to realise its true potential and profit from it. We certainly were not aware at that stage that Murray's business tactics would end up in law courts with the validity of their triumphs being seriously questioned. McCann's turnover was more organic. He had impeccable grassroots credentials, that extra tough variety which sustained itself in exile and that saw him emboldened to save an institution for people like himself, devoted to the club. Although someone else saw it differently. Michael Kelly in his 1994 recollections, *Paradise Lost,* writes wistfully of that last night the power was handed over:

> I could hear the crowd outside chanting 'Michael Kelly's on the dole!' before they made their way back to their peripheral houses. McCann greeted them about 10.45pm and they dispersed tooting their horns uncaring that they had seen the last of the real Celtic.

This was echoed in the vitriol directed at McCann by a not insignificant number of Celtic supporters who regarded him as a carpetbagger, which I suppose was implicit in Kelly's last sentiment. When Celtic won the Scottish League Championship in 1998, McCann was roundly booed by a substantial section of the crowd on that flag-raising 1 August day. Even now I can still feel the mix of astonishment and embarrassment some of us felt at this almost humiliating treatment. It was an interesting take on the Good Samaritan story. The mass of critics on the terraces viewed McCann at that moment as a man who had stopped and helped a badly beaten traveller, only to be accused of pickpocketing his shekels. Although some prominent journalists were suspicious of McCann's motives, there were also staunch defenders, particularly from the business world. One of them, financial consultant David Low, put it this way in a feature he wrote for *The Herald* in February 2004:

> It is convenient for many to forget that when McCann arrived, Celtic were essentially homeless with a turnover of £8.7 million

compared with the £15.9 million for Rangers. By the time he left, the stadium had been bought and paid for, Celtic had won the SPL [Scottish Premium League] Championship and Celtic's turnover had grown to £33.8 million against Rangers' £36.5 million.

The scene was set for an entirely new power struggle between these two clubs based very largely on the personalities of two men who, although different in character, could both be abrasive, dictatorial and uncompromising, but with different financial strategies, which would eventually bring one of them into disrepute even among his own supporters. Once McCann had fully installed himself, and the blueprint for a new Celtic Park began to emerge, I sensed a mood arising that was akin to the emergence of Stein in the '60s, at that time when the stadium in the East End could have been named The Doldrums.

You could feel a transformative era emerging which we would all grasp eagerly. Financially, there now seemed a gradual levelling of the playing field and the prospect that Celtic, infused with new cash and more stable, would produce competitive Old Firm games. But I doubt if these two men now enjoying power of control gave a moment's thought to the fact that a ball deflected off George McCluskey's boot finding the net in a Scottish Cup Final, thus initiated a chain reaction which led to the circumstances that sat them on their thrones.

Murray, of course, had a 6-year head-start on McCann, and in that time you would have thought he would have made many a clinical appraisal of the commercial status of Rangers in a world where Presbyterian footballers of merit were likely to become rather thin on the ground around the world in future. But he was certainly bringing them in from a' the airts, particularly from England where the ban on European football for their clubs made raids across the borders reverse a trend that had diminished the Scottish game for decades. At the time we felt that this new dimension might infuse the Old Firm fixture with a healthier, more cosmopolitan feel. But take the iconic English international Terry Butcher, later to become Rangers captain, and how he felt about taking on this new culture in a country of which he knew blessed little:

I got caught up in the atmosphere far too much. My wife said I went from one extreme to the other, from being a naive

Englishman not knowing anything about it into someone sucked into the hatreds too much. I ended up with an immense hatred for Celtic, not on religious grounds, but just as our greatest rivals. Your hackles would flare up whenever you saw a Celtic jersey. My wife said, in that respect, I had become not a very nice person. I had ended up like a supporter. You just didn't like being at Celtic Park surrounded by all that lime-green colour. You just wanted to be out of the place as soon as you could. It became a habit to walk into Celtic Park and make sure everybody wiped our feet on the Celtic crest which lay on the floor there. We weren't instructed to do it. It just happened because you could feel the animosity as soon as you walked in there, and that was our way of dealing with it. And in general we bonded well in working up the belief that everybody was against us, so the hell with them, just beat them!

Butcher ended up in an infamous game whose outcome was greatly influenced by the images that were carried of Hampden 10 May 1980, even in the minds of Scotland's judiciary. If that riot had not happened I am sure I would not have ended up in a courtroom gazing at Old Firm players who were in a state of incomprehension, and sat in front of a judge who looked like an old blackbird which had lost its ability to sing. Even for a man who had experienced much in European football life Souness had never come across anything like the afternoon of 17 October 1987.

CHAPTER 16

# No Ordinary Trial

ONE GAME WAS to speak a startling truth to the new Rangers player/ manager about the Scottish environment which eclipsed any assumptions he had ever made about it. Even on that brightly sunny, early autumn day, Hampden of 10 May 1980 cast its shadow over it, in an almost eerie way. Politics made that connection. Or, perhaps more pointedly, Margaret Thatcher did again. It was the Old Firm game at Ibrox. Souness was now no longer the individual I had spoken to in Santa Fe in New Mexico on his appointment to the job, when he wished to be considered a fresh new face, with an even fresher attitude to the parochial squabbles of the Old Firm, and had actually told me he wouldn't mind losing to Celtic four times in a season, so long as Rangers won the title. One game against Celtic in the Glasgow Cup, in one of his first outings, turned him from peacenik to warrior.

He had come across a distressed club which had factors to consider other than Celtic. The Old Firm were having to take into account the emergence of a new force: Alex Ferguson. Aberdeen winning a league, then three Scottish Cups in a row and lifting a European trophy meant the Old Firm were being challenged seriously for the first time in living memory. The problem was bigger for Rangers. Their self-designated catchment area of talent was diminishing in size and quality. Celtic could go anywhere they liked to hoover up talent. Rangers simply did not. Souness was becoming more painfully aware of that. Despite his self-confidence and his obvious worldliness, I did not believe that Souness knew what he had let himself in for.

The background to that October day in 1987 was stormy in a variety of ways. On the Friday, the day before the game, a hurricane ripped its way through the south of England causing millions of pounds of damage, defacing some of the most beautiful areas in the country and cutting off power from the City of London and its financial centres.

Later that same day, on the other side of the Atlantic, a commercial cyclone hit Wall Street with millions of dollars being written off the value of shares. Black Friday in New York paved the way for Black Monday in London, where share prices plummeted so dramatically that one dealer was moved to comment that the only reason people were not jumping out of windows was that they were all now double-glazed. Sandwiched in between these cataclysms was a game which seemed to fit perfectly the pattern of cosmic disturbances. The turbulent meeting of Rangers and Celtic at Ibrox, October 1987, was to provoke outcry, moral indignation, weighty editorials, fierce public argument, that was to rage on for months, and put me in a Scottish law court as opposed to a commentary platform, after being asked to make a contribution to a bizarre Old Firm battle.

At that time the political attitude to football in the UK was one of outright hostility. The tragedy of Heysel Stadium in 1985, where many people lost their lives after extreme disorder as Liverpool were playing Juventus in the European Cup Final, had seen the personal intervention of the Prime Minister. With characteristic decisiveness she had immediately summoned to 10 Downing Street the media witnesses to the events in Brussels, so that she could at least demonstrate that there was concern at the highest level. My old friend and colleague, Peter Jones, the BBC radio commentator who broadcast from Heysel, was one of the guests and recounted for me what ensued. He was asked if the conduct in Belgium reflected crowd behaviour in England. He let loose. He simply catalogued the disasters he had witnessed as English supporters cut swathes as damaging as the October hurricane through the towns and cities of the country. He listed trains wrecked, cars overturned, shops pillaged, houses near grounds boarded up almost permanently for safety, displays of weaponry that would have been the envy of any terrorist group around the world and the constant intimidation and frequent assault of innocent bystanders. He was in full spate and being an eloquent Welshman nobody could draw a picture better than himself. His final sentence to her was like he was taking a knife, not a brush, to the canvas he had just painted. 'I see society breaking down every Saturday.' Mrs Thatcher was so appalled that she actually asked Jones to repeat what he had just said. It staggered her, and she admitted that she had failed to be aware of what was going on. She then said, with some resolve:

We must do something about this. We may have to take un-
popular measures but something will be done.

And so began her personal involvement in the campaign to cleanse
football of what had become known throughout Europe as 'the English
Disease'. Now, in that month of October, to compare the Scottish
football environment with what was happening south of the border
would be like comparing croquet to a bullfight. But you have to think
back to the Hampden riot. Since then, although the bitter atmosphere
around an Old Firm game had not resulted in anything remotely like
that violent occasion, the images of that sordid final had not faded from
political minds. You have to recall that it was a fixture which provoked
unprecedented debates in both Houses of Parliament. Yes, politicians in
the south were aware of the sectarian issues in general terms, which up
till then they viewed with a disapproval, but only at the 'tut-tut' level.
There was an almost logical indifference to a situation they regarded as
purely parochial. No longer. The crowds attacking each other on that
day in May had lifted the veil from eyes in the south. If you add that new
feeling to the fact that Thatcher was including the whole of UK football
in her ominous threat of action, the Old Firm were in the political firing
line in an unparalleled way, but with little awareness of it. After all, the
world had not spun off its axis after 10 May 1980. So they went into
that 17 October match little realising what was in store for them.

For the record, here were the teams that October day:

RANGERS: Woods, Gough, Phillips, Roberts, Ferguson, Butcher,
Francis (Cooper), Falco (Cohen), McCoist, Durant, McGregor

CELTIC: McKnight, Morris, Whyte (Rogan), Aitken, McCarthy,
Grant, Stark, McStay, McAvennie, Walker, Burns (Archdeacon)

As Rangers had not agreed to take to the field at the same time as
Celtic, I suspect to adhere to Souness's desire to be unconventional, it
did suggest a certain nip in the air, even though it was October. The
incident for which the game will forever abide, not just in the memory,
but in legal writings, occurred approximately 17 minutes into the game.
Inspector James Moir was on duty at the Celtic end of the ground. His
statement to the Procurator Fiscal of Glasgow reads:

About 3.15pm as I was patrolling near the west end of the stadium my attention was attracted to an incident near the Rangers' goalmouth. I saw that the Rangers goalkeeper Christopher Woods had come out of his goal and had been challenged by the Celtic player, Francis McAvennie. I saw McAvennie quite deliberately strike the Rangers keeper Woods with what I would describe as a slap on the face. The Rangers keeper in turn seemed to put his right forearm against McAvennie's face and push him away. The next thing was that the Rangers centre-half, Butcher, joined the other two and they then began to jostle each other. I was then aware of the Rangers football player Graham Roberts running across from the opposite side of the park and I then saw him quite deliberately punch the Celtic player McAvennie on the side of the head, causing McAvennie to fall to the ground. The whole attitude of the crowd was very volatile and it seemed to me that we were in grave danger of a pitch invasion by the football supporters.

Note the 'pitch invasion' image. Hampden 1980 was still imprinted in many retinas. High in the press-box area, Sergeant Thomas Wylie was operating the video camera:

As a direct result of this [the incident on the field] I saw there was obvious crowd disorder in the west end of the enclosure immediately under the main stand. I also saw that there was crowd trouble in the Broomloan Road stand. Because of this I then panned the cameras in on these two sections to view the disorder. This would automatically mean those scenes of disorder would be filmed on the video cameras.

When the melee petered out on the field the referee booked Woods and McAvennie for violent conduct and then ordered them from the field. There is no report anywhere of any police observation about the reaction of the crowd to the actual ordering-off, although it is significant that referee John Duncan's statement contains the following:

As a result of all this action on the field there was a terrific volume of noise from the spectators and there was obviously a great tension in the atmosphere, but I can personally say that I never felt in any way threatened. To be perfectly honest I was not too conscious of any crowd reaction and the police seemed to have the situation under control.

The police themselves though were stating clearly they had been worried about the danger of invasion. They still felt sore about criticism they had endured seven years previously at Hampden. Perhaps they were being over-sensitive and if they were, it was certainly going to matter at the end of the day. The field was ablaze with incidents. In the second-half Terry Butcher was judged by the referee to have deliberately struck Alan McKnight, the Celtic goalkeeper, in the back, as they rose from the ground after a clash, and he was booked and sent off. This merely ensured that the general reporting of this game by the media would be in terms of discipline and conduct, rather than the score line. Celtic had been two goals up; Walker had scored after 33 minutes and two minutes later Butcher had deflected the ball past his own goalkeeper. The fact that McCoist pulled one back halfway through the second-half and a nine-man-Rangers saved the game through Richard Gough, in the last few seconds, was dramatic enough, but certainly not sufficient to drive off the front pages the news that three experienced internationals, expensively acquired by the clubs, had apparently disgraced themselves. The reverberations seeped through to ears not normally attuned to the cadences of football. And the two clubs suddenly became embroiled in an entirely new game which produced the startling phenomenon, for them, of complete unity.

Immediately after the game, perhaps with a sense of foreboding, the chairmen of the two clubs, David Holmes of Rangers and Jack McGinn of Celtic, met for a solid three hours to discuss the implications of the field disturbances. They were certainly not to know that, by the beginning of the next week, there would be quite unprecedented intervention in the matter from an unusual source. The rerun of the game on Scottish Television on the Sunday might have given a wider audience the opportunity to ask a question which was now beginning to formulate on most lips: 'What is all the fuss about?' There had been no invasion. The incidents on the field, by comparison with some other Old Firm encounters, did not look like inducing cardiac arrests. But then the political atmosphere around this game had completely altered after that Downing Street showdown, as we were to find out. And it should be pointed out that the Strathclyde Police were very reluctant to take any action and would have let it pass. However, there was a significant intervention.

The Procurator Fiscal of Glasgow, Sandy Jessop, who had not been at the game and had not even seen the recording, had nevertheless been alerted to the matter. The principal legal officer for the area decided he would ask the police for a report on the field events, given the scale of the publicity they had received. Eventually, at the beginning of November, four players – Terry Butcher, Chris Woods and Graham Roberts of Rangers, and Frank McAvennie of Celtic – were summoned to appear at Govan police station where a charge was to be made against them. The two clubs, having agreed to a joint defence, in the matter, employed one of Scotland's foremost criminal lawyers, Len Murray, to represent the players. They were charged with 'conduct likely to provoke a breach of peace amongst spectators'. Len Murray's first objective was to approach the Procurator Fiscal in the hope that such a charge might be dropped and the players 'given another chance'. On 5 November he had a cordial meeting with Jessop, characteristically the soul of courtesy. But he was also firm. He admitted to having an open mind on the matter of pursuing the charges further, but then ominously the conversation took another tack. Whereas the initial charge related to the specific few seconds just after the 17th minute, the Procurator referred to other incidents. David Holmes, the Rangers Chief Executive learned that Jessop had itemised the following, which had disturbed him, and to which he had to pay some attention.

1.  McAvennie, before the major incident, had recklessly bundled Woods into the net.
2.  Falco had tackled McStay crudely in the opening minutes.
3.  Peter Grant had made the provocative sign of the cross to his supporters after a goal had been scored.
4.  Graham Roberts, who had gone into goal to replace Woods, had provocatively 'conducted' his own supporters in a sectarian song after Rangers had equalised late in the game.

He then went on to say, had he wished, he could have brought charges against Grant and Roberts on these two specific matters and been confident of obtaining convictions. This line of thinking suggested to Len Murray that the Procurator Fiscal was being influenced not only by a strict examination of the incident related to the charges but also by the current political atmosphere arisen around the sport. In short, a critical and perhaps punitive eye was being brought to bear on contemporary football conduct. This seemed to be a different angle altogether. Murray's gut reaction, despite the pleasantries, was that the charge would be brought to its conclusion, especially since the Procurator had been annoyed by an article which had appeared in the *Rangers News* purporting to be by Terry Butcher, in which he had played down the incident involving Graham Roberts 'conducting' the sectarian singing. This had given the Procurator Fiscal the impression that the matter was not being taken seriously enough, and Len Murray thinks that article had a big influence on the final outcome. At one stage David Holmes told the solicitor that he would resign his position if it went to court, so solicitor Murray met with Jessup again to stave off the final move.

To Murray's astonishment he learned that Jessup had brought in others and told him he had watched the video of the incident in the company of the Solicitor General of Scotland, the Lord Advocate and two Advocates Deputes. This was now big time, and had the appearance of major legal figures who had taken Margaret Thatcher's warnings in Number 10 to heart and wanted to act on them. It was opportunistic. On 20 November the acting Assistant Procurator Fiscal, Sam Cathcart, issued the following complaint against the four players in these words:

> The charge against you is that on 17 October within Ibrox Stadium, Edmiston Drive, Glasgow, while participating in a football match, you did conduct yourselves in a disorderly manner and commit a breach of the peace.

The charge had changed from that issued at Govan Police station back on 1 November when it had been on the basis of conduct 'likely to provoke a breach of peace amongst spectators'. The trial was set for 12 April 1988.

I sat at the back of the court. Since I knew all four players well, Len Murray had asked me if I would be there as character witness for them in their defence, if called. I was willing to do so, since I thought the whole procedure was like something out of a Gilbert and Sullivan comic opera. Graeme Souness did add his opinion to the proceedings, pre-trial, when he came into the Ibrox boardroom in his training gear, during discussions between the board and Len Murray, lounged back in the chairman's chair, put his trainers up on the desk and proclaimed, 'This is all a load of fucking shite'. Many around the land would have concurred, with perhaps less colourful language. Then, as sure as the River Clyde flows to the sea, sectarianism wormed its way into proceedings. David Holmes received phone calls prior to the trial, from within the legal profession warning him that Len Murray was a Roman Catholic. Indeed he was; and a devoted Celtic follower, who, had events not brought Fergus McCann to Parkhead, might have gained the chairmanship of the club. Then Murray heard that reservations were being expressed in his own circles that Sam Cathcart, the Assistant Procurator Fiscal, was a well-known Rangers supporter. To top it all, it emerged from those people who are obsessed by these matters, that the Sheriff chosen to preside over the court, Archie McKay, was a Cushendall, Northern Ireland-born Roman Catholic. Conspiracy theorists proceeded to make a mediaeval banquet out of this.

Unaccustomed as I am to court of laws, and expecting something akin to Perry Mason, I was unimpressed by the mumblings that went on between the four barristers and the Sheriff. One of the barristers kept making a mistake over the names of Butcher and Roberts and had to be corrected repeatedly by the Sheriff. Len Murray sat near me at times and I could see from his expressions that he was not thrilled by proceedings, and probably could have performed better himself, as he is a renowned public speaker as well as being a distinguished lawyer. Although the charge had been changed, the thrust of the revised accusation was the provocation of the crowd. Herein lay a certain naivety. The supporters had apparently given the impression that they wished to invade the pitch when the incident took place. But I have seen an Old Firm crowd reacting in a similar manner, on merely seeing the opposition run on to the field for a warm-up. Reaction to the vagaries of the game, while it can take ugly forms, is part of the necessary theatricals of the fixture. There had in fact been no riot, and for those with even a modicum of familiarity with this fixture there had been no real danger of such. Hampden 1980 was still obviously the spectre. Seats, regrettably, had been broken but, without wishing to sound blasé, considerably fewer than the average at this event. But the Crown simply did not wish to see it that way. Then there was the control of the match by the official. This fixture is admittedly a notoriously sensitive game to referee. Nevertheless, had Mr Duncan, taken firmer action earlier in the game for the even more reckless actions of Falco and McAvennie, it is entirely feasible that the players, knowing that he wasn't there merely for decoration, would have exercised rather more caution.

The sadness one felt watching the proceedings from the back of the courtroom was compounded by the irresistible conclusion that these four players, far from possessing a threat to law and order, were being made scapegoats in a politically hostile environment. The way the trial was proceeding Murray felt that a character witness would not be relevant, so I wasn't called. That was admittedly disappointing for me since I had prepared a strenuous defence of these men that Clarence Darrow or Cicero himself would have admired. I felt, and I suspect Murray did too, that it wasn't going to work out well. After exhausting replays and examinations of the incident on tape and listening to both sides of the argument, Sheriff Archie McKay delivered his verdict. He found Frank McAvennie not guilty on the basis that in slowing-down of the tape it appears he had made no real contact with Woods. He found 'not proven' for Graham Roberts, as it could not be clearly seen from the tape what the extent of his contact with McAvennie had been. He found Chris Woods guilty of breach of the peace, for in the Sheriff's view the pictures had shown the keeper deliberately elbowing McAvennie. He found Terry Butcher guilty on the same charge, having seen again, from the video his action of shoving the Celtic player forcibly backwards. Both players were fined and an appeal was lodged. Allan Heron of the *Sunday Mail* wrote a piece which blamed McAvennie squarely for starting the incident and was threatened with legal action by the player's agent Bill McMurdo, who ironically, was a staunch Rangers supporter. Nothing came of that.

This was no ordinary trial. Had it not been Rangers and Celtic, with the riot at Hampden still in the minds of those who prosecute these matters, had Thatcher not shortly before this issued her war cry against football and had encouraged the lawmakers to set some example, this case would never have come to court. Her next trick in Scotland would be the Poll Tax.

The two Rangers players lost their appeal almost one year later. The Court of Appeal judges were split two to one. Lord Ross again stressed the reaction of the crowd as a valid reason for the charge and conviction. But Lord Murray, in a dissenting judgement, while deploring the conduct of the players, stressed that there was

a heavy responsibility upon the prosecution to exercise special caution and restraint when decisions to prosecute are taken in marginal or sensitive cases. If abused, or overused, the offence could readily bring the criminal law into disrepute.

Many thought it had. The defence solicitor, Len Murray, put it just as succinctly afterwards, when he said:

There is an old Turkish saying which goes, 'an Englishman will burn his bed to catch a flea'. The Crown burned its bed.

At the heart of it of course was the sectarian divide which had insinuated itself even into consideration of the tribal loyalties of those representing the law. Nor, at that stage, did there seem to be any likelihood of Rangers discarding Protestant absolutism. But could they possibly go on into an uncharted future and a changing society any longer with the same rigidity? On asking that question of David Murray, in an early stage of his ownership, I received an expletive-filled response which brutally indicated that nobody would bully Rangers into changing their ways. Then one day in 1989 an apparition appeared at Ibrox in front of myself and colleagues which carried the impact on us as if we were watching an alien stepping out of a spaceship, uttering the words, 'I come in peace'.

# CHAPTER 17

# Indian Rope Trick

MAURICE JOHNSTON'S NEW Rangers blazer was too big for him. For whom it was intended in the first place I know not. So as this Catholic-born ex-Celtic player stepped into the Ibrox blue-room on 10 July of that year, for the press-conference, as Rangers' first publicly acknowledged signing of a Catholic, he looked like a wee boy on his first visit to a museum, wearing something handed down to him by a bigger brother. And like a wee boy he wore the bewildered expression of a kid who had got separated from his parents in a maze of corridors, and had come out unexpectedly into the glare of someone else's publicity fanfare. Although he was there in front of our very eyes it was still difficult to comprehend. The fact that his blazer was a full size too big for him, accentuated the feeling that this was not real, but some kind of charade. I had been taught that water could never flow upwards, so this was like watching a fundamental law of physics being turned upside down. Indeed, earlier that morning, I had been phoned by my own son at home, as I was preparing to go off to the BBC for an ordinary day at the office, to tell me that there was a strong rumour going around the city of Glasgow, that Mo Johnston had signed for Rangers. He said his office colleagues were crowded around him waiting for me to respond for verification. My reply then now falls somewhat into the disastrous category of Michael Fish's mild weather forecast in 1987, when he told people not to worry, that a storm was not coming, before England was half-destroyed by exactly that. Suspicious of the adventurism of the press in general with some of their stories, I replied with great confidence: 'Tell them there is more chance of the Pope signing for Rangers than Mo Johnson.' In one office at least, my credit-rating was to plummet.

In my defence I was not alone in being caught out. The BBC news department was as ignorant as I was. When they did contact me to head to Ibrox they were still clueless as to why such a one was being called. My recollection is that the name Johnston was not mentioned in that conversation. It was simply a case of 'Something's happening. Get there as quick as you can'. So admittedly the *Sun* had startled and scooped everybody. They had heard whispers. Ian Scott, who went on to be sports news editor of the *Daily Record,* was then assistant to the sports editor of the *Sun.* He was becoming frustrated with the rumours he was hearing, linking Johnston and Rangers, however improbable they seemed to him. He knew his editor Jack Irvine was a personal friend of Souness and asked him to contact the Rangers manager and put it to him bluntly was he interested in the former Celtic player? All he got were noncommittal responses which were certainly not outright denials. Scott listened to the tape of that interview and was aroused, as he told me.

It was then I discovered what a 'pregnant pause' meant. To that first question of the editor, there was silence. Souness was in his car heading back to Edinburgh. He asked Irvine to call him back when he got there, which he did. We listened again to the conversation. Jack asked him several times different questions, in different sorts of ways, and although he never at any time said yes or no we could feel something was on. 'I think he's signed him,' I said. Jack agreed we should rip out what was being prepared for the paper and devote a whole 16 pages to debatably the biggest story we ever had, even though we had received not a single piece of encouragement from Souness. It was just the fact that he had not denied it that prompted us to believe we were on to something big. He could still have been stringing us along, of course. But we took an enormous gamble.

You can now understand why Souness was proceeding with a stealth that a professional abduction gang would have envied. He was fully aware of the sensitivity of such an episode within the Ibrox support. Had it really leaked out in advance it might have provoked a much wider protest from within their ranks which could easily have turned into a protest group. It was vital not to allow anybody any time to muster any significant opposition. It had to be a *fait accompli.* No going back. Done and dusted. He was successful in as much as even the rival journalists to the *Sun* were scoffing at them for this preposterous suggestion which they believed they had started. So when eventually I dashed off with a BBC camera crew, only pursuing a possibility, but saw the crowds around the entrance to the stadium, I realised something special was afoot, but still could scarcely believe it all, until Johnston came through the door of Ibrox's inner-shrine the Blueroom, and faced the music.

There was no riot, nor even a single ringing vocal dissent outside in Edmiston Drive, but a kind of sullen incredulity among the almost reverential crowd, as if at the last minute it simply wasn't going to happen. Sign a Catholic? Pull the other one. Indeed, one man alighted on me and quietly asked if 'HE' was really in there signing on the dotted line. It sounded so much like the boy who, according to legend, confronted his hero the great Chicago White Sox baseball player 'Shoeless Joe Jackson', who was said to have been involved in his team's bribery scandal for taking money to throw the World Series to the Cincinatti Reds, and begged him plaintively, 'Say it ain't so, Joe'. That air of disbelief eventually dissipated and the crowd then gave the hovering camera crews exactly what they wanted. They were not looking for voices of a charitable nature to underscore the coming of the new age of reason. They were after the hardliners. They were willing and able. There were no screaming rages but a simmering anger, made clear in most of the interviews. Think of it. Here was the year 1989. The Berlin Wall was about to be dismantled. De Klerk in South Africa initiated the first steps to end apartheid. A man with a shopping-bag would stand defiantly in front of a tank in Tiananmen Square. Set against these great social upheavals around the world it was a reflection of the kind of riven society we had tolerated for decades, that we were making a sensation of a player signing for a football club. How small and parochial it must have looked not just to the foreigner, but to ourselves, wakening up to the fact that perhaps our lack of resolve on this matter made us all complicit in its survival for so long.

Of course, some of the broadcast vox pops deliberately played up to this and we learned later that some of them were actually paid to burn their Rangers' scarves in protest, in front of cameras. This was all good theatre, but there was something more relevant taking place. Away from those queuing-up like actors auditioning to be villains, there was another vast Rangers public making an alternative assessment.

Here was Johnston, a renowned goalscorer, a Scottish international, flamboyant, a pest from hell for any defence. Here was someone who only two weeks previously had seemed to suggest he would sign for his first love, Celtic. Here was someone who only a few days earlier had Celtic manager Billy McNeill standing with him in the tunnel at Celtic Park for the benefit of the photographers, expressing his expectation of Johnston leading the line for him. And yet here were some people telling the cameras they didn't want him. They were the ones who retained in their minds the scenes that took place on 26 October 1986 at Hampden Park in a towsy Old Firm Scottish League Cup final, which ultimately had the Celtic manager Davy Hay complaining that the refereeing was so poor, and by that token so biased, that Scottish football should import foreign referees for his club to have any sense of fairness established. One of the most dramatic episodes was watching Johnston being sent off. When he left the field he made the sign of the cross on himself, not out of a fit of religious remorse, but as a nifty bit of tribal identification that was hardly likely to placate the very people he, in future, was going to represent. Incidents are protected with care in the vaults of the Old Firm memory bank. So we imagined there could be a massive revolt against someone seen as a provocateur. We were wrong. What overwhelmed the potential for any toxic backlash was that the Rangers manager was rightly perceived to have cuckolded, shafted, humiliated and indeed destabilised their great rivals, and with such audacity that any deep sense of loss at ditching an old, if shabby, tradition was made to seem, to the vast majority, like a veritable coup. For Ibrox, despite the efforts of some in the media to portray significant dissension, continued to be packed to capacity.

Souness and Murray had achieved what the old board could not have. I certainly believe that some of them would have loved to ditch the past, they just didn't really know how to go about it. They could not have enjoyed watching others in public life criticising them for this, ridiculing the whole preposterous nonsense of their self-imposed purdah. Although it was comedy, they could not have found it comfortable to watch actor Ricky Fulton, in front of a greatly amused TV audience, including from their own ranks, playing the part of a Rangers manager trying to get out of a contract they had just signed with a player, because, to their great chagrin, he let out that he had just been to Mass. The former Ibrox board had neither the chutzpah nor the commercial swagger and success of the modern duo to pull off the equivalent of the Indian Rope Trick.

'The Sash' was not to lose any of its resonance. The vilification of Rome was not to disappear overnight from the terracing liturgy. The signing of Johnston was very quickly accepted and seen as it surely was, a technical switch that would benefit the club hugely in their great rivalry, not some profound moral statement to the rest of the world. I sensed a suspension of judgement on Johnston among the supporters around me when I commentated on his first game in a Rangers jersey. But then in later months, when he scored the only goal of the game against his former club at Ibrox on 4 November 1989 and ran towards the crowd like a new-born Bluenose, he was seen by those at the other end as effectively sealing a pact with the devil. That in itself cemented his relationship with the Ibrox support.

There is little doubt that Celtic were shaken by this. This was a new phenomenon. There was no one within Celtic Park at the time who thought they would see this in their lifetime, as much as any diehard on the other side of the city. They could hardly extend their congratulations to Ibrox for turning on its head a policy that, particularly after the Hampden riot, White had laid bare in turning the tables against Rangers. Now they had to face up to a club which previously was intensely, parochially Scottish and Protestant. And it hit Johnston's ex-colleagues particularly hard. One was Sky's Andy Walker who felt he was double the player when playing alongside the blond striker.

> When Mo firstly signed for Celtic I felt the club was given a great lift. We all felt a surge of confidence because we knew we had somebody special coming to play for us. And so it was. I was always a better player with the likes of Frank McAvennie and Mo playing alongside me. And he was Celtic through and through. So you can imagine the shock I felt when I took a phone-call from my father when I was abroad on holiday, who told me he had signed for Rangers. At first I didn't believe him. It was difficult to take in. All his ex-colleagues were shocked to the core. Roy Aitken used to room with Mo when they were on Scotland duty and that's when you get to really build up a relationship. But that would never occur again. It just couldn't. But I'll tell you when it hit me worst of all. Now, as you know, losing to your great rivals

is always painful under any circumstances. But when Mo scored the only goal of the game against us at Ibrox, it took me about three days to recover from it.

Johnston in fact was the catalyst that led Rangers to inflicting on their rivals one of the most wretched eras in their history, the nine-in-a-row title dominance of Ibrox. Perhaps not exactly the scary legacy that was associated with the Curse of the Bambino when Babe Ruth of the Red Sox left for the New York Yankees and the Sox were not to win a World Series for nearly a century. But there were times during that period when to some Celtic supporters it began to feel like they were heading in that direction. At the centre of this business was his agent Bill McMurdo, an ardent supporter of the loyalist cause in Northern Ireland, whose home just outside Glasgow was festooned in all things red, white and blue, but who nevertheless did business for Celtic for both Johnston and his other Parkhead client, Frank McAvennie. Celtic were dealing with someone with clear Rangers sympathies and obviously suspected he had particularly engineered this move to Ibrox. However, he himself put the blame squarely on the Celtic board. The *Scottish Sun* of 10 December 1994 reported him as saying:

> I didn't want Mo to sign for Rangers, you know. But in the end he opted for Rangers and I knew he would handle Ibrox all right because he gives 100 per cent to whoever he is with. The Celtic directors tried to save face by blaming me for it all. But the truth is they knew what was happening. Anyway, around that time none of them understood the workings of freedom of contract.

McMurdo was a sharp operator, as his clients would attest to, and Johnston always maintained his move was all about money and nothing else. Ibrox had more of it then than Celtic. You have to take into account that the player was a likeable, roguish wee Glasgow fella who liked a good night out, could be great company and knew more about the train stations around Europe than the Stations of the Cross. He was not enlightening himself by studying the sociology surrounding the Old Firm. Nor was he to become a Trappist monk. Indeed, a year after he arrived at Ibrox he was involved in an altercation with Mark Hateley and had to be sent home from the training-camp in Italy. He arrived back in Glasgow with bruises on his face, accompanied by the excuse that he had flopped rather heavily down on the bare springs of a bed. That was as believable to the tabloids as a sighting of the Loch Ness monster in the Broomielaw. His value to the manager saved him from draconian action, as measured by the fact that he was the club's leading goalscorer with a total of 40 goals in two seasons.

Andy Walker and Johnston were to meet up again when both were invited on to the panel to discuss the Celtic-Rangers Scottish Cup semi-final match of 2016. But only just. For Sky, having flown Johnston over from the States for this, were stunned when the former Celtic/Rangers player informed them, on the morning of the game, that he wouldn't appear because of threats made against him from unnamed sources. Since his apostasy he was now painfully aware that, at least in Scotland, there were some nasty people about who did not embrace Christian forgiveness. Huge pressure was put on him to appear, since a non-appearance, after massive promotion, would have caused huge embarrassment to the television company. Finally, he relented. That incident indicated the depth of bitterness that was exacerbated, not reduced, by Rangers committing themselves to moving away from their much reviled signing policy.

This dramatic manoeuvre by Souness put the Old Firm relationship on to a new footing, light years away from that day at Hampden in 1980. I sensed, though, the inevitable tension that springs from one club having overall supremacy. Rangers ruled at that time, reminding me of what it had been like in the early '60s. The *angst* among the Celtic followers was a compound of frustration at what Souness and his successor Walter Smith would be achieving and disgust at the antics of their board, which seemed amateurish by comparison. That Skol Cup Final I mentioned, with the sending off of Johnston, was as bitter an encounter as I could recollect for some time. I would put it well up there on their toxic Richter scale.

This animosity was to have a dramatic tipping-point, though not on the field. It centred on an incident that caused Superintendant Hamish MacBean, match-commander at Hampden in 1980, to reflect back on the words he had used at the end of the riot, years earlier. In that empty stadium, surrounded by exhausted officers, he had uttered a sigh of relief by declaring: 'My God, we were lucky. Nobody was killed.'

In all the helter-skeltering on the pitch, the alternate charges one way then the other, the occasional mauls, the throwing of bottles and the horses pitching into battle, I only had a fleeting notion of a death occurring. I was so completely absorbed by the sheer spectacle of it all that I suppose, as a broadcaster I had lapsed into a kind of detached *It's A Knockout* mode, on an afternoon to be lapped up by the inherent voyeurism of the television audience. It was a single death years later that reminded me how culpable I had been in ultimately only thinking of it as broadcasting scoop.

CHAPTER 18

# The Avenging Angel

NOT EVEN THE scriptwriters of *Peaky Blinders* could have dreamed it up. On 7 October 1995 a Catholic boy wearing a Celtic scarf had his throat slashed and died at the hand of a man in the area where the ultra-Protestant Billy Boys once reigned. It was a revolting act that was almost archetypal of the whole morass of sectarianism which had not abated since Hampden 1980 but seemed to have intensified. Mark Scott, a 16-year-old, a Catholic, was simply walking back from watching his team play Partick Thistle when he was attacked from behind by Jason Campbell. The attacker, as was later shown, had family connections with Loyalist terrorist groups in Northern Ireland. So? Would this not be enough to convert universal revulsion, as there was, into some credible positive social action to purge us of this scourge? Could this not be seen as a turning point? Anyone with any shred of humanity would have thought so. But I had enough experience to know that, for a start, there are terrible forces of allegiances in the streets that would simply be wholly indifferent to such a heinous crime. And that, in any case, the political will to intervene in a positive manner had always seemed lukewarm. But then my orthodox mindset was to be challenged from what I thought was a distinctly odd source and I began to realise that, at the very least, fresh thinking had arisen which would not easily be dismissed or intimidated.

Its first manifestation came in the form of a letter to *The Herald* on 4 June 1999, at the time I was a columnist for the paper. The address of the sender intrigued me, St Hugh's College, St Margaret's Road, Oxford – 2 June 1999. It was a long letter which took up two full columns of the page and might, for me, have been given only a cursory read, had it not been for her phrase in her fourth paragraph, 'Mark Scott, my friend, the 16-year-old Glasgow Academy schoolboy...' There, at least, was identity. The writer was Cara Henderson, a law student at Oxford

University. She did not miss her primary target:

> On Saturday night, Donald Findlay QC, the then vice-chairman of Rangers Football Club, was attending a private party alongside players and fans to celebrate his team's triumphant season. During the course of the evening Findlay sang a medley of Protestant anthems which featured anti-Catholic lyrics. The significance of such an act can only really be appreciated if one fully considers the backdrop of hatred and violence that so forms the history of this society and continues to shape and blight the present.

The evening of 29 May 1999 in the Edmiston Suite, the social club that existed beside Ibrox at that time, was triumphalist in nature, as her letter recognises. Someone videoed the proceedings, for whatever reason. The songs did not refer specifically to the recent success, but to an event in 1690. The words of the 'The Sash My Father Wore' were well known around the stadium. But Findlay had added another to his repertoire, which ended with:

> We're up to our knees in Fenian blood,
> Surrender or you'll die,
> For we are the Brigton Billy Boys.

Some who would never dare to sing it, nevertheless did not stamp their feet in protest, but might perhaps have even tapped their toes instead, to a rousing tune associated with Protestant supremacy. And, since Rangers had just won the Scottish Cup that same day, and completed another treble, it might have seemed perfectly appropriate for a rousing rendition, fuelled by a few beers, or more. Except that it wasn't purely about Protestants then. Two Catholics were sitting in the audience. Two players who had helped Rangers beat their great rivals Celtic that afternoon. There was the Italian captain of the side Lorenzo Amoruso, and Neil McCann, a man brought up in the west of Scotland who knew full well the implications of the song. Indeed, the transformation in the way that their club now signed players at that stage, was so startlingly different from the past, that at Tynecastle one day, in a game Rangers were playing against Hearts, I could hear the mass of home supporters chanting derisively at the away fans, 'You've got more Tims than Celtic!' to the tune of 'Guantanamera'.

Indeed, even those who would have been the loudest in joining in the choruses were also lining up to get pictures with, and buy drinks for, the two Catholics who were now being baptised into ways of men, who despite the loudness of their choruses of support for the singer of the song, couldn't give a damn about who Rangers signed now. After all they were picking up league titles one after the other. This was the post-Mo Johnston era when supporters had wakened up to the fact that world society had not disintegrated when he had breached the unwritten code. In that sense, these songs of yore were being rendered meaningless, nay, almost comically inappropriate in terms of the new policy of the club. But at the same time they realised that these ditties, poisonous to others, gave the support to an identity that they dared not challenge and occasionally would give succour to. The songs were regarded as culturally 'theirs' and meant nothing more insidious than a confirmation of identity. As when David Murray on one occasion told a group, 'They're trying to take away our songs'. Indeed, the former Celtic manager Jock Stein, once said to me, of both sets of supporters:

> Let them sing what they like. Let them get it out of their system. Then on Monday morning they'll be back working with each other again on the same job.

Although I hung on virtually every word he ever spoke about the customs connected to the Scottish game, I also knew that even many, who had the greatest respect for the man, would have taken issue with that belief.

But one thing is certain, the singing of 'The Sash' and other songs, by one man that night, videoed and made public by someone, was as if he had just lit a fuse. Findlay is a respected QC who, according to those in his profession, has a keen legal brain and never has had any shortage of clients. Those who have to confront him in court face a daunting prospect, as his interrogations give the impression he is stripping the recipient to the bare bone. In his brief associations with me, I found him charming, and his laconic, softly spoken and pipe-smoking image gave you the impression of a thinker, a man who carefully plotted his way through life. But there was another Donald Findlay. There was the man who would suddenly appear in public, as if he were the twin brother of the advocate, but who was the actual black sheep of the family, and only let out of the attic from time to time. For instance, he was in much demand on the after-dinner circuit. And hearing him one night speaking at a Variety Club Dinner in honour of the ex-Rangers manager Walter Smith I began to understand why. He told crude stories, with aplomb it must be said, that might have come out of the mouth of Roy Chubby Brown at his most lurid. So much so, that you could feel ripples of stifled embarrassment spreading through the audience. He did not seem to mind that Smith's grandchildren were sitting directly in front of him. He didn't blink and was so apparently unperturbed that some of us were thinking of hiding under the circular dinner tables just to get away from it all. It revealed, that when rid of the advocate's wig, he could let loose as if it were some sort of therapy which, he imagined, bonded him with the common herd.

But, what pained the law student from Oxford was the fact that with perfect entitlement, and with little sensitivity, Findlay had appeared as defence advocate for 23-year-old Jason Campbell who had slit the throat of and murdered Mark Scott on his way home from a Celtic match at Bridgeton Cross. And, using as much as he could of a hopeless situation, Findlay had pleaded that Campbell had just intended to slash his victim. Scott, a Celtic supporter, who had even tried to hide his colours in the streets, on the advice of his mother, was nevertheless identified for what he was and attacked. The murderer was nevertheless sentenced to life, even though he had remained insensitive to the end, given that it was claimed, in court, that he had said to someone beside him, during an identification line-up, 'Long live the Not Proven verdict'.

It was three years after his client had been sentenced to life imprisonment for that loathsome crime, that Findlay got up to sing his song. The resultant publicity skewered him. He was forced to resign his position as vice-chairman of Rangers after his good friend David Murray eventually distanced himself from him in public, and the Dean of Faculty of Advocates at the time, Nigel Emslie, filed a complaint against him, alleging, 'serious and reprehensible misconduct, bringing the Faculty into disrepute'. He was eventually fined £3,500 by the body. Perhaps if Findlay had not got up to sing, or that his cavalier insensitivity had not been revealed publicly, then Cara Henderson would not have appeared from left field, as the Americans would say, nor would the anti-sectarian group Nil by Mouth have been formed . So perhaps, paradoxically, he did society a favour by removing cataracts from many eyes. However, for the young student from Oxford, the complexities of Roman law she surely would have encountered in her law studies, would be but plain sailing compared to what she now considered taking on, the massive evils of sectarianism that actually had driven a stake through her heart in a most personal way.

\* \* \* \* \*

Cara, having practised law in London for years, lives just outside Geneva in Switzerland with her husband and small child. She talked to me at length about those earlier times. I admit that both of us utterly forgot that we had crossed swords (although cardboard stage swords, to be honest) almost 20 years previously, such is the depredations of the passing of time. But we will come to that. She first wanted to slightly clarify her friendship with Mark:

> I think there was a bit of romanticising about our relationship.
> Yes, I suppose you could call him my boyfriend in the sense that
> we went to the pictures together, for example. But really it was
> kids' stuff, nothing more than that. Nevertheless, I knew him
> well through sitting beside him in class at Glasgow Academy. We
> sat together in fours, in the English class, two boys, two girls and
> I must say that this was the early stage of a mixed school as I had
> been at another private girls school Westbourne, and I principally
> recall how I found the boys quite intimidating. But I got on well
> with Mark. However we were not as close, or going out together,
> when he was killed.

She had heard an announcement on her radio that a boy had been murdered on his way back from a Celtic game. They mentioned his name in the broadcast. But her recollection is that it didn't register with her right away because she thinks they got the name wrong and used a middle name instead of his Christian name. It didn't strike her until the following morning:

> I was lying in my bed, just having woken up when my mother

came through and told me Mark had been murdered. She had actually known late that evening but had decided to sleep on it before she told me. I was shocked, of course, but I just lay there like I was on autopilot for some time. I did not get over this well. For whatever reason I felt a sense of guilt mixed in with a whole load of other feelings and its only in the last three or four years that I've got over that. I think setting up the charity itself maybe affected me in that way. I think that's why I've been haunted by it for so long.

But it was Findlay's contribution which really riled her:

Here was a man representing the establishment, the educated middle class, in a profession that was supposedly to protect us, singing a provocative song, and the same man who had defended the murderer. But do you know, I think to be fair to him, others had been doing this often and it had seemed acceptable, until it wasn't. Like getting away with fiddling expenses until it's found out. He was the one who brought it into the limelight, and in that sense I think he was something of a fall guy. However, I couldn't stand that. So I wrote to *The Herald* in protest. And do you know there was something very odd about the way they handled my letter. Admittedly it was long. I wrote it over two pages of foolscap. And for some reason I can't quite understand, *The Herald* published it back-to-front. They put the second page first. But to be honest, maybe that made it even more effective.

It was unquestionably effective in stirring the minds of many. In the letter itself, she was explicit as to why four years after the death of her friend she found herself compelled to write it:

The grumblings of this swollen underbelly of a bigoted sub-society are becoming louder and more frequent. Men such as Donald Findlay must therefore stop feeding the old sectarian chants and Protestant anthems, which this thuggish and most violent element choose to digest literally. In a week in which we bear witness to the ongoing agony of the families of the IRA families, who have not yet been granted the final dignity of recovering their bodies, our attention should focus on the latest victims to be added to this history of hatred.

You could tell this letter was on a plane much higher than 'Disgruntled, Duntocher' Her intelligence clearly shone through, as did her awareness in mentioning the IRA's brutalities to broaden the perspective of her attack. I therefore have to place a *mea culpa* on the record. I didn't absorb the contents of it the way others might have. Firstly, there was the fact that, even then, I was a veteran of the sectarian debate, and I felt I had heard all this before. Certainly what was new was the source. Fresh and original. But my world-weary cynicism about her entrance into the fray, stemmed principally from when I first set eyes on Cara. It was outside Ibrox prior to an Old Firm game, Sunday 26 November 2000. I think I only noticed her standing in Edmiston Drive because she was posing for the posse of photographers surrounding her. By that time her campaign, Nil by Mouth had got off the ground and the publicity surrounding her was now intense, particularly on this occasion. She was to see her first Old Firm game, at the invite of the Ibrox board, who now, like Celtic, were keen to associate themselves with her initiatives.

Looking at her, against the immensity of the stadium, and the rising crescendo of the habitual sectarian uproar inside, she looked almost as if she was about to swallowed up in the maw of this infamous beast and never be seen again. Her task, at that moment, seemed to me to be both thankless and hopeless. She is in no way frail. But she simply looked dwarfed by the milling physical environment she was in. I must have felt then, how climate change deniers regard the Swedish teenager campaigner Greta Thunberg. Indeed within the stadium, even in the plush seats, it is claimed she was subjected to dog's abuse by one individual, supplementing the remark thrown at her outside the ground, that Michael Stone, the Protestant loyalist and murderer, was looking for her. Perhaps in jest, but of unsurprising bad taste. So, blithely, I targeted her for naivety, in my weekly column and wrote:

Even though Stanley Kubrick got in there before me with the title 'Eyes Wide Shut' it is the best I can come up with to reflect on Cara Henderson's visit to Ibrox. Such an innocent abroad at an Old Firm match treads the fine line between being a saint and voyeur. Christian charity, we could have told her, has never been much in attendance at the Old Firm match.

She did not wait long to rebut me in the letter pages of *The Herald* again:

I write in response to Christopher Morgan's letter (29 November) and Archie Macpherson's column (27 November). Both accuse me of naivety in so far as I chose both to attend the recent Old Firm match and then afterwards to speak out against the sectarian filth that I both witnessed and experienced first-hand. It would certainly have been naive of me to expect it to have been any different and unfortunately it wasn't. But I do believe that there is an important distinction to be made between expecting and accepting something. I did expect that the sectarian sickness, which continues to be incubated in our society would disfigure the game, and it did. But just because I expected it, did not lead me towards accepting it. And, if for that reason I then stand accused of being naive, then I gladly accept that. Archie Macpherson thought that the title 'Eyes Wide Shut' would have been a more appropriate than Nil by Mouth for the 'naive' campaign; perhaps he is right for our eyes have been too long closed to this problem. Meanwhile some young men continue to pay the price for our society's ongoing acceptance of religious division and at least one of them is at the moment in intensive care fighting for his life.

I am sure, for the readership of the paper, her last reference to a serious incident, which took place after that game she had attended, put me firmly in my place as purveyor of plodding orthodoxy. I hadn't been taking on a wee lassie from the sticks, but a mind being honed in the forensic legal skills she was acquiring at an Oxford college. From my reading of history it was clear to me that she would have been a dynamic figure in the suffragette movement given the sturdy sense of purpose she demonstrated to everyone she encountered. She clearly had personal abilities, but her background supplemented that. She had supportive middle-class parents, with her father a lawyer, who had had enough wherewithal to send her to private schools. Thus, she was provided with the classic and privileged middle-class ingredients to produce a self-confidence that, as a former teacher myself, I understood could clearly be identified with such a background. So the girl, who can vividly recall being taken to a Rangers match with her father, wearing a green jacket, and in the playground certainly knew the words of sectarian anthems, without an awareness of their meaning or potential aggravation, started a movement that still exists to this day and of which she is still rightly proud:

> Nil by Mouth? It was my mother who suggested that name to me. I know it's a phrase that comes from advice to nurses in a ward about administering medicine to patients but I'm not sure if that is what was in her mind. Thinking back I was aware myself that I had absorbed some anti-Catholic rhetoric without being fully conscious of it. At the outset my ambition was simply to start a billboard campaign. So we got our message on the sides of buses, and boards, just to establish awareness of what we were about in our campaign against sectarianism. And that's what we achieved at the start, not with the notion yet of setting up a charity. We fundraised. But eventually we felt that we were really making solid progress in publicity, so I was advised we should now set up Nil by Mouth as a proper charity. Then after I graduated from Oxford I took a year off to go back to Scotland to get really involved in all of this. And I have to say I don't recall any serious threats made to me, or anything like that. Remember this was in the days before the social network. I'm not sure if I could have withstood all the pressure in that kind of culture.

Although that is so, when she did relinquish her prominent role to get on with her life in pursuit of a legal career, she had to fend off accusatory stories that she was using the money raised by the charity to subsidise her travel and studies. But she left behind her a well-established organisation whose initial *ad hoc* adventurism, in taking their views to schools, churches and colleges, propagating their views on their core subject, gradually evolved into something much more organised and professional. She won a variety of awards and commendations by Scottish society for not just winning the hearts of people, but for driving cynics like me into new ways of thinking. However, in the cruellest way possible, fate could only deliver her something nearer martyrdom, in return.

On the 23 May 2012, at the time of the suicide bombings in London she was walking along a pavement in the city when it exploded directly beneath her feet. Not a terrorist bomb, but a freak gas explosion which engulfed her and which still haunts her:

...my hair still burning and the back of my dress blown off and my tights evaporated into the smoke-filled air and the skin on my hands, arms and legs continuing to bubble and melt – is a moment frozen in time, because it is a moment of feeling completely and utterly alone in the world.

In a lecture she delivered at Webster University in Geneva, on 29 April 2018 she showed the same amount of courage she had applied to her stance on sectarianism, by being brutally honest about the lasting effect the explosion had on her mental health, in order to help other sufferers of post-traumatic stress disorder. An overwhelming sense of disorder in her life affected her, with her mind occasionally in turmoil, as can be seen in this extract for her speech, where she admits Mark Scott still lives in her thoughts, principally because of that explosion:

I also started to feel as if my reaction to his death had been inappropriate, as if I didn't have the right to grieve the way I did. And worst of all I felt as if I had been wrong to do what I did afterwards, which was to set up a charity to campaign against sectarianism. Although the charity has undoubtedly been a driver behind a significant cultural shift in Scottish society, the fear that I didn't have the right to do what I did, or worse, that I had somehow been a fraud in speaking out about sectarianism, haunted me, sometimes to the point where I felt that I could no longer live with myself.

These are the words of a woman who at one stage was in a state of mental disorder that could be traced back to the streets of Bridgeton in Glasgow. However, she now gives the impression, that she had surmounted that stage of depression, although life would never quite be the same again. On that basis she is working on another campaign to encourage the United Nations to declare an International Day, dedicated to raising awareness about the damaging effects of trauma on our physical and mental health. Which obviously means there are some UN people in New York who will soon discover how life is going to change for them, when they answer her knock on the door. As an important political figure in Scotland did one day.

# CHAPTER 19

# 'Scotland's Secret Shame'

JACK MCCONNELL WAS a student at the University of Stirling in 1979 when he took a trip to London for the Auld Enemy game. He travels regularly there now as Lord McConnell of Glenscorrodale. His journeys are more benign than they were that year when citizens of the UK capital were made to despair that Hadrian's Wall no longer could contain the hordes. It was an experience which made a great impact on the future First Minister of Scotland:

> I went down with two mates looking forward to the game. We travelled one day on the underground. Some of our supporters pulled the emergency chord several times causing the train to be stopped, until everybody was told to get off the train and the whole line was closed down for the rest of the day. Then there was a riot in the station and my mates and I got into a waiting-room and hid, while supporters were ripping the station apart. The mayhem they caused in London that year was a turning point for me. I had made my mind up I would never go back to that game again. And anyway the fixture was eventually abandoned. However, the following year, in 1980, which I remember well, since that's when I won my first ever election, to be President of the Students Union at Stirling, I thought that the riot at Hampden would be a similar turning point and that something fundamental would alter its status in some way. But of course it didn't.

So, by the time he was in his late 30s and had become Education Minister in Henry McLeish's Scottish Labour administration at Holyrood, and as a football lover who had first stood on the terracings at Cappielow as a boy, he was fully aware of the hatreds which provoked the problems facing the game's administrators:

We used to play Rangers–Celtic games in my primary school on the island of Arran. But I never really got into that culture. But I was quite shocked when I went to University in '77 and heard people trying to find out what school anybody went to, and talking about the 'other kind' the 'them and us' conversations, meaning Catholics and Protestants. Coming from Arran I had never heard the likes before. It really hit me hard.

But like many of his ilk, he admits that although he was concerned with the problem, he was simply part of the political paralysis surrounding it. That is, until he met Cara:

I'll always remember that. She was brought into my office by Peter McLean, who had started the Bhoys against Bigotry campaign along with Fergus McCann at Celtic. I can never forget the way she started, when she looked me straight in the eye and said, 'You've got to do something about this. And if not, why not?'. Now, to be honest I felt the way you reacted to her when you first came across her. Maybe not as strongly as that at first, but I just felt how nice it was for her to get involved, but that's about all. Then when I listened to what she had to say I realised I was dealing with someone very intelligent and much more realistic and mature than I had previously given her credit for. And she was making it clear that somebody like myself had to pick up this issue and run with it positively, since she couldn't do it on her own. So that very day we committed to funding Nil by Mouth.

Cara's sincere and articulate intervention had deeply affected McConnell, who admitted that although he wanted to move on it, he wasn't quite sure how. Neither did parliament as a whole. A gauntlet had been thrown down to Scottish politicians by the Old Firm, in the very month the new Scottish Parliament was founded.

On 2 May 1999 Celtic met Rangers at Celtic Park. It was in effect a league decider. Rangers won the game and the title, amidst mayhem. During the match a handful of Celtic supporters invaded the field and the referee ended up with blood running down his face after being struck by a coin. As passions ran high, a spectator was hospitalised after plunging from a high tier in the stand to a lower level. There was the customary outrage afterwards. But they had to play a Scottish Cup Final only a few weeks ahead. So on reflection, and thinking of the distorted image it might convey to the world with the new Scottish Assembly in Holyrood, only a few days away from sitting for the first time, I wrote the following in my column for *The Herald*, 12 May 1999:

> The fixture should not be cancelled, but only television cameras and the media should be allowed entry. A football match in a deserted stadium might be like an opera without the chorus. But, as a first step, it might indicate to the watching millions throughout the world, that we at least have taken a first step in the right direction, and that we are saving Glasgow from a night of chaos, one way or the other.

I was immediately set upon by the silver-haired security official for Celtic, the normally genial ex-policeman George Douglas, former Divisional Commander, who was almost incandescent with rage and dismissed my suggestion as ludicrous. He was obviously speaking for the entire club itself. But, I knew that in the higher echelons within UEFA, this kind of punishment was receiving credible backing. West Ham had been forced to play behind closed doors at Upton Park against Castilla, only five months after the Hampden riot, in a European Cup Winners' Cup tie, because of the behaviour of some of their fans in the previous leg. And I recall, for instance, commentating on an Inter Milan–Rangers European tie on 29 September 2005, in an empty San Siro stadium, because of previous crowd trouble there. Strict liability was rearing its head. My clash with the former policeman at Celtic Park, hired to keep crowd matters fully in his ken, showed how resistant they were to any kind of interference. That is why I have no doubt that within Parkhead and Ibrox in May 1999 they were chastened by what had occurred, but also dismissive of any proposal that would disturb the duopoly. On that, they would undoubtedly have been united. They assumed, confidently, that this suppurating boil of a fixture would never be lanced but simply be treated with that emollient called money.

An influential force, of course, was the fact that many of the politicians at Holyrood were avid football supporters themselves, and many nursed deep-rooted passions for the Old Firm. In the past I had friends, even among Labour cabinet ministers, who would crawl over broken glass not to miss a Celtic match, particularly against Rangers. Whether our politicians sat at Parkhead or Ibrox, they had a positive allegiance to that fixture which made them seem like a kind of Praetorian Guard for its tradition, many of whose aspects they openly deplored, but whose presence lent it a kind of sombre credibility. McConnell did not sit in either camp, and perhaps his detachment from identity with the fixture made him aware of political impassivity:

> I was very conscious of the fact that politicians didn't want to change much. There was acquiescence. Nobody was really wanting to change the status quo. And that was the same throughout all the political parties.

That frustration supplemented by the new devolutionary powers produced a sense of liberation which eventually swept him into action. This led to an unprecedented political declaration. For within a year of Nil by Mouth being set up, McConnell became First Minister. The inspiration he had felt as Education Minister, when he met Cara, was transformed into positive action in his new status. In December 2002 he was to deliver the most important speech of his life. He delivered it in St Mungo Museum in Glasgow which was particularly identified with one phrase he used, and was emblazoned across many media outlets, 'SCOTLAND'S SECRET SHAME'.

He recollected the day of the speech for me in his home in Stirling which is only a short drive away from his alma mater, and where he now proudly sits as the university's Chancellor:

> I never thought I would become First Minister at my age, 41 at the time. And I thought I might only get a couple of years at this. You just never know how long these things will last and was I going to miss the opportunity to do something about a subject that I had been concerned about for years? The cross-party talks on what to do about sectarianism had produced some recommendations, so we were prepared to change the law to make offences that were motivated by religious hatred an aggravated offence. Now my predecessors as First Minister, Donald Dewar, Henry McLeish, were not prepared to do that, since they felt the law was adequate as it was. But I felt we had to lift these offensive

actions up the scale and turn this into law. So we issued a report detailing our proposals. That's when I decided to speak up and use the words, 'Scotland's secret shame', although, of course, it was hardly much of a secret, was it? But I had to use a phrase that would catch the imagination. But I tell you I had MSPs phoning me not to do it, because they felt the political backlash would be too strong. It would divide communities. It would lose votes. Did we? You know for every vote I lost I think I gained more. And in any case I was going to do it regardless, given that I didn't know how long I would be in this job. Besides that, I had Cara Henderson continually in my ear asking, 'What are you going to do? What are you going to do?'.

It was certainly given a dramatic airing when he told his audience of this move towards new legislation:

This is a very important day, not just this year, but in the history of Scotland. It is a day when Scotland can grow up and move away from the divisions of the past. These measures signal our determination that Scotland will no longer tolerate acts of religious hatred. We will act to toughen the law so that the courts can more severely punish crimes motivated by sectarianism. The report also proposes that football clubs, the police and prosecutors systematically identify and ban people spreading religious hatred inside and outside football stadiums. It is time for Scotland's secret shame to be put in the past.

The first barrier to that was selective deafness. Who would have thought that overnight deep remorse would be felt on the back of such candour, and that some visible change would be in evidence in the rancour at these fixtures? The naivety behind the notion that instantly there would be a positive reaction was perhaps exemplified most of all by an editorial in the *News of the World*. It interpreted events at the Old Firm fixture only a couple of days after that speech, in which there was an effort at globalisation of their enmity, with Celtic supporters waving Palestinian colours and Rangers with Jewish flags.

Where were the police and the stewards when the flags were unfurled? Where were they when the songs started up? They were turning a blind eye. Taking a softly, softly approach. Yesterday both the police and the Ibrox stewards made a mockery of the First Minister's words.

Habitual acceptance of this environment contributed to deafness on the terracings and among the police. What was required to back it up was a legislative process to lend confidence and legal strength to any policing. That was to come a year later.

One man who was in on the development of the First Minister's speech was Dave Scott, a Catholic from Lisburn in Northern Ireland, a graduate of Stirling University, who continued to live in Scotland and contributed advice to McConnell on the writing of the speech. He was a lover of football and still vividly recalls the first game he ever saw in Scotland, Ayr United against Hamilton. Having been born and brought up in an area where he personally knew people who had been killed in deliberate sectarian attacks, he was also a graduate of the street of hard knocks. After he left university, in his role as political adviser to Labour MSP Bill Butler, he was very close to all the cross-party discussions on sectarianism which were held in Holyrood and still regrets the transference of power that took place in 2007:

> There was a dramatic change. Alex Salmond's approach was totally different. The whole issue was put further down the political agenda. Funding was cut for many of our community projects and you could tell that the First Minister was not happy answering questions about these problems. A generous man might want to say that Salmond wanted to sell Scotland as an appealing place, talk up Scotland as a great country. A more cynical, and perhaps more practical interpretation, is that the church might have got in his ear and told him to stop talking about these things, not to play up the social problems so much, since to be honest Salmond was keen on winning over the Catholic vote.

However, it has to be said that the Labour Party itself was not unaware of attracting such support.

Section 74 of the Criminal Justice (Scotland) Act established under

McConnell in 2003, actually emerged from cross-party group meetings and was shaped by the Liberal MSP Donald Gorrie. It meant that, for the first time, any crime that could be linked to sectarianism, much of which revolved around the Old Firm, would carry a heavy tariff in the courts. It was the first time that sectarian offences had been quantified. Scotland's 'secret' shame was being made more public. Since its onset thousands have been charged under that law.

So what had to accompany a legal stance, were the efforts of non-governmental organisations like Nil by Mouth to try to bring communities together, to look each other in the eye, and talk frankly about this issue – even to the extent of bringing the Orange Order to sit across the table from Irish Republican sympathisers. This lay at the core of Cara Henderson's approach to the problem, which even from the comfort of a Swiss back-garden, with infant sounds and the clatter of domesticity in the background, she still spelled out with conviction:

I didn't want to go down that road of accusing anybody of bigotry. I wanted to introduce as many people as possible to the subject and make them think about it. I wanted to bring people together and achieve some consensus about a serious social problem. We wanted to have facts and figures to show, if indeed, it was one way more than the other. And remember when we started out nobody was amassing statistics on sectarianism. Everything was anecdotal. We changed that.

Her personal charisma inspired others to help her movement move on from simply sloganising to being an actual body with an organisation that could proselytise in the community. In December 2000 they reached an agreement with the Catholic Church, the Church of Scotland and Glasgow City Council that encouraged the Millennium Commission to award them £400,000 to set up a project aimed at encouraging individuals and communities to come up with anti-sectarian schemes. However, they certainly were not winning over everybody. My early reservations, which I still regret, were puny compared to the objections of those who thought Nil by Mouth was applying sticking plaster to a cancerous growth. One of the most prominent critics is Jeanette Findlay, a lecturer of Economics at the University of Glasgow, a passionate Celtic supporter, and a member of the Celtic Trust which stresses the value of the club as a social institution. She herself took on the Celtic Board in later years on their reticence to accept the Living Wage norms. She told me bluntly:

> There is no such a thing as sectarianism. The reality is that we face continuing anti-Catholic bigotry. That's what it is. To try to define it as sectarianism is providing a false equivalence, as if it is all balanced. It is not.

Although she was to be upbraided at one stage by the club itself and even the by Celtic Supporters Association for her defence of some IRA songs heard occasionally at Parkhead, she firmly believes that an institution like Nil by Mouth has the wrong end of the stick. However, someone who obviously would have agreed with her, and himself not disinterested in the progress of Celtic in football was nevertheless an unashamed admirer of Cara Henderson.

James MacMillan, a Catholic by background and identity, and globally acclaimed Scottish composer wrote a composition dedicated to Cara. 'The Birds of Rhiannon', a dramatic concerto for orchestra lasting 25 minutes, was conducted by himself at The Proms in the Royal Albert Hall, 26 July 2001. The honour he had bestowed on her was compounded by the fact that a previous composition of his had been dedicated to Nelson Mandela. Thus Cara was elevated to almost saintly stature on the wings of music. MacMillan clearly felt a spiritual link to the young Protestant, and now, as it so happens, atheist woman. For exactly a couple of months after Cara's letter had appeared in *The Herald*, MacMillan delivered a speech at the Edinburgh International Festival which he must have anticipated would produce shock-waves. And it did. He claimed that bigotry was still rife in Scotland. He was articulate and passionate. He aroused discussions among those of us in pressrooms attending games, when journalists and broadcasters assembled to hear the verdicts of the mighty. As workers in the industry, we felt we knew something about the assembly line of sectarianism associated with this fixture. But did we really know all about it? Was a composer from the concert hall, actually telling us that we were blind to its wider manifestations? One sentence in his speech summarised his views:

> In many walks in life – in the professions, in academia, in politics

and sport – anti-Catholicism, even when it is not particularly malign, is as endemic as it is second nature.

His background explains much of his attitude. This was a Catholic man from the mining area of Cumnock in Ayrshire where even if you did not have his musical ear, you would certainly have known what Orange flutes in the streets could mean. He recalled vividly the hatreds expressed during his schooldays because of his religion.

But in truth, whether Protestant or Catholic in these huddled chats, all having experienced explosions of bigotry, my pressroom colleagues were nevertheless puzzled. As I looked around me in my own professional environment in the media, I couldn't perceive that social advancement had been stymied by any particular religious background. Although others who had been around for some considerable time they could readily testify that it had existed in times gone by. Many people around me in Labour circles who had come through the ranks in civic or political life and held significant posts in public life were practising Catholics. I found myself starting to wonder if the Old Firm game distorted our perceptions of bigotry, in making a too-ready assumption that the juices of hatred dried up after 90 minutes and that we could leave them behind in a stadium. This is the '90-minute bigot' concept that perhaps we accepted too readily.

Gerry PT Finn of the University of Strathclyde, in *Scotland's Shame?*, an anthology of writings on bigotry edited by the historian Sir Tom Devine, himself a Catholic, touches on that perception:

Sporting contests can exaggerate the nature of ethnic conflict. But it is equally a mistake to believe that sporting contests and society are somehow unconnected.

It certainly suggests that those of us who thought we were in the eye of the storm at an Old Firm game, and that it would abate in one afternoon, were perhaps, totally ignorant of the real magnitude of the problem, as defined by MacMillan. Were we blinded by the excesses of the Old Firm culture to the extent that we didn't realise that in multifarious ways the malignancy was more widespread? My personal experience didn't square with that, and 'personal experience' is the basis upon which Devine bases his own scepticism over the extent of the problem, as was described by MacMillan.

The historian summarised the writings. What he provides us with is a degree of dubiety, the real difficulty of arriving at a neat conclusion over the conflicting arguments about the extent of bigotry, when he writes:

> Catholic writers like Patrick Reilly ('To ask if there is anti-Catholicism in Scotland, is like asking if there are Frenchmen in Paris') and Bishop Joseph Devine, who would argue that James MacMillan's lecture is 20 years out of date, take up radically different divisions. To some extent this disagreement must stem from different personal experiences as so many of the issues in the debate come down to subjective judgements.

Certainly, a man sitting now in the House of Lords will never forget the personal judgement he had to make on that. Jack McConnell encountered a kind of pincer sectarianism in 1999 when he was set on becoming MSP for Motherwell at the start of his national political career:

> This issue crept into my selection process within the Labour Party to become their candidate for Motherwell and Wishaw. I had both sides at me. One side knew that my wife Bridget had been born a Catholic. The word was I had married, quote-unquote, a Catholic. So one side wouldn't vote for me because I had married that way. And the other side wouldn't vote for me because I wasn't a Catholic. It was madness, but it was there. There was that undercurrent throughout the whole selection process. Now I had known of the sectarian problems of North Lanarkshire, but I was astonished to encounter it personally, in the middle of an internal political process. Even when I won, I had graffiti plastered over the walls of our house indicating somebody's displeasure at having been selected.

Against that perennial background, both clubs were now having to prove their credentials in the stand against sectarianism. Fergus McCann's first appointment, in the summer of 1994, after he had firmly established himself, was a former SFA referee Peter McLean. He had always made it clear that, while he respected other people's religious faith, he had none himself, and felt he was an ideal figure to help create and promote an entirely new Celtic campaign, Bhoys Against Bigotry. It contained a charter that included a distinct social mission, and also set out to discourage songs which reflected the republican side of Irish history particularly about the IRA. It was not universally accepted amongst the Celtic community. McLean admitted that life was not entirely tranquil afterwards:

> I lost count of the number of times I was spat on by both Celtic and Rangers supporters as soon as I became identified with this enterprise. And make no mistake there was also internal debate. I remember one individual speaking up and stating that if we went through with this we would lose up to 20,000 supporters. To which Fergus retorted, 'Good. They wouldn't be the kind of supporters we would want in here. They'd be replaced by another 20,000 who weren't coming because they don't like some of the songs being sung here'.

It prompted a Celtic supporters group to pen their own song which had a touch of mockery to it:

> Fergus has said no,
> so those tunes will have to go,
> these Rebel songs no longer can be played,
> so we've made our self's a pact, to polish up our act,
> so don't you sing 'Boys of the Old Brigade'.

But more than mockery came from the mouth of the much beloved Celtic manager Tommy Burns, who at first completely supported the initiative, and stated at the time that:

> Bhoys Against Bigotry has helped and I have noticed a huge reduction in sectarian singing at Parkhead.

However, he had deeper feelings. And, just before his sad death from skin cancer, had written to Celtic supporters:
Something happened at the club around Fergus's time, they

seemed to want to embark on a sort of crusade to change aspects of the club. I told Fergus that we don't have bigotry here.

This later statement would have chimed with the view of Jeanette Findlay's belief that one-way bigotry directed at their club was the actual reality. But it certainly commanded more attention than any Rangers initiative, although that would have been misleading because as Jack McConnell admits he got on splendidly with Rangers secretary Campbell Ogilvie: 'They put on a presentation for us which was outstanding'. In it they showed how they were inviting schools into the stadium to work at different schemes. This included Catholic schools, as the club tried to put out feelers to people who might have thought there was no place for them in that establishment. This was the precursor of what developed into their Everyone Anyone campaign in 2020 which states its principle of fostering openness that is meant to effectively shut the door on the past.

This is why, years earlier, the Nil by Mouth organisation meant so much to any hope of progress and was confidently funded by government and other businesses. Cynicism may have surrounded it, with some critics still trying to portray their people simply as do-gooders who, in blunt terms, were farting against thunder. But anybody who has met with Dave Scott, who was to become its director in 2011, is made immediately aware of his dynamism and crusading spirit that energised not only the entire organisation but also who came in contact with him. He took over the post just after it had just been announced that the Scottish Government was to introduce the Offensive Behaviour at Football and Threatening Communications (Scotland) Act, and with the news that parcel bombs had been sent to Celtic manager Neil Lennon and the Celtic-supporting Trish Godman, then Deputy Presiding Officer of the Scottish Parliament. At that time politicians were certainly being challenged by the crime figures which had been released in November 2011 which revealed that there were 693 charges aggravated by religious prejudice, 58 per cent anti-Catholic, 37 per cent anti-Protestant. Significantly, 88 per cent of these offences were recorded away from football matches, which suggests the problem was far from just a stadium phenomenon. This is something Scott well understood and he took this baptism of fire in his stride. He made it clear that he supported many in the legal profession:

I gave an interview [about the Offensive Behaviour Act] in which

I said this was a bad idea, that it would run the risk of breathing flames into the situation. Alex Salmond got up in parliament and criticised me. He said I was only opposed to this because I had been a former employee of a Labour MSP.

But there was a long list of figures utterly opposed to this, including leading lawyers. Sir Tom Devine called it: 'a stain on the reputation of the Scottish legal system for fair dealing'.

*The Herald* on 15 December 2011 was entirely sceptical in an editorial which declares:

> Lack of clarity in the current bill risks criminalising fans for something closer to muscular enthusiasm than bigotry and for the use of songs and symbols that would not be considered offensive elsewhere.

In any case, that act was eventually repealed in March 2018. Nevertheless, with some eruptions of sectarian chants and what was considered wild behaviour at the Old Firm game at Celtic Park on 31 March 2019, Scottish Police Federation Vice-Chairman David Hamilton jumped in and voiced concern about its repeal:

> Personally I believe the repeal of the Offensive Behaviour Act has had an impact, because I think some people feel wrongly legitimised to behave in a way that they wouldn't otherwise behave.

Now that sounded eminently sensible. Everybody understands and sympathises with the problems that the police have had with Old Firm crowds before and since the Hampden riot. But we also have to pay attention to law and its application. The Law Society of Scotland was unequivocal about this Act. It pointed to the figures that clearly indicated that the 287 fans charged with offensive behaviour could have been dealt with under previously existing laws. And its punchline could not have been more emphatic: 'it follows that the 2012 act has not been fundamental to tackling sectarianism'.

Nor had it been likely to do so. This legislation was a populist move, good on the eye and suggesting toughness on the spot, and whose authors imagined that sectarianism could be crushed by bobbies arresting people for singing songs in crowds of up to 60,000. For instance, at one stage Roseanna Cunningham, charged with the responsibility of steering the act through parliament, announced that singing the national anthem would be an offence. Then she changed her mind and said it wouldn't. They were twisting themselves into knots. In short, the act was a fig leaf to cover the authors' inability to comprehend the true complexity of the problem. But, in terms of exacting punishment, the SFA had overwhelmingly voted against the concept of strict liability, which could mean clubs losing points, or closure of a stadium, in part if not entirely, if their fans were found guilty of various crowd offences, including, of course, sectarian chants.

By that stage, Dave Scott of Nil by Mouth, had covered the length and breadth of Scotland, conducting sessions in schools and a variety of other meeting places explaining the issues to both children and adults, and was qualified to say to me:

> Sectarianism isn't just about violence. Of course, it's there. But more endurable is attitude. I think Scotland is becoming a less violent society and there is less sectarianism around connected to that. But it is about attitude.

That attitude I know from personal experience is still framed in that sometimes sleekit question, 'Which foot does he kick with?'. Scott's stress on obdurate mindsets was certainly behind the thinking of James Kelly: the MSP who successfully campaigned for the April 2018 repeal of the Offensive Behaviour Act, and talked up what Nil by Mouth had actually been engaged in for over two decades, when he declared the way to attack the problem was necessarily long-term and stressed where the emphasis should take place, 'in classrooms and community groups'. So I am reminded of two eye witnesses who were actually on, or close to, the pitch at Hampden at the height of the riot in 1980. A television personality and a photographer used words that still resound with me.

## CHAPTER 20

# A Changing Landscape

PRESENTER DOUGIE DONNELLY and *Scotsman* photographer Donald McLeod were jolted by the suddenness of the violence after that 1980 final, and still distinctly recall their feelings. They were both professional enough to make quick assessments of who was doing what to whom. One thing caught their attention. From Donnelly I heard this:

> And, do you know, I've always found this interesting. All I saw were young neds. There were no sorts of mature men there. They were like kids. And the bottles were being thrown by them.

And from McLeod, an echo of that when he told me:

> One image really struck me. It was the gear they were wearing. With the kind of jackets and the cut-off jeans they wore, on both sides, it was like being at a Bay City Rollers convention.

Much closer to the action than I was, they could paint an accurate picture of youthful disorder, of dangerous capers, of unbridled hatred coming from boys, many of whom were clearly not old enough to be recruited into the armed forces, or were indeed still learning about algebra or how to spell words properly – like 'violence', for example.

It appeared that no hardened veterans on either side of the divide were present on the field, perhaps because their bones were not up to making it on to the pitch, even though some of them may have had that inclination. For let us not forget that, long before the entry of the gladiators, from the outset, the animosity between the factions was taking place in the best seats in the stadium, where they were actually coming to blows. We can safely assume that the vast majority of those on the field would not have been born when I was making my first observations on Old Firm hostility in the '60s. So where did they get all this fire in the belly from?

Where else but the oral tradition, that flow of sectarian rituals passed down from one generation to another. It floods through the peer groups with their self-sustaining chants and songs. It is gang culture with a special remit.

I know from experience that a huge gulf can exist between classroom and playground. It is in these separate playgrounds, where attitudes can thrive wholly immune from the good intentions of the educators, that traditional enmities are fostered. You can perhaps identify that in the rebellious Green Brigade and Union Bears, youthful groups at Celtic Park and Ibrox respectively, who can sometimes be inventive and amusing in their declared role in life of being constantly irreverent and frankly troublesome at times. Of course, they are not in awe of authority, and indulging in crude aggressive sloganising is unlikely to earn them a standing ovation in directors' boxes. Although they wouldn't exist, or make any impact, if they were simply orthodox. But they sometimes reveal a clear understanding of some of the issues surrounding the clubs and played a notable part in advertising their opposition to the Offensive Behaviour Act by their street demonstrations. They are not simply indulging in fan banter as might happen anywhere in the world. They echo social division. And I am sure not absolutely everybody disapproves of some of their actions. Indeed, many sitting near them might echo the jokey endearment of the late comedian Dick Emery, 'Oh, you are awful, but I like you!' But comparing them to disruptive Ultras in other countries would be like contrasting choral evensong with bullfighting. And so the traditions of hatred go on. I have seen kids, particularly at Old Firm away games, mouthing the old slogans as fluently as I suppose their fathers and grandfathers did. In the years they have travelled the country, analyst Andy Walker and commentator Ian Crocker of Sky Sports have constantly taken the temperature of Old Firm fans, who still air their feelings freely around them. Walker, experienced as a player in Old Firm games himself, was emphatic about the atmosphere in 2019: 'Things haven't got better. The bitterness is much worse than it's ever been'.

This view was endorsed by the powerful journalist of *The Scottish Sun*, Bill Leckie, who wrote in his paper in January 2020:

I've been immersed in Scottish football all my life, have written about it for close on 40 years and never has the atmosphere around this fixture been quite as hateful, as vile, as petty, as sinister.

Indeed, in one extreme case, in September 2019, a 14-year-old was arrested during a clash in Glasgow between Irish Republican supporters and Loyalists. The police said he was armed with a weapon no less. All this seems to imply 'attitude'. That word, stressed by Dave Scott, is simply a synonym for 'bigotry' which is still prevalent amongst those still swayed by the culture of the Old Firm. It suggests that the great effort of schools to preach tolerance and understanding of the 'other kind' faces resistance from an element immune to reason. This does not discredit the valiant efforts of such organisations as Nil by Mouth, because the alignment among all the people I have met in pursuit of this dilemma, from Cara Henderson onwards, including everybody who voted to repeal the Offensive Behaviour Act, stresses the need for an educational solution. This leads you, inevitably, into territory that can have an incendiary effect on passions. As long as I can recall, our society has been hotly, passionately, opposing or defending the effects of separating kids from the age of five on the basis of religious belief. It is something that MacMillan has referred to, in terms of the trials and tribulations he came through, as a Catholic pupil in Cumnock. I know little about North Ayrshire. But I do know North Lanarkshire well, and the estrangements that exist in communities there would be familiar to MacMillan anyway.

The village of Glenboig near Coatbridge provided supporters to that 10 May final. Two buses left for the game, one Rangers, the other Celtic. They were heading for their traditional stances on opposite terracings. Their separation when they arrived on the southside of the city of Glasgow was essentially no different from their separation in their clay-mining village. It was less obvious in the village than it would be on those terracings, where they would wish to flaunt the republican tricolour, or at the other end, the Union Jack. Nevertheless, the separation manifested itself clearly and distinctly in other ways. You didn't need to scratch beneath the surface to detect the cleavage. It was there in almost iconic form. At one end of the village there was the Catholic school, at the other end the non-denominational one, or Protestant school, to give it its common usage. Both umbilically connected to the two churches. In the centre street was the main pub, the social focal point – but there was no coalescing there. The pub was a stockade of sectarian rigidity. It had two entrances, one strictly for Protestants, the other for Catholics. Tradition determined that they would drink in their own territory at either end of the bar. You would find that the locals talked almost affectionately about the split as if it were a quaint custom that might even have tourist appeal. But they would add, distinctly, that there never was any trouble, no fighting, no aggression, just separate drinking.

Indeed, there is no evidence that when the fans returned to the village after one of the most dramatic sectarian outbursts in the history of Scottish football, that any act of provocation occurred. From what I learned, they drank, as they regularly did, in that conditioned stand-off, some with glee, others obviously desolate. That did not surprise me as I knew the community well, having taught in a school there, and having married a local girl. But, a fissure of division did run through it. I think this was represented most notably by the two schools, the palisades of social division. But, of course, this was not unique. Glenboig was not perhaps the exact microcosm of working-class industrialised Scotland, but it was greatly representative of the spread of villages around North Lanarkshire which I got to know well in my teaching years. Sectarianism there could be boisterous, noisy, sinister, and much of it with dark humour. But nobody would dare ask, 'Why are there two schools, when one would do?'. And, why two entrances for a pub, based on where you were baptised? Instead there was, to use the word Jack McConnell uttered to me in another context, acquiescence.

Two cultures ran parallel to each other. Of course there was occasional social overlap and some mixed marriage, but that was minimal. Ignorance of each other's religious sensibilities could easily be a breeding ground for intolerance, as elsewhere, where such division was obvious and even in the most part, like Glenboig, benign. 'Them and us' was part of daily expression.

People in many areas in the west of Scotland accepted the divisive norms of daily life as if they were simply reflecting what nature had ordained, unchallengeable, immutable. Particularly when it came to the schools. What school you went to did have real meaning about almost any aspect of life and was no great advantage to Catholics in the job market in those earlier eras when prejudice was thick on the ground. 'Irish need not apply', if not placed as signs in windows, was certainly in the minds of those who would openly practise bigotry in those times. Although, in explaining the importance of schools in maintaining the Catholic identity, the late Professor Patrick Reilly of the University of Glasgow, writing in *The Herald*, poured scorn on the notion that potential discrimination be used as an excuse to end separation of schools:

> We must distinguish between a demand that newcomers become exactly like the host culture and a welcome without conditions or stipulations. Forsake your identity or suffer the consequences; it is what the Christians said to Shylock. Today it sounds suspiciously akin to one of those notorious Mafia offers that are so perilous to refuse.

Amidst all the contrasting and clashing views that surfaced from time to time, it was in North Lanarkshire, in my other life, before broadcasting, as a teacher and then headmaster of a school, that I developed my educational views. I started to harbour the desire to preside over a school which would house children of all faiths or none under the one roof, quite separate from any solution to the sectarian issue. It was simply the right way to educate children in a cohesive society. I knew it was something of a pipe dream. Whenever I brought this up in public, the reaction of those around me was as if they were listening to one of those dewy-eyed contestants in the Miss World competition inevitably declaring a wish for world peace. Mild amusement and glazed looks would ensue at one end of the spectrum. At the other end was an anger that stemmed from believing that such thinking was an attack on faith itself. I would have thought that the inclusivity of different beliefs was about social consolidation and possibly helping to end the mystery that shrouded each other's faiths, and in fact regenerate thinking about religion which surely had the confidence and resilience to sustain its role in society. The corollary to all this was that anyone challenging the status quo was in effect simply stoking sectarianism itself.

In addressing schooling, I return to Cara of Nil by Mouth and the lecture she gave to a university in Switzerland and in which, again, she made the candid admission about the youthful relationship with the victim of sectarian violence:

> Mark was my boyfriend and yet when he asked me out on a date, and in spite of how excited I was, I hesitated before saying yes, because I knew he was Catholic and for some reason I thought he was lesser than me.

So, here was a supposedly well brought-up middle-class girl infected by the cultural disdain of another person's identity, which reflected an attitude which existed at many social levels in Scotland. But looking back at the murder, something built up in her mind that was to traumatise her. She began to realise that the killer had undoubtedly seen Mark in that same alien vein. But, in Jason Campbell's case, that difference had risen to the level of perverted brutality. She agonised for years over the thought that she had something in common with the murderer, that they were both 'shaped by a culture of division based on people's ethnic and religious heritage'.

But it was school, albeit a fee-paying independent one, that had brought she and her Catholic boyfriend together, and had forced her to admit that sitting at adjacent desks with someone from the 'other side' opened her eyes to the prejudice that had infected her.

Seven years after Mark's murder it was interesting to note a report in *The Herald* on 20 December 2002. One of the most respected figures in the history of Scottish football, Billy McNeill, captain of the triumphant Lisbon Lions team of 1967 and a practising Catholic, had offered this observation on sectarianism in the Celtic fanzine *The Alternative View*:

> For me the solution is schooling. To achieve that solution kids must go to the same schools regardless of their religion. Maybe, with that, in a hundred years or so, the nonsense that is sectarianism will be over. I know my opinions will upset some people but it is what I believe after thinking about this subject a great deal.

*The Herald*, aware this statement followed calls for a debate on the issue from First Minister Jack McConnell and broadcaster Kirsty Wark and noted the view of the fanzine's editor, Matt McGlone, that 'Billy is entitled to his thoughts just like anyone else'. But, McNeill's views were summarily dismissed by his church's spokesman, Peter Kearney:

> Sectarianism, intolerance and bigotry are bred in homes not schools... Billy McNeill is respected as a sportsman, but he is not experienced as an educationalist.

It certainly is a valid point to bring up the home factor. Everything starts in the home, from potty training to how to handle a knife and fork, and, we would hope, learning respect for people of different cultures. And undoubtedly there is the antithesis of that, where hatreds are nurtured in a home. The murderer of Mark Scott was obviously not brought up in a household adhering to the values of the Good Book. But it is also about the way you develop outside the home, and being inside a school can be seen as an effective staging post in learning how to relate to others of contrasting beliefs. It is a fact, though, that increasingly more people started speaking up about a subject that certainly can inflame. Michael Kelly, formerly of the Celtic board, wrote in *The Herald* in 2000:

> First, change the law. That means addressing the question of separate schools. Abolition will never receive the necessary political support. But at least debate will force religious leaders to accept that defining children of five by religious denomination implants that factor in developing minds.

The Salmond administration is to be commended for ploughing money into different anti-sectarian schemes and commissioning a report by Professor Duncan Morrow from Northern Ireland, in which he concluded that in itself the ending of separate schools would not stamp out sectarianism. We were certainly to learn how difficult it would be to alter the status quo in education. When Lord McConnell was Education Minister at Holyrood, he was the architect of change which brought children closer together, in a rephrasing of the famous political slogan from the Bill Clinton electoral campaign, 'It's the education, stupid'. But, it faced him with an existential battle that was as bitter as any he had ever fought in his political life, as he recounted to me:

When I got down to business I knew that this simple idea of ending segregation by eliminating Catholic schools was a non-starter because of their ongoing success academically, apart from anything else. So I thought of one positive step that could be made. I didn't like the idea of kids walking to school separately. I wanted them to be together. So we built into our development programme joint-campuses where they would walk through the same gates and share the same playground facilities, although educated separately. There was deep, deep anger about it. I was lobbied about it strenuously. Many church people were not at all happy with the joint-campuses. But we persevered with that. We just had to. And I'm proud of that, for there are so many examples of communities which were deeply divided and are now much more harmonious. For example, in the 1990s there was actual fighting in the streets of Wishaw about priorities for the new primary schools between the Catholics and the non-denominational community, after the local council had agreed plans to build a new Catholic primary school. Actual fighting. But we passed legislation to build a school with a joint-campus on that very site, and to this day that school has been a great success. The kids eat together, they play sport together, they walk to school together. They are in contact with one another on a scale that's so different from the past in these areas. They might get taught in separated classrooms but I think it is a model that respected the different traditions. It would not be my ideal choice, but ultimately I have no difficulty with that.

Glenboig now has a single joint-campus school serving the area, as of the McConnell blueprint – one of over a hundred around Scotland now, brought about by sheer economic necessity. Pragmatism has brought children closer together. The pub in the main street has also had a facelift. It's been replaced by a roadhouse of one single ecumenical entrance, with the door permanently shut on the old days of separation. There is the hush of compromise about the village, as there is about the changing educational status.

And so it is clear that the Minister was telling kids who were either green or blue that they could share so much in the precincts of a school. Although the average Scottish child spends only 15 per cent of their waking week in school, this togetherness he pursued clearly spilled over into more social contact. You would think most minds would be open to that as a potent move forward. But some of their elders were never quite as amicable when the crunch came to accepting this joint-campus concept. When he was First Minister, in conjunction with the churches, McConnell developed a three-school integrated campus within one building in Midlothian. The night before the opening ceremony he received a phone call to his office to tell him there was a problem. There had been intervention in the building: some people had put religious artefacts on the walls, then others took them all down again. Folk were trying to mark out their territory before the official opening. There was agitation in the council about this, amounting to uproar. McConnell stepped in vigorously to what was developing into an unseemly clash of cultures:

> I told them that I would pull out of the ceremony if this was not sorted out and I would tell the press exactly why I was doing that. Well, a compromise was reached and common sense prevailed, but I tell you there was a photograph taken of the platform party of all the officials at the opening, and you could see the tension in their faces about it all.

The photographer who snapped this probably did not require any of the skills demonstrated by the photographers on the Hampden pitch on 10 May 1980. But, ultimately, they were at either end of the spectrum of the same problem. The children at the centre of this sociopolitical religious facedown probably knew nothing about what was going on around them, even though there is little doubt that many in the school would be followers of the Old Firm, given their widespread appeal of the two clubs. And, indeed, with the coming of Stein in particular, there was an increase in Celtic sympathy in the non-denominational schools, in keeping with that club's historic openness. And it has to be said, the vast majority of both sets of young supporters would never misbehave in any way at a game.

By contrast, they were to see some of their heroes in a bad light, sometimes dramatically. Like waking up on the morning of 3 March 2011 and seeing two angry Old Firm faces on some front pages, or being able to watch a particularly graphic scene on the television screen that was to bring Hampden 1980 back to my own doorstep.

\* \* \* \* \*

The setting was Celtic Park at the end of a Scottish Cup replay which Celtic had won 1-0. The two men were Neil Lennon and Ally McCoist. One a manager, the other an assistant to Rangers manager Walter Smith. Their raging postures and spluttering mouths got them so close they might have been exchanging body fluids. Angry, fuming, bitter, an ugly brawl. Men of two completely contrasting personalities. Lennon with a volcanic temperament that tended to camouflage the fact that he suffered severe depressions at times. McCoist with a bubbling sense of humour which could brighten up any dressing room and made Craig Brown, as Scotland manager, regret not having taken him to the World Cup in 1998. Lennon, the subject of disgraceful, incessant sectarian abuse and actual physical violence, which almost became a regular item in news bulletins, to our shame. McCoist, chosen to be the successor to Walter Smith. Both of them born supporters of their respective clubs, which may have sparked something primeval in them on that occasion. Seen, of course, by those who think along these lines, as Protestant and Catholic warriors.

They certainly illustrated how circumstances had changed since 1980 when McNeill and Grieg, both of whom could erupt with ease, would never have acted as cheer leaders for the crowd. I saw this altercation at Celtic Park as cheap indulgence, playing to the crowd, mimicking the terracing rage, showing your colours, to be as one with them. I have to admit that I found it slightly risible. It was like one of those brawls which start off apparently with vicious intent, but never a punch is actually thrown, in the hope that those intervening will stop it anyway. That's exactly how it concluded. Admittedly it did not look pretty, and I knew immediately we were in for another bout of public soul-searching, as the scenes were being beamed around the world by the television people with a 'Heigh ho! Here they go again!' alacrity. The statistics certainly suggested the game had been more bloody than the death scene in *Hamlet*. There had been three red cards and ten yellows handed out to Rangers players. It was ripe for indignation. The Tory leader at Holyrood, Annabel Goldie, was top of the pile with words straight out of the textbook: 'Repugnant, disgraceful and utterly unacceptable'.

But the whole scene was beginning to develop for me in a very personal way. Various outlets were queuing up for me to comment on the incidents of the evening, because of my link to the 1980 riot. Two sham pugilists jousting in the technical area? A mere *pas de deux*. Why, I had had hundreds down in front of me on that day, really going at it. Quotes from my commentary on the riot day slipped back into view in the press. In the interviews I gave, I also regurgitated an old refrain of mine. 'Ban the cameras, not the fixture.' The script I had written all those years ago. As far as role-modelling was concerned, I made the point that the tussle would be as useful to a young audience as instructing them on how to moon the headmaster. The Hearts manager at the time, Jim Jefferies, not surprisingly, offered the macho explanation, telling the *Daily Record*:

> How was it a disaster for Scottish football? It only showed to the world how much it means to Celtic and Rangers.

He probably hadn't been given the crime statistics, which showed there were 33 arrests at the ground, and afterwards, 200 violent and anti-social crimes and 40 incidents of domestic violence, all linked by the police to the event. This simply added to the toll through the years which was associated with innumerable assaults, many a woman being battered, and of course deaths. One study reported that through the decades 15 murders could be linked to the Old Firm game.

First Minister Alex Salmond, right on cue, called another summit involving the clubs and the SFA obliged. I had covered so many summits in the past I felt like I had been bagging Munros. We knew it would have as much influence on the harsh reality of conflict as a meeting of the Scottish Ornithologists' Club. Then, two major issues were to drag me into some of the most bitter disputes ever to surround the Old Firm clubs, affecting the whole of Scottish football. Both of them were existential problems. Both of them were about transforming the landscape. One was about the very future of Scotland itself. The other pointed to the distinct possibility that the Old Firm fixture, which had withstood condemnation from many sources throughout the decades, might in fact, become as obsolete as bear-baiting.

# CHAPTER 21

# New Territory

EVEN THOUGH I could not possibly have understood its implications at the time, in 2003 I heard an odd story in Manchester. I realise now, this was like someone revealing to me the existence of a time bomb secreted under the layers of apparent prosperity. United were about to play Rangers in a Champions League game. They were under the management then of Alex McLeish, who had taken over from the Dutchman Dick Advocaat. On the eve of the game I was relaxing in the hotel with my co-commentator Andy Walker, sharing a sherbet or two. A man in the official Rangers hospitality party wandered across to talk to us. He was a stranger, but when you work in this business you are public property. Sometimes it is pleasant and other times you want to duck under a table to get out of the way. On this occasion we engaged in a pleasant chat, about the state of the game in general, as he was interested in our views. Then the conversation turned to Rangers. I never did find out if he was a supporter or not, but his connection with the club was in a construction project. As it turned out, he was a civil engineer, in charge of a new development at the stadium. I can't recall how it arose but he began to tell us something that was supposed to have been kept under wraps. Rangers were in the process of building a hotel which would be attached to the Copland Road end of Ibrox, and, by the way he talked, it seemed like a viable and probably highly profitable undertaking.

One day, when the thunderous clatter of test pile-driving was going on, he had been confronted by John Greig, in his new role as Rangers' PR man at that time. He told the engineer to stop the proceedings immediately. At first he imagined that since there were meetings taking place in the Ibrox boardroom it might be the horrendous sound that was bothering those people up the marble staircase. However, when he pursued the matter further with Greig, it was made clear that when Greig said 'Stop!' he meant the whole project was finished. The engineer was taken aback, since much work had already been undertaken. But, no. It was over. Greig, at first, was reluctant to expand on that, but eventually, revealed, almost graphically, what had happened. He explained to the astonished engineer that at a board meeting there had been a confrontation between David Murray, the chairman, and the manager Dick Advocaat, in which the Dutchman had threatened to leave the club immediately if they did not put an end to this work. He wanted the money spent on a new training facility. Or else.

Clearly, Advocaat had won the day. So the Dutchman, who had been at Rangers since 1 June 1998, could have been added to the historical soubriquets like Attila the Hun, Vlad the Impaler and Ivan the Terrible, and be known for ever after as Dick the Profligate. He used a cheque book like it was his Excalibur, drawn, not from a stone, but from his chairman's ready paw. Greig firmly cautioned the engineer to say nothing to the press about it. I think with the Dutchman out of the scene, the engineer felt he could loosen his tongue to us. That he did volunteer that snippet of information, allows me to identify the day of the silencing of the pile-drivers, as a tipping point for the club. From that very day the superb Murray Park training complex did emerge, ranking with the best in Europe, but built on the gurgling sound of Rangers' remorseless descent into huge and crippling debt which was estimated in 2004 to be £80 million. At a dinner one evening in a Glasgow hotel Murray actually said to me, 'Murray Park is a burden to us'. A fit of remorse, or simply an excuse for not being able to buy more players at the time?

Nine years later, on 13 June 2012, the *Daily Record* had a sombre black and white front page totally given over to an event that suggested it was reflecting a national tragedy. To the background of a photograph of the Rangers team which played in the club's first ever Scottish Cup Final in 1877, they offered this stark condolence. 'R.I.P. RFC.' It was the day after Rangers Football Club had been plunged into liquidation. It had been on the edge of the precipice since David Murray had sold off the club to businessman, Craig Whyte, for £1, after Lloyds had had taken over from the Bank of Scotland and abandoned the previous bank's policy of continuing to support the club for fear that a major Scottish institution would go out of business altogether. Lloyd's demanded the debt should be paid off. It all brought to mind the time when Celtic were on the brink. Nobody, outside the inner sanctums of both clubs in their days of peril, really knew what was occurring above their heads. But, with Celtic, there eventually was an upfront and clearly identified scheme to save the club. With Rangers there was, first of all, sleight of hand. For into the scene stepped a man who obviously had the talent to sell Edinburgh Castle to a tourist.

The first time I set eyes on Craig Whyte was the day Rangers had won the Scottish Premiership title in their last game at Kilmarnock on 15 May 2011. Into the Football Writers Annual Dinner on that same evening came the new Rangers owner surrounded by a bevy of hangers-on, lending the impression of some new dynamic force come among our midst. It was a scene as inspiring to the Rangers community as the gift of a wooden horse had been to the ancient Trojans. But, of course, there was no faculty I possessed that could have foretold what it was leading to. This contrasted with my first sighting of Fergus McCann who suddenly appeared at the back of the Celtic stand, well after the final whistle of one of the games and began to talk to my colleague, Hugh Keevins, on the commentary platform. Like Whyte, that evening at the dinner, there was no way I could predict the outcome of his entry into the fray. But there was a difference. As the little man spoke I could feel something that was intimately connected with the Celtic fraternity. (Not that he was allowed to speak all that long because a steward suddenly appeared and make it clear that no interview was to be allowed with this 'intruder'. So the interview was conducted in a broadcasting van in the carpark.) After all, although I did not know it at the time, he had been an official with the Croy Celtic supporters club in his earlier days. Hopeless though his task of saving the club might have appeared at that time, there was an authenticity and sincerity about his appeal that I knew would strike a chord with the support because, although he had a transatlantic twang, his voice was pure Celtic.

Of Whyte I knew nothing. Indeed, within a very short space of time we learned that there was no major figure in the Scottish business community who had heard of Craig Whyte, and even a cursory examination would have shown that he had previously been banned as a company director for seven years. As I absorbed the *Daily Record*'s front page, I thought of the times I had come across Murray, particularly in his handsome headquarters, in a palatial building in the Gyle, the commercial complex on the west side of Edinburgh. He was immensely self-assured and spoke in a way that suggested he had his finger firmly on the pulse of Scottish commercial life. And yet he had consorted with a shadowy figure with little credibility. After Whyte, almost inevitably, had pushed the club into this abyss, with schemes that were luridly delusional, Murray told the *Daily Record*:

> I was duped. My advisers were duped. The bank was duped, the shareholders were duped. We've all been duped. Is duped the right word? Duped IS the right word! I deeply, deeply regret selling the club to Craig Whyte.

I would find it easier to write a sentence of belief in the existence of the tooth fairy than to accept that this entrepreneur was 'duped'. Even at the time, I recorded my incredulity in *The Herald* column:

> For the cavalier way he discarded Rangers, he at least owed the supporters due diligence in assessing Whyte. Whom did he hire for that? Inspector Clouseau? The only publication I have read recently that has not discovered something unattractive about Whyte is *Garden News*.

The odour of subterfuge still lingers. I could not imagine that Murray had collapsed into a weeping heap on knowing the club was no longer his. On the face of it, it is more likely his sigh of relief was picked up by earthquake sensors in Hawaii. For, although the debt had been hugely diminished, the club he left behind was simply nothing the 'saviour' could cope with, such as 276 creditors left baying for blood. The level of degradation the club had reached is perhaps better reflected in some of the simpler bills they owed: £567 to a newsagent, £70 to a florist and, believe it or not, £40 to a face-painter. Whyte had walked away from a place that seemed not even to have a cupboard to be left bare.

We were now into new territory in the relationship of the two clubs. It was no longer to be a head-to-head of the Old Firm in this existential crisis, as Rangers through various strands of financial mismanagement were to be isolated by an alliance across the whole width of Scottish football. It was one of the most astonishing transformations in the history of the game to see a previously mammoth institution rendered vulnerable. And it was time for us in the media to go back to night school to swat up on new lingo.

For the whole farrago was difficult to comprehend. Since the moment Murray had confessed to Rangers' financial difficulties, there had been a wholesale addition of terminology to the jargon of the media. We were now talking Employment Benefit Trusts (EBTs), company volunteer agreements, 'big tax case', NewCo liquidators and most of all, (trippingly off the tongue), HMRC. Not much then about bigotry or trouble between fans. We were now at a higher altitude where some of the terms were beyond my understanding, even though I tried to write and speak about these matters as if I was a player in the stock exchange. Murray used EBTs to reward players by a system that benefited them and club alike and was widely practised in that shady world where evading the tax system is to the cost of the rest of us. I knew nothing about the legalities of such, but, to me, the system appeared grossly unethical. Eventually, the legal system judged it to be beyond the pale. It laid him open to the accusation that, quite simply he had cheated. Ironically, Murray hadn't needed to go down that route. He could still have acquired these same stars and paid them lavishly in the manner to which he was accustomed. He was being too devious by half.

In the time between the liquidation in June 2012 and Rangers becoming an actual working football club again, a bevy of characters passed through the Ibrox boardroom who would have graced the pages of Damon Runyan, not to say Bram Stoker. The internal machinations and the comings and goings within Ibrox enthralled us all, perhaps principally, among the Rangers support whose loyalty to the club was equalled only by their bafflement as to what was going on.

Politically, Murray and I were poles apart and consequently he always left me feeling queasy. I think I had made a safe assumption that he was not a subscriber to *Tribune*. And all the dubious dealings that caused the taxman to pursue him, and afterwards succumbing to the louche Whyte, who got the club for a song, you were seeing clear evidence that Murray and Whyte cared little for the concerns of largely working-class people about to be deprived of one of their basic enjoyments in life. Brian Dempsey, the former Celtic board member who had been prominent in the battle to save the club he loved, spoke to the *Daily Record*, 5 March 2015, with a sensitivity that rose well above the knee-jerking of many:

I feel for the thousands of fans who are loyal to their club and who were innocent of any wrongdoing. The ones who have suffered most have been the Rangers fans and with my Labour background I find that unacceptable and appalling.

The clash was clear. 'Sporting Integrity' took to the field against 'The God of Riches, Mammon'. Commercial considerations meant nothing in a sport if you cheated to take advantage of your opponents. This was not just fought out in boardrooms but on the airwaves. I recall sitting beside the powerful investigative Channel 4 journalist Alex Thomson, in STV's studio discussing the issue and listening to him state the case for the most draconian measures to be taken against Rangers, and became aware of how history was not about to come to the aid of the club. He was, perhaps unintentionally, conflating the sectarian issue with the financial mess. Inferring Rangers had a reputation that would not induce ready sympathy. Nobody was going to nominate them, retrospectively for a Nobel Peace Prize, because they had signed Mo Johnston and a subsequent trickle of Catholics. Then, not surprisingly, came a voice in support of Mammon. In exile then, Fergus McCann offered his views on his old adversaries. He told the *Daily Mail* on 29 August 2016:

> Expelling Rangers from the league. How smart is that? Everybody gets hurt. The people doing it get hurt. It was driven by fans, driven by emotion. Not a smart move.

And eventually, they faced the question of continuity. There are those who continually obsess even yet, with profound satisfaction, about this 'new' Rangers having no history at all now. The club died. Full stop. Their timeline had been broken. All kinds of graffiti were suggested, as to what they should be called, Sevco 5088, or Club 12 or Zombie FC, not to mention a whole host of names that were decidedly x-rated. Those who continually drone on about it disregard a more important reality. On two occasions in season 2018/19, Steven Gerrard's team at Ibrox, beat Celtic twice, after a long and painful series of defeats and then on 30 December in 2019 triumphed over their old rivals for the first time at Parkhead in nine years. The Celtic supporters I knew weren't exactly overjoyed by that. The pain registered, as I could gather from talking to people and reading social media, was no different from the generations preceding them. Why? Because they were playing against Rangers. None other. As Shylock said, 'If you prick us do we not bleed?' Celtic fans bled, all right, after these three games. It was pain with historic depths.

In his globally praised book, *Sapiens,* Professor Yuval Noah Harari writes this:

> Unlike lying, an imagined reality is something that everyone believes in, and as long as this communal belief persists, the imagined reality exerts force in the world.

In other words, in football, a club's existence depends not only on the pages of history, but in its firm establishment in the minds of people who will, under any circumstances, constantly identify with it, from cradle to grave. That is something that is much more difficult to erase from the records. So when Rangers started playing again in the basement league and suffered the indignity of Annan Athletic, from the Scottish Borders, where much more was known about the oval ball, to Govan on 9 March 2013, and beating them 2-1 in front of a 40,000 plus crowd, they were certainly booed off the park, but a couple of weeks later the same numbers were there to watch again. This was no longer just football. Attendance was an act of defiance. Kevin McKenna, the respected columnist for both *The Herald* and *The Observer,* and devoted Celtic follower, wrote under the *Thunderer* byline in *The Times* on 6 November 2015:

> If Celtic had gone out of business, as it almost did 20 years ago, we too would have fought for our unbroken history. Rangers have wandered in the wilderness for four years now. It's time to forgive and move on.

However, no matter the historic evidence that showed how the two clubs benefited from each other commercially, the Celtic board could not ignore the emphatic stance of an element, if not the huge majority of their supporters, that they ought to let Rangers wallow in their own misery and submerge without trace. They could hardly ignore a banner raised from one group of their support on 29 April 2012 which proclaimed, 'Rot In Hell' to their opponents at the other end on a day in which Celtic won 3-0 with ease. It is a safe bet that their rivals would have thought the same under parallel circumstances, and indeed expressed similar views when Celtic were on the edge of the precipice. At some of the public meetings I attended, among supporters groups, at which the prime subject was the Rangers dilemma, a combination of OJ Simpson's lawyers, Johnnie Cochran and Alan Dershowitz could not have put up a defence for Rangers. It was a veritable tsunami of terracing hostility towards the club. Or put another way, it was like some opponents of theirs, who had to fight for decades at welterweight against a heavyweight, suddenly discovering their opponent was suffering from the worst case of osteoporosis and could hardly stand. So, perhaps understandably, they waded in. Particularly on social media. This is the most dramatic change in public communication since I began watching football. I recall the days when I saw pigeons being released at Old Firm games to carry the message back to perhaps the mining communities which were always well-represented at these games. These digital messages were clear enough. They would not allow their boardrooms to let Rangers off lightly.

John Boyle, for instance, who owned Motherwell, at that juncture, and was at the centre of the heated discussions about the future of Ibrox, stressed an emotional factor to me, in saying:

Of course, there were many who thought that Rangers got what they deserved. However, there is no doubt there was an element of vindictiveness in the process! Too many people wanted to settle old scores with Rangers.

He took that approach as he went into the various discussions within the Scottish Premier League, but not completely free to act of his own volition. He had his own fans view to think about, who were not in a charitable mood. And as Boyle recalls, the SPL made a pre-vote decision of great significance:

As soon as the proposal to have a secret vote failed, Rangers were pretty well doomed. Some people who may have supported Rangers on the quiet, could not do this publicly, if they were to oppose the views of their own supporters. Now, of course, Aberdeen, Hibs, Hearts, these sorts of clubs just wanted Rangers out of the way. It meant they could advance themselves in their absence. There's always been resentment about the dominance of the Old Firm. Even down to the belief they got the majority of refereeing decisions. So, of course, that meant there was a majority to expel Rangers. But what about us? It was not in Motherwell's interest that Rangers should go down to the bottom league. We would lose something in the region of £150,000 by Rangers not coming to Fir Park, if not more. Now I am not against self-interest but when it harms the common good it is a nonsense. I was in favour of heavy restrictions on Rangers, like banning them from European football for a spell, measures like that which would hurt them, but still keep them in the top league.

But there was, in fact, no immediate Armageddon. Some other clubs in the Premier Division actually showed an increase in attendances, although eventually gaps were to appear around the stands at Celtic Park. Although, there was more to it than profit and loss in a club's balance sheet. Boyle, who had a volatile business career himself, and for which he has attracted sometimes very hostile criticism, could not ignore the voices from the terracings whose 'sporting integrity' banner was unfolding like a Salvation Army crusade against sin. He, and others, could not ignore this, even though Corinthian values had always seemed less evident in Scottish football than downright self-interest.

This movement, though, gathered strength on the basis that a club, which had manipulated the transfer market to tilt the playing field in their favour, did not deserve any special consideration. The path they had followed was deeply flawed and laden with hubris. So sympathy began to disappear like 'snaw aff a dyke'. They deserved no special consideration.

It followed logically that the lower clubs of the separate Scottish Football League voted 25 to 5 to put Rangers down to the Third Division. They did so with gleams in their eyes. They had just voted themselves manna from heaven. Rangers supporters would squeeze willingly into towns and small grounds to the great financial benefit of the locals. So for the first time in 120 years there would be no Old Firm fixture. Some people thought we were in now for a period of sanity and thank God it was out of the way. But with Celtic supporters constantly reminding Rangers of their degradation, understandably, under the rules of traditional hostility, resentment was only going to be stoked away for further aggression.

After having been drawn back from the brink, few of us in the media doubted that Rangers would eventually grind their way back eventually to the top rank, despite continuing rumours about their finances. Celtic supporters were aroused by that prospect, given the falling attendances at their stadium and with even season tickets holders not taking up their options at times, absenting themselves in great numbers. As Andrew Smith of *Scotland on Sunday* on 29 December 2013 put it:

> It will probably be only 18 months before there is a Rangers to ridicule and lord it over in the Premiership. Without that promise of ding-dong derby days, most of these fans would probably chuck their tickets.

Even though Celtic would go on to trounce their rivals, in the manner of a turkey shoot, it did not diminish the fervour of the event. The Rangers fans would troop up in big numbers, only to be trounced again. It demonstrated that the bitter rivalry was enough itself to bring Rangers folk back to a game, simply to demonstrate remarkable resilience and loyalty. Masochism now seemed an enduring feature of their support. It pointed to the massive cultural change between the two clubs. In my boyhood days, and well beyond, Rangers ruled the land and pulled along much of the media with them, like they were adherents to the idea of continuing supremacy, thus leading to the view from the east end of the city that they could never get a fair deal from the leading newspapers of the day. And prompted Stein, when he entered the scene, to tell me:

> Even when somebody says something positive about us I suspect they're just patronising us.

Now it is reversed. Celtic have achieved the kind of respect and influence that Rangers once enjoyed around the media. They have plundered trophies in Rangers' fall from grace, as their great rivals would have done in similar circumstances. They exert barometric pressure on practically anything of significance that happens in Scottish football; as Ibrox once exercised in days gone by. They are reflecting simply the power of relative wealth, as is now evidenced around Europe. Money not only talks, it sings the 'Hallelujah Chorus'. Up to and including season 2018/19, Juventus had won 8 titles in a row. Bayern Munich, for instance, have now won the Bundesliga a record seven times in a row. Dinamo Zagreb have now won their title 13 out of 14 seasons. Even in smaller leagues the principle still applies, when you identify Dundalk winning their Irish title five out of six times. Real Madrid and Barcelona, of course, still dominate, as they are accustomed to, but their percentage of wins by three goals or more had increased from 20.5 per cent in the '90s to a staggering 37.8 per cent in the last couple of seasons. Wealth, in football, commands now, in an unprecedented dimension. Recently we have had the first German treble, the first Italian treble, the first English domestic treble, three French trebles in four years, all emerging from clubs who, financially, continue to consolidate their advantages. Which is why, in parallel with all that, Celtic in achieving their trebles, have a financial stockade built around them which, although certainly not impregnable, is certainly well prepared for assaults of any kind. Add that to the fact that Rangers' old recruitment policy now seems simply a relic of mediaeval times and you don't need to be an astute historian to identify that as the biggest change in the footballing culture in Scotland since I started out with the mic.

But, in the fluctuations that have taken place over the decades, it is significant to note that, by the end of 2019, the atmosphere had changed. For almost a decade Rangers could have travelled to the games in a tumbrel for the guillotine, rather than a team bus. But, by the end of that year, their role as hapless victims of their great rivals, seemed, at least temporarily, to be over. The fear of losing was now being shared by both communities. It almost had a nostalgic feel to it.

Yet, despite an upsurge in interest and rivalry, both clubs are not immune from the powerful influence of our neighbours in the south, which has made the Old Firm seem more parochial than they have ever been. The great levels they both have achieved in European football look beyond their grasp. Europe, and particularly England, is now awash with astronomical sums of money linked to players, and against which they cannot compete. Martin O'Neill who took Celtic to the final of the UEFA Cup in Seville in 2003, told me bluntly in an interview at the beginning of that following season, 'A Scottish team will never win a European trophy again'.

Sky television might rightly proclaim that an Old Firm fixture can swell their audiences. But, apart from the Old Firm global support bolstering the figures, many others are simply attracted by its notoriety. From my experience of working among broadcasters in the south, that is a recognisable factor. They certainly have always been in awe of the spectacle of sound and fury. As Des Lynam, the former presenter of BBC's *Grandstand* once said to me after I had taken him to one of those games, 'Watching English football now, is like watching silent movies'. But you have to wonder if their credit is gradually slipping, with comparisons constantly being made now with glamorous figures elsewhere. For out in the streets, and in public parks, what was I beginning to see but an increasing number of English club jerseys being worn by kids: Man U, Liverpool, Chelsea, Arsenal and even Barcelona. That has multiplied over the years. A friend of mine, a Celtic supporter who organises dinners for fans, took some Celtic friends to Belfast and, out of interest and curiosity, trawled through those areas so closely associated with the Old Firm, the Falls Road, and the Shankill. Not once did he see a kid wearing an Old Firm jersey.

From time to time I admit I grew tired of all the animosities. Angry at all the indignation which would lead nowhere; painfully aware that 10 May 1980 was the start of a Groundhog Day process where, year after year, you could have picked out any particular comment I had broadcast, or article I, and others, had written and superimposed them on all the ruckuses through the years and nobody would have noticed many differences in the words, despite the passing of time. As the French have it in their old aphorism: the more you change, the more things seem exactly the same.

And the hostility can take various shapes, as if the virus can jump species, as I learned one day during the Scottish independence referendum.

# Epilogue

THIS REFERENDUM ACT had been passed by the Scottish Parliament in November 2013 and into the fray many Old Firm fans had dived with relish. I was doing radio commentary during that whole campaign but, before it had gathered a head of steam, I had been hospitalised. Shortly after the announcement of the referendum I had a major cancer operation. I wrote about my experience in *The Herald* to warn others of early detection and of how such an initiative had helped me. I received an inspiring and greatly sympathetic letter from Alex Salmond, the First Minister, which ended with words of encouragement,

> On behalf of the people of Scotland, I wish you continued good health and look forward to hearing your words of wisdom as the 'voice of Scottish football'.

It was deeply affecting. I doubt if any politician had ever made such an impact on me as he did at that time. I replied graciously and even though I didn't share his political views I admitted that he stood head and shoulders over most at Holyrood for political savvy. I was asked to make a short film in support of the Union case for STV. I simply couldn't bring myself to take part after such generosity of spirit from a man who stood at the other end of the referendum spectrum from me.

I let this feeling lie dormant for a while as I identified the familiar Old Firm division developing. I noticed outside Ibrox there were pamphleteers promoting support for the Union and the NO vote, to the question, 'Should Scotland be an independent country?' Outside Celtic Park there were those punting support for YES. That was the general and strong impression you could gain; of course, largely on an anecdotal level. I certainly saw little evidence of the reverse of that. Of course, there were notable exceptions. One in particular was Brian Wilson, whom I have known since his days as a prominent Labour Minister in the Blair government, and now Celtic director, who was eloquently anti-nationalist. The Rangers-supporting playwright and novelist Alan Bissett was fervently a nationalist. I recall him telling me enthusiastically of a play he was writing about his hero, Jim Baxter, and listening to his lyrical description of the nationalist movement; and of his marked disappointment immediately after when I told him how I was going to vote. But, generally, you could feel a significant number of Old Firm fans were on either side of the divide. And politicians were certainly aware of that.

Currying favour with a particular constituency was nothing new, since we had seen at the time of the 1978 World Cup, how the disaster associated with the national side in Argentina might have stalled the mood for nationalism around then. But it showed that people passing through the turnstiles really mattered and their support was of significance. That referendum campaign, for as much as I experienced it in North Lanarkshire in particular, was a boisterous time all round, with elements of hatred occasionally surfacing, which was far from pleasant. Listening to some heated arguments you could have felt you were in a pub after an Old Firm match. To be fair, others might have experienced it differently in other regions. I suppose it depended on the company you found yourself in.

But the preponderance of feelings between the two factions were of distinctly polarised views. Of course, they had already existed in the context of historical division. As Tom Gallagher, Emeritus Professor of Politics at the University of Bradford, underlines in his book *Scotland Now*:

> A strong sense of anti-British nationalism had existed among that segment of Scots Catholics mainly preoccupied with Ireland, a place from which many of their ancestors had originated. For many years, Celtic football club in Glasgow has been the main repository for that Irish consciousness. A large segment of the fan base cultivated Irish nationalist symbols.

Indeed, the former Lord Provost of Glasgow, Alex Mosson, and season ticket holder at Celtic Park, let his views be known to a senior political journalist, 'I'm voting YES to help the boys over the water!' This was as much to do with the potential break-up of the British state rather than simply independence for Scotland.

Gallagher also noted the influences on the other side:

...the religiously-orientated Orange Order felt compelled to make a public affirmation for the Union, by organising a march through Edinburgh on 13 September which drew 15,000 people. (Protestants would vote 60.1 per cent in favour of the Union, while less than 40 per cent of Catholics would.)

And undoubtedly there would be many Rangers supporters in that Orange march, or from whom there was occasional aggression to bystanders. All of this is continually seen as threatening and toxic for Catholics. So, a division was definitely there on the traditional lines, to a significant extent. What annoyed many in the Scottish media was the attempt by outsiders to characterise the obvious sources of heated division as a developing Ulsterisation of Scotland. For instance, Tom Bradby, then ITN's political editor, and a former Northern Ireland correspondent, said in a broadcast that the referendum reminded him of his days in Ireland. That would have suggested wide-scale violence, disorder, fear. There was none of that. But there was noise, caterwauling and bitterness in certain areas, and in these torrid political times the division was spreading to the terracings and stands. I could hear 'Rule Britannia' blasted out by Rangers supporters, and with social media effectively organising opposition from varied supporters around the land, the strains of 'Flower of Scotland' challenged that. That alternated with the repetitive rebuke, to the Rangers fans, 'You're no' Rangers anymore!'

Politicians had always been aware of terracing sympathies. Even after the referendum when Jim Murphy was elected leader of Scottish Labour (and after his '100 streets in 100 days' campaign for Better Together, which had the appearance of a wagon train trying to fight off the Sioux, and which led eventually to the Little Big Horn of Labour's massacre in May 2015) he was painfully conscious of making sure that the Union he had fought for, was not the same as that championed by the distinct majority at Ibrox. Even before he got to the main thrust of his acceptance speech on the podium, he was hinting to the audience that he supported a team in the East End of Glasgow, and since Bridgeton Waverley had folded in 1962, it narrowed down the options. Without mentioning it by name, this Celtic fan was trying set out his stall in terms that the followers of that club would sympathise with, that he was no terracing Unionist.

Then several months into the campaign and continually being asked to offer public support for the NO vote I succumbed and agreed to speak at a meeting in Dundee along with former Prime Minister, Gordon Brown and former Chancellor, Alistair Darling. I suppose the sheer novelty of my presence on a political platform took the fancy of some newspapers, and the *Daily Record* played up my speech prominently on front and inside pages of the paper. To follow this up they wanted to take some pictures of me in my home neighbourhood, Shettleston, in the East End of Glasgow. Off I went, with the cameras, and alongside the local Labour MP Margaret Curran and the future leader of the Labour group in Glasgow, Frank McAveety, to pump flesh and display comradeship with the community; a community I had left decades ago but wondered if the old divisive beliefs might still flourish in the area. Before the end of the day I was having to make a dramatic judgement on that, as a volley was directed towards me, in a surprisingly innovative way.

We arrived at Shettleston Road and stood directly under the window of the very room where I had first seen the light of day. It was there I had sat so often and watched the crowds flocking to Celtic Park, on Old Firm day, like they were responding to the distant sound of a bugler. I had come full circle and felt the desperate need for some kind of recognition for being back among my ain folk.

As we looked upwards we saw an elderly gentleman sitting at the window of that very room, staring down at us. I could see the dawn of recognition appearing on his face. I'd been spotted. We all three smiled back up at him, as he stuck his head out and shouted at me,

Fuck off ya English cunt.

Ah, well. Not an Undecided, for sure. So much for my Dundee oration. Being divested of my nationality was at least a startling novelty. His words seemed to air with the same venom that sprung from the football tribalism that had echoed in my ears all these years. I couldn't help but feel that the Orange or Fenian tag had simply been abandoned temporarily for identity of another kind during the referendum, but which seemed to carry the same sectarian stamp. And, yes, I didn't see it coming, although my home neighbourhood had always been capable of robust views on any subject. This was the first time I had been back there in decades. And even in the early 21st century, Shettleston had been designated as one of the most disadvantaged urban areas in the whole of the UK. So it was perhaps not too surprising that rage was an underlying seam that was easily tapped into, by people who might have watched the outside world pass them by, with lofty indifference, and that I was being seen simply as a voyeur, about to beat a hasty retreat to a much better world. That I could understand. But I was so inured to the sounds associated with bigotry that I found it difficult to distinguish him from the fray I was accustomed to. He wasn't an irate voter to me. He was a football man screaming at a colour which inflamed him. It was how you could behave to the 'other kind'. But, in retrospect, it still makes me wonder just how prevalent this ancient bitterness still is, especially in a period when political debate seems to be becoming just as strident and recriminatory as the howls from the terracing.

Now I am behind my own window. I am sitting here looking out on a world petrified by COVID-19. I am self-isolating because for the first time in my life I am being advised I am old and vulnerable. Therefore, I tend to clutch at things which appear timeless and make life still seem safe and permanent and full of events that are within the grasp of understanding because much else connected with the virus is incomprehensible. Nothing is more important than avoiding the horrible fate that is afflicting others because of this diabolical scourge. So, I want to be constantly reminded of normality, despite it all. The Old Firm are helping me out with this. Or at least the arguments surrounding them are. The Premier League of 2019/20 like many tournaments around the world has been suspended. Had it been played to a conclusion Celtic would have won it. You don't need to be gifted with second sight to have worked that one out. But the maths does not discount another possibility, however remote that would appear. And any league competition needs to be played out to the full, as a true reflection of status. Hence, the impasse, and the flux of arguments surrounding it. Hence my familiarity with this kind of Old Firm conflict lends me this odd feeling of gratitude that, thank God, there are matters in life which will not change all that much.

Throughout these pages I have shown how this kind of stand-off between the two clubs has occurred in succeeding generations. This time it is set against the deaths of potentially hundreds of thousands around the world. This time it is also about the survival of Scottish football itself. The eventual vote to end the season for the Scottish Leagues outwith the Premiership, award titles and allocate badly needed funds to the stricken clubs still leaves the question of the top league's conclusion unresolved. This is at a time when the league authorities and SFA are at issue with UEFA's desire for all European league seasons to be completed. As I write in the middle of April 2020, we still await the outcome. In the background, the Holy Grail of ten-titles-in-a-row is nearing the grasp of one club and being fought against by the other like the beleaguered corps defending the Alamo. I have already touched on how tragedy has prompted many of us to hope a new atmosphere might be generated among Old Firm followers: the Ibrox disaster of 1971 and the murder of Mark Scott in 1995. Both incidents inspired hope but were followed by disillusionment. So, a tragedy on the scale of COVID-19, might make footballing enmities appear pathetically trivial and encourage the belief that emerging from this current pandemic the Old Firm followers will embrace the Bard's 'shall brothers be for a' that'.

I bear too many personal scars to lapse into that romantic mode. After the Hampden riot of 10 May 1980, after the indignation and scorn that was heaped on the Old Firm Cup Final, I have shown that the sectarianism at the core of the fixture has a resilience that seems impenetrable. So separating cynicism from optimism is a difficult task for me. But I also acknowledge things ain't exactly what they used to be.

I have to return to the words of Sir Tom Devine who stresses that our views on sectarianism could be shaped largely by personal experience. My experience suggests that there seems to be less concern about who is Protestant or Catholic than there was back in my boyhood days when there were still tramcars running up and down the East End of Glasgow. Obviously there have been great social improvements since the 1950s and hence the emergence of a better-educated population, with increasing numbers upwardly mobile in society, leaving behind old shibboleths and, of course to the regret of Christians, abandoning churches in significant numbers. The old identities are more blurred.

But we are still left with too many assumptions about that trend. Bitterness can still lurk round any corner. Thus, I am still as perplexed about it as I was on that bus heading to Carntyne on that hot August day in 1949 when I saw men fighting over the incident at Ibrox when Sammy had kicked Charlie. But, unlike the bus, the passion aroused by such Old Firm controversies, apparently has no terminus.

# Some other books published by **Luath Press**

## Singin I'm No a Billy He's a Tim
Des Dillon
ISBN: 978-1-908373-05-2 PBK £7.99

What happens when a Rangers fan and Celtic fan are locked in a prison cell together on the day of an Old Firm Match?

It is through Billy and Tim that Des Dillon explores sectarianism, bigotry, how it becomes part of one's identity and is inculcated by family and society. However, the book is not limited to Scotland but refers to every peace process in the world, where common ground and a shared humanity is found through responding to the needs of others. Now it is up to these two fans to start their personal peace process to find some common ground to slowly let go of their bigotry.

# Stramash: Tackling Scotland's Towns and Teams

Daniel Gray

ISBN: 978-1-906817-66-4 PBK £9.99

Fatigued by bloated big-game football and bored of a samey big cities, Daniel Gray went in search of small town Scotland and its teams. At the time when the Scottish club game is drifting towards its lowest ebb once more, *Stramash* singularly fails to wring its hands and address the state of the game, preferring instead to focus on Bobby Mann's waistline.

Part travelogue, part history and part mistakenly spilling ketchup on the face of a small child, *Stramash* takes an uplifting look at the country's nether regions. Using the excuse of a match to visit places from Dumfries to Dingwall, Gray surveys Scotland's towns and teams in their present state. *Stramash* accomplishes the feats of visiting Dumfries without mentioning Robert Burns, being positive about Cumbernauld and linking Elgin City to Lenin. It is as fond look at Scotland as you've never seen it before.

## Barcelona to Buckie Thistle:
## Exploring Football's Roads Less Travelled

Mat Guy

ISBN: 978-1-913025-35-9 PBK £12.99

'When my playground cohorts began falling in love with the FA Cup winning Tottenham Hotspur side of 1981 and that stupendous Ricky Villa goal, or the all-conquering Liverpool, or their near neighbours, Everton, whose league win in 1985 made all the kids want that vibrant blue kit for Christmas – I found myself falling for non-league Salisbury, my grandfather's team, absorbing all its charm, warmth, meaning.' MAT GUY

Mat Guy is not interested in the big names of football: the likes of Barcelona and Bayern Munich and Manchester United, with millions of fans and millions of pounds. Instead, in this book, he tours the little leagues of the footballing world, charting this global phenomenon through some of the least known football teams.

Looking at the grassroots movement from the grounds themselves, this is a manifestation of love for the sport at a different level to the one we are accustomed to seeing. From the highlands of Scotland to Azerbaijan, Liechtenstein and Andorra, Mat focuses on the heart and soul of the beautiful game.

## Should've Gone to Specsavers, Ref!

Allan Morrison

ISBN: 978-1-908373-73-1 PBK £7.99

The referee. You can't have a game without one. The most hated man (or woman) in football but you have to invite one to every game.

Enjoy a laugh at the antics and wicked humour of Scottish referee Big Erchie, a powerhouse at five foot five, and a top grade referee who strikes fear into the hearts of managers and players alike as he stringently applies the laws of the game.

But Big Erchie is burdened with a terrible secret... He's a Stirling Albion supporter.

Details of these and other books published by Luath Press can be found at:
**www.luath.co.uk**

**Luath** Press Limited

*committed to publishing well written books worth reading*

LUATH PRESS takes its name from Robert Burns, whose little collie Luath (*Gael.*, swift or nimble) tripped up Jean Armour at a wedding and gave him the chance to speak to the woman who was to be his wife and the abiding love of his life. Burns called one of the 'Twa Dogs' Luath after Cuchullin's hunting dog in Ossian's *Fingal*.
Luath Press was established in 1981 in the heart of Burns country, and is now based a few steps up the road from Burns' first lodgings on Edinburgh's Royal Mile. Luath offers you distinctive writing with a hint of unexpected pleasures.
Most bookshops in the UK, the US, Canada, Australia, New Zealand and parts of Europe, either carry our books in stock or can order them for you. To order direct from us, please send a £sterling cheque, postal order, international money order or your credit card details (number, address of cardholder and expiry date) to us at the address below. Please add post and packing as follows: UK – £1.00 per delivery address; overseas surface mail – £2.50 per delivery address; overseas airmail – £3.50 for the first book to each delivery address, plus £1.00 for each additional book by airmail to the same address. If your order is a gift, we will happily enclose your card or message at no extra charge.

**Luath** Press Limited
543/2 Castlehill
The Royal Mile
Edinburgh EH1 2ND
Scotland
Telephone: +44 (0)131 225 4326 (24 hours)
email: sales@luath. co.uk
Website: www. luath.co.uk